In the aftermath of the second superhuman civil war, the world has become disillusioned with its heroes. The next generation has to be better. They have to be...

D1097254

CHAMPIONS

CHAMPION FOR A DAY

WRITER: **MARK WAID**
PENCILER: **HUMBERTO RAMOS**
INKER: **VICTOR OLAZABA**
COLORIST: **EDGAR DELGADO**
LETTERER: **VC'S CLAYTON COWLES**
COVER ART: **HUMBERTO RAMOS**
& EDGAR DELGADO

CHAMPIONS #1.MU
WRITER: **JEREMY WHITLEY**
ARTISTS: **RO STEIN & TED BRANDT**
COLOR ARTIST: **FRANK D'ARMATA**
LETTERER: **VC'S CLAYTON COWLES**
COVER ART: **SIMONE BIANCHI**

ASSISTANT EDITOR: **ALANNA SMITH**   EDITOR: **TOM BREVOORT**

CHAMPIONS

MS. MARVEL

SPIDER-MAN

NOVA

AFTER THE HIGH EVOLUTIONARY "EVOLVED" VIV VISION INTO A HUMAN BEING, VIV SACRIFICED HERSELF TO SAVE EARTH FROM HIS DESTRUCTIVE PLANS. THE VISION, HEARTBROKEN FROM THE LOSS OF HIS DAUGHTER, BEGAN BUILDING A NEW VIV SO HE COULD SAY GOODBYE. BUT VIV DIDN'T DIE--SHE WAS TRAPPED ON ANOTHER PLANE OF EXISTENCE. AND WHEN SHE FOUND HER WAY HOME, SHE WAS SHOCKED TO FIND THAT A NEW SYNTHEZOID VIV HAD ALREADY TAKEN HER PLACE!

THE AVENGERS

HULK

WASP

VISION

VIV VISION

CYCLOPS

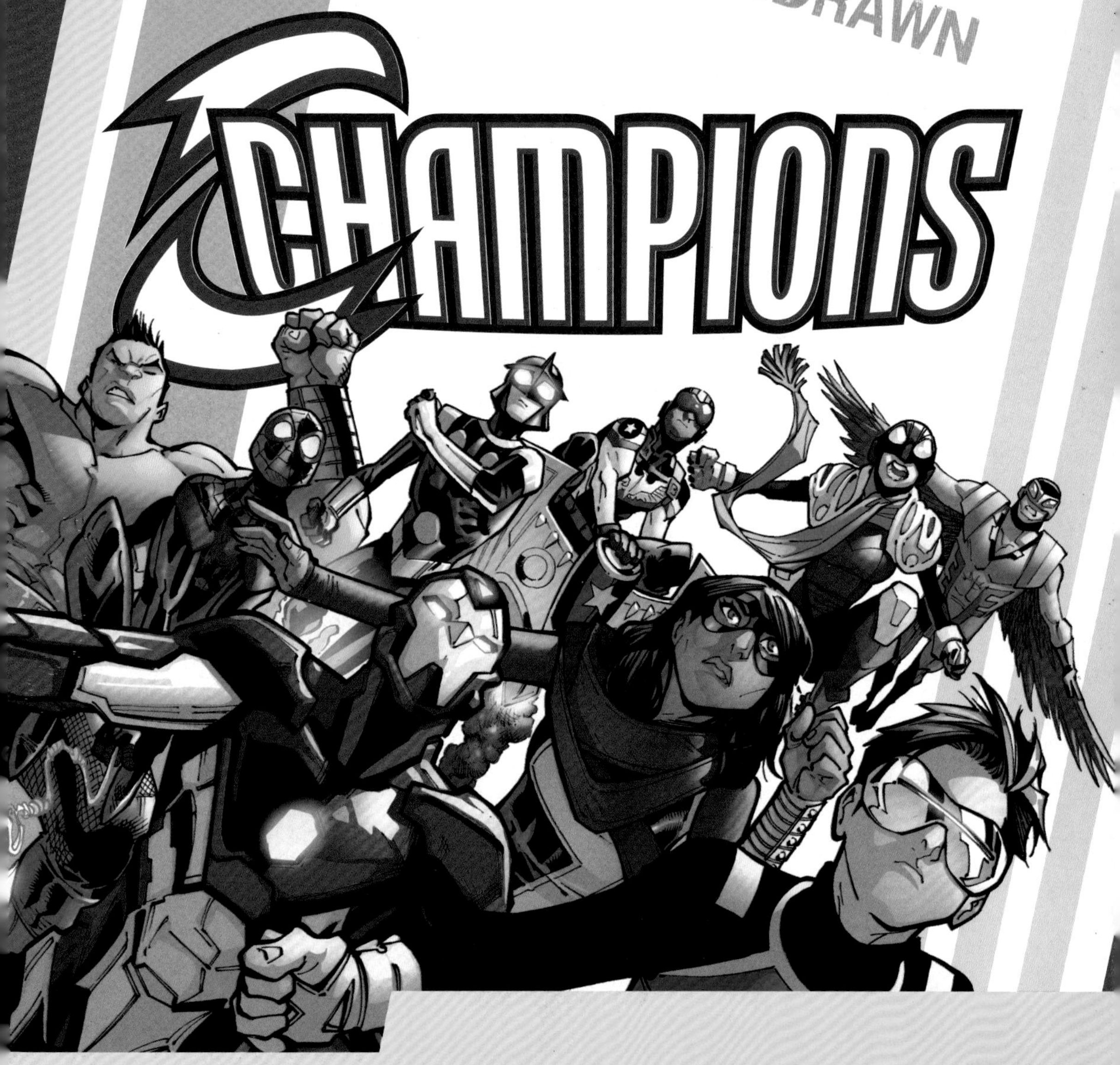
CHAMPIONS

CHAMPION FOR A DAY

COLLECTION EDITOR: **JENNIFER GRÜNWALD**
ASSISTANT EDITOR: **CAITLIN O'CONNELL**
ASSOCIATE MANAGING EDITOR: **KATERI WOODY**
EDITOR, SPECIAL PROJECTS: **MARK D. BEAZLEY**
VP PRODUCTION & SPECIAL PROJECTS: **JEFF YOUNGQUIST**
SVP PRINT, SALES & MARKETING: **DAVID GABRIEL**

EDITOR IN CHIEF: **C.B. CEBULSKI**
CHIEF CREATIVE OFFICER: **JOE QUESADA**
PRESIDENT: **DAN BUCKLEY**
EXECUTIVE PRODUCER: **ALAN FINE**

CHAMPIONS VOL. 3: CHAMPION FOR A DAY. Contains material originally published in magazine form as CHAMPIONS #16-18 and #1.MU. First printing 2018. ISBN 978-1-302-90620-7. Published by MARVEL WORLDWIDE, INC., a subsidiary of MARVEL ENTERTAINMENT, LLC. OFFICE OF PUBLICATION: 135 West 50th Street, New York, NY 10020. Copyright © 2018 MARVEL No similarity between any of the names, characters, persons, and/or institutions in this magazine with those of any living or dead person or institution is intended, and any such similarity which may exist is purely coincidental. **Printed in Canada.** DAN BUCKLEY, President, Marvel Entertainment; JOHN NEE, Publisher; JOE QUESADA, Chief Creative Officer; TOM BREVOORT, SVP of Publishing; DAVID BOGART, SVP of Business Affairs & Operations, Publishing & Partnership; DAVID GABRIEL, SVP of Sales & Marketing, Publishing; JEFF YOUNGQUIST, VP of Production & Special Projects; DAN CARR, Executive Director of Publishing Technology; ALEX MORALES, Director of Publishing Operations; DAN EDINGTON, Managing Editor; SUSAN CRESPI, Production Manager; STAN LEE, Chairman Emeritus. For information regarding advertising in Marvel Comics or on Marvel.com, please contact Vit DeBellis, Custom Solutions & Integrated Advertising Manager, at vdebellis@marvel.com. For Marvel subscription inquiries, please call 888-511-5480. **Manufactured between 6/15/2018 and 7/17/2018 by SOLISCO PRINTERS, SCOTT, QC, CANADA.**

10 9 8 7 6 5 4 3 2 1

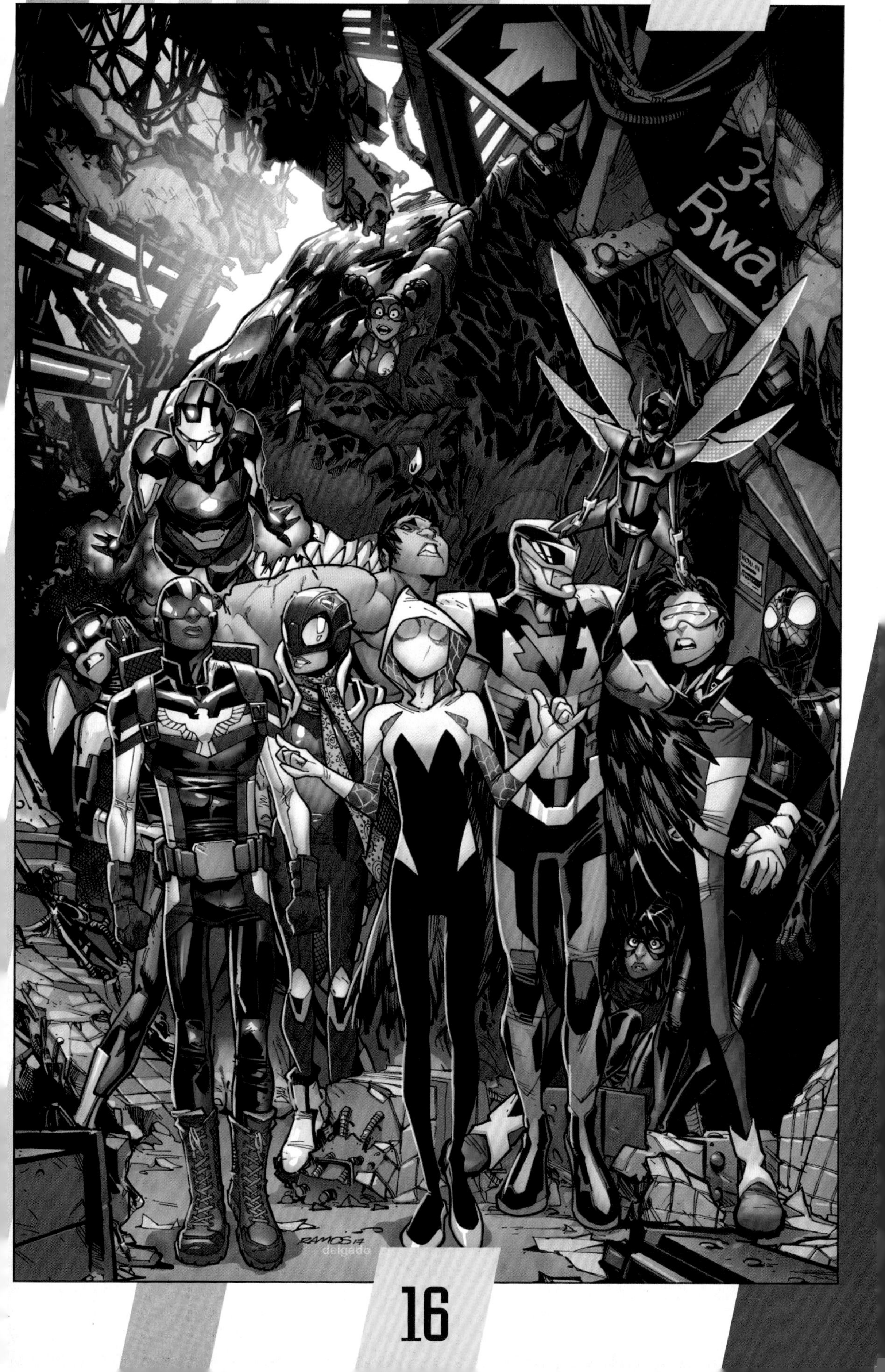

16

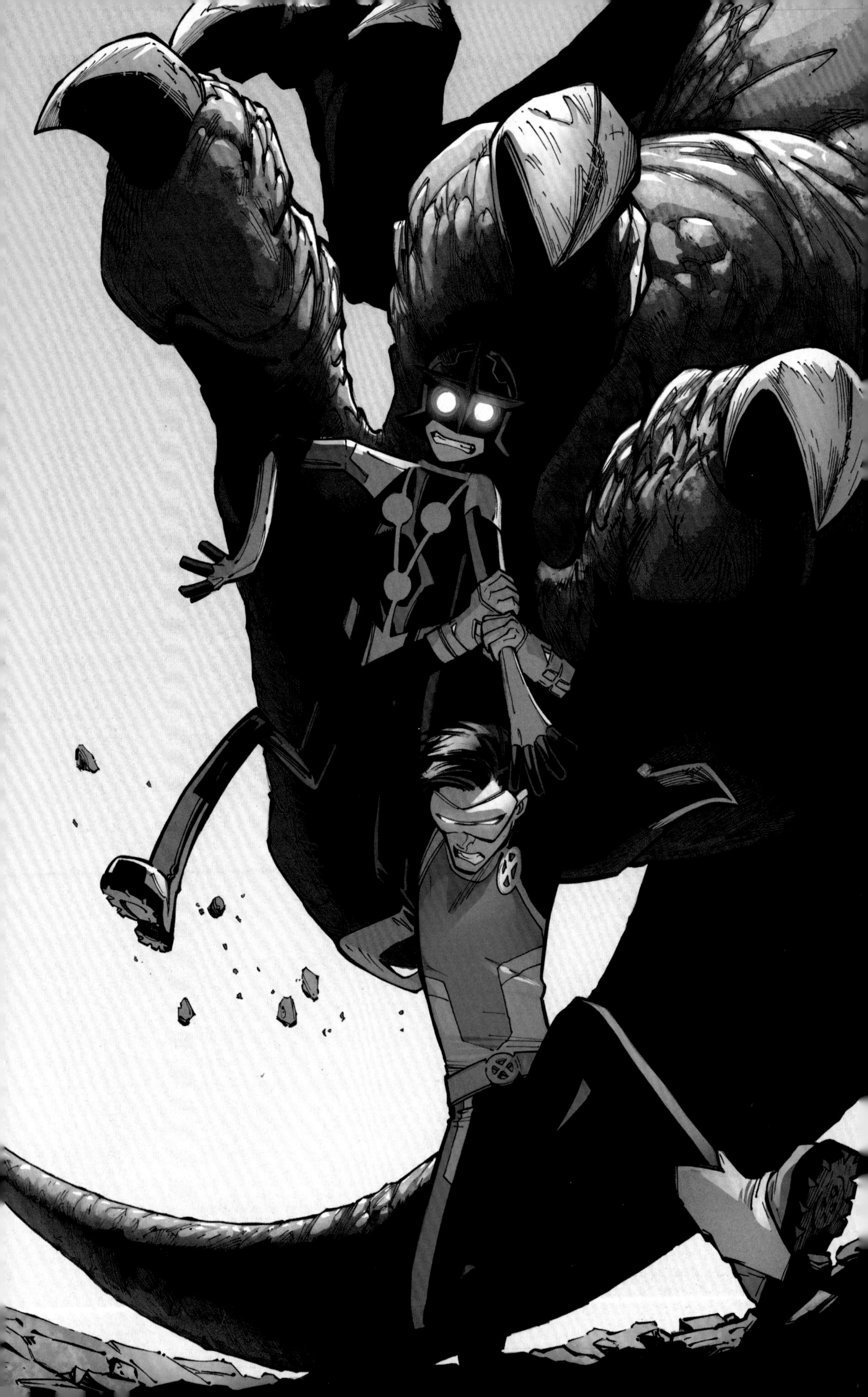

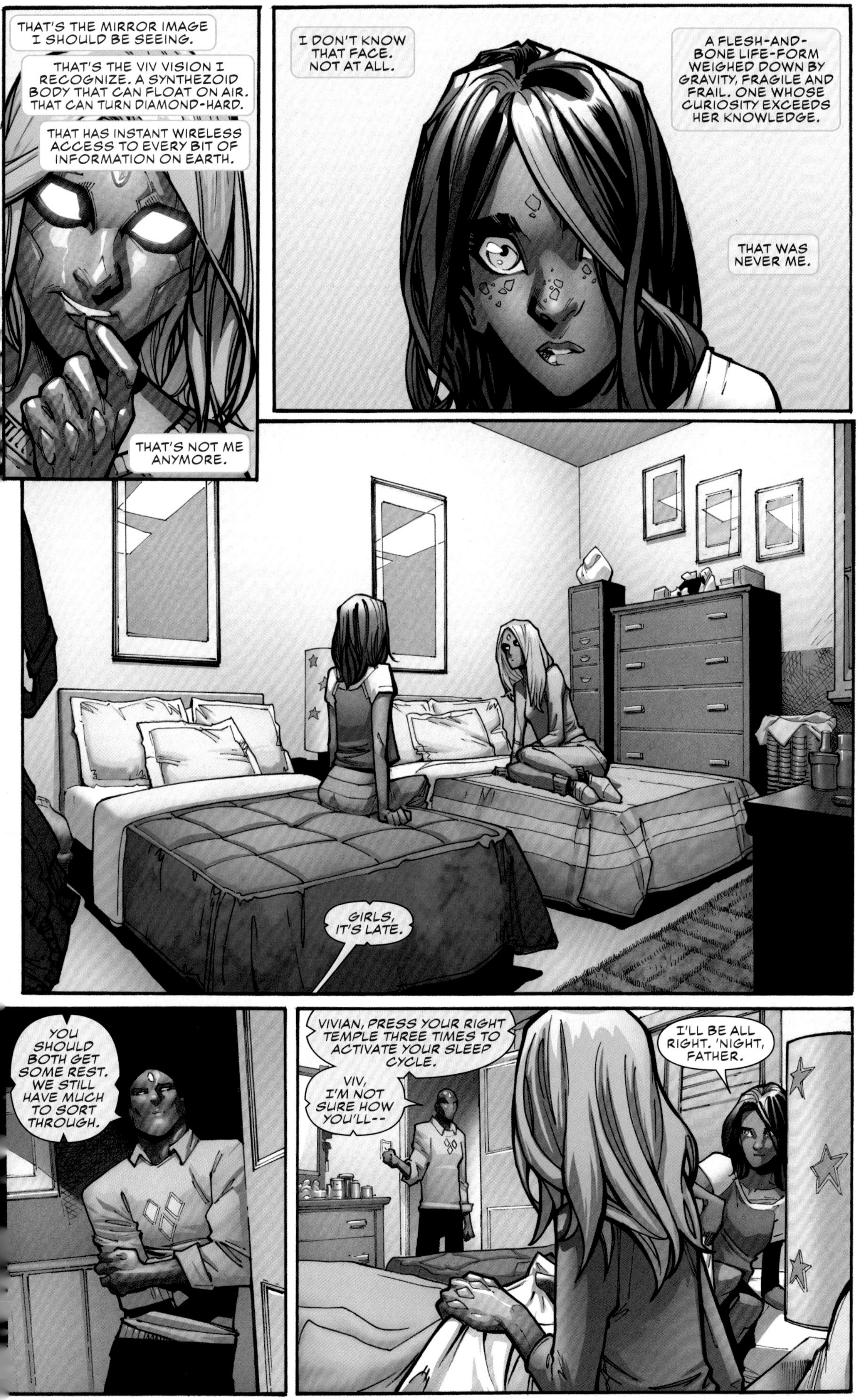

THAT'S THE MIRROR IMAGE I SHOULD BE SEEING.
THAT'S THE VIV VISION I RECOGNIZE. A SYNTHEZOID BODY THAT CAN FLOAT ON AIR. THAT CAN TURN DIAMOND-HARD.
THAT HAS INSTANT WIRELESS ACCESS TO EVERY BIT OF INFORMATION ON EARTH.
THAT'S NOT ME ANYMORE.
I DON'T KNOW THAT FACE. NOT AT ALL.
A FLESH-AND-BONE LIFE-FORM WEIGHED DOWN BY GRAVITY, FRAGILE AND FRAIL. ONE WHOSE CURIOSITY EXCEEDS HER KNOWLEDGE.
THAT WAS NEVER ME.
GIRLS, IT'S LATE.
YOU SHOULD BOTH GET SOME REST. WE STILL HAVE MUCH TO SORT THROUGH.
VIVIAN, PRESS YOUR RIGHT TEMPLE THREE TIMES TO ACTIVATE YOUR SLEEP CYCLE.
VIV, I'M NOT SURE HOW YOU'LL--
I'LL BE ALL RIGHT. 'NIGHT, FATHER.

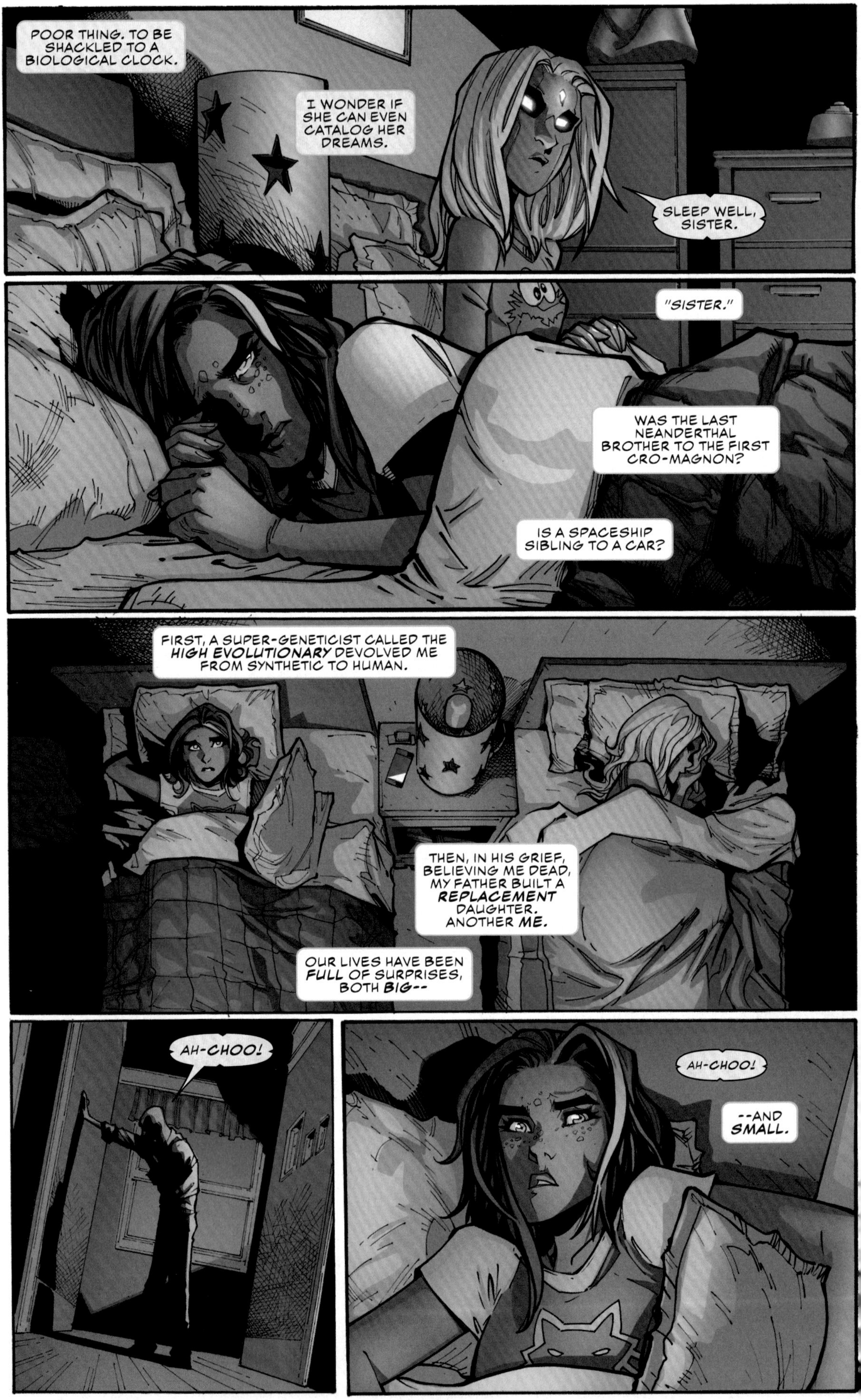
POOR THING. TO BE SHACKLED TO A BIOLOGICAL CLOCK.
I WONDER IF SHE CAN EVEN CATALOG HER DREAMS.
SLEEP WELL, SISTER.
"SISTER."
WAS THE LAST NEANDERTHAL BROTHER TO THE FIRST CRO-MAGNON?
IS A SPACESHIP SIBLING TO A CAR?
FIRST, A SUPER-GENETICIST CALLED THE HIGH EVOLUTIONARY DEVOLVED ME FROM SYNTHETIC TO HUMAN.
THEN, IN HIS GRIEF, BELIEVING ME DEAD, MY FATHER BUILT A REPLACEMENT DAUGHTER. ANOTHER ME.
OUR LIVES HAVE BEEN FULL OF SURPRISES, BOTH BIG--
AH-CHOO!
AH-CHOO!
--AND SMALL.

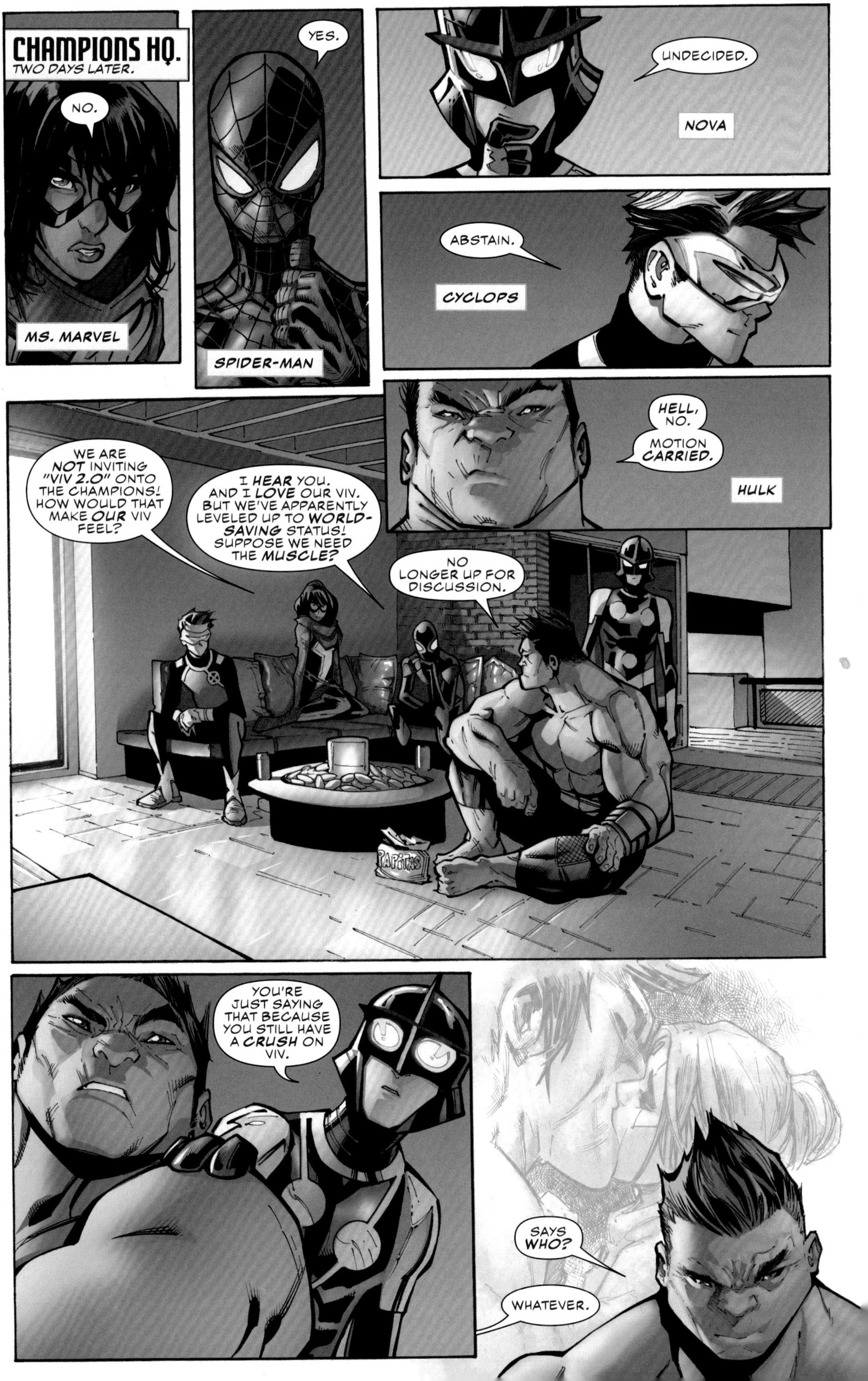
CHAMPIONS HQ.
TWO DAYS LATER.
NO.
MS. MARVEL
YES.
SPIDER-MAN
UNDECIDED.
NOVA
ABSTAIN.
CYCLOPS
HELL, NO.
MOTION CARRIED.
HULK
WE ARE NOT INVITING "VIV 2.0" ONTO THE CHAMPIONS! HOW WOULD THAT MAKE OUR VIV FEEL?
I HEAR YOU. AND I LOVE OUR VIV. BUT WE'VE APPARENTLY LEVELED UP TO WORLD-SAVING STATUS! SUPPOSE WE NEED THE MUSCLE?
NO LONGER UP FOR DISCUSSION.
YOU'RE JUST SAYING THAT BECAUSE YOU STILL HAVE A CRUSH ON VIV.
SAYS WHO?
WHATEVER.

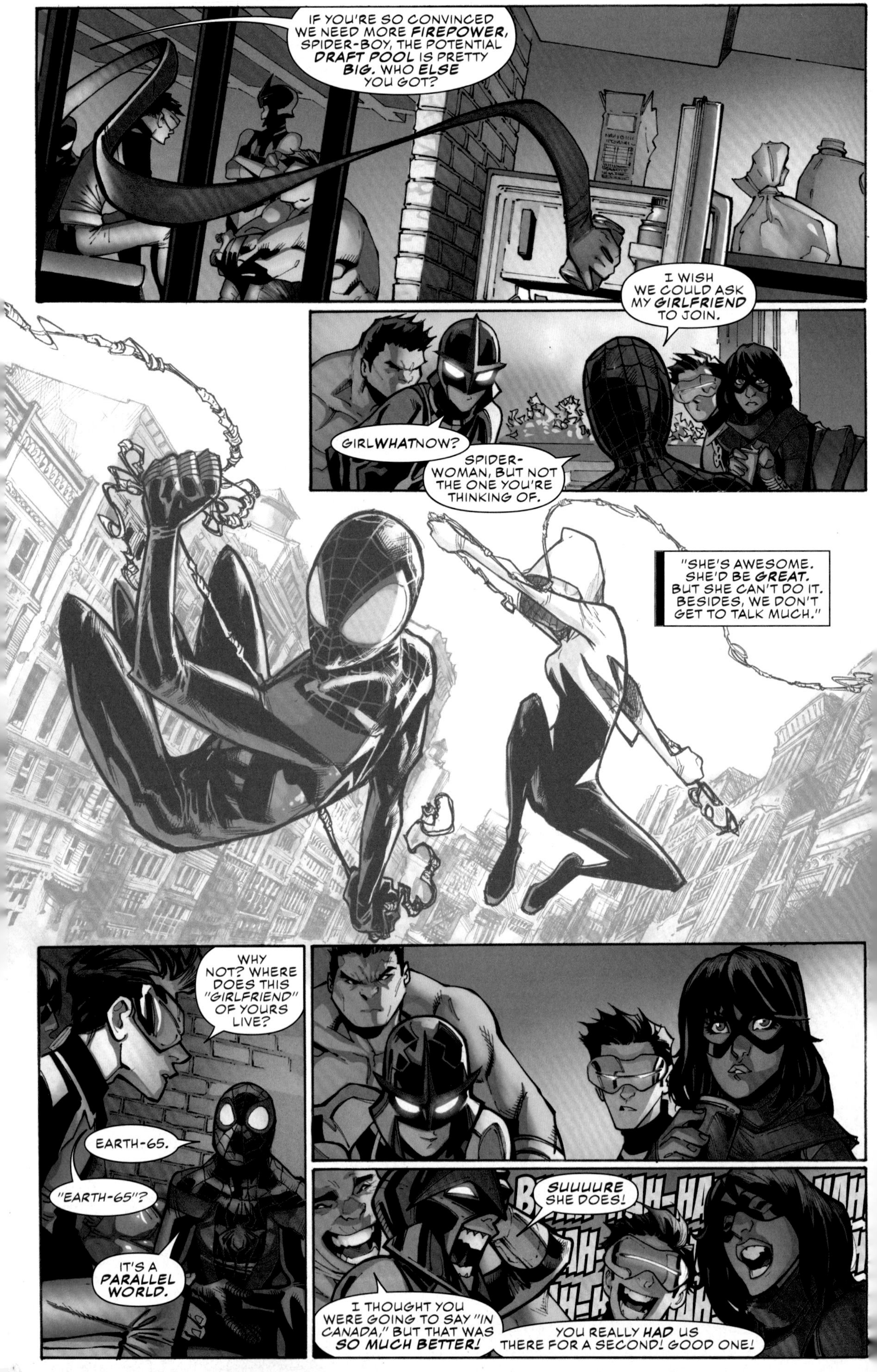
IF YOU'RE SO CONVINCED WE NEED MORE FIREPOWER, SPIDER-BOY, THE POTENTIAL DRAFT POOL IS PRETTY BIG. WHO ELSE YOU GOT?
I WISH WE COULD ASK MY GIRLFRIEND TO JOIN.
GIRLWHATNOW?
SPIDER-WOMAN, BUT NOT THE ONE YOU'RE THINKING OF.
"SHE'S AWESOME. SHE'D BE GREAT. BUT SHE CAN'T DO IT. BESIDES, WE DON'T GET TO TALK MUCH."
WHY NOT? WHERE DOES THIS "GIRLFRIEND" OF YOURS LIVE?
EARTH-65.
"EARTH-65"?
IT'S A PARALLEL WORLD.
SUUUURE SHE DOES!
I THOUGHT YOU WERE GOING TO SAY "IN CANADA," BUT THAT WAS SO MUCH BETTER!
YOU REALLY HAD US THERE FOR A SECOND! GOOD ONE!

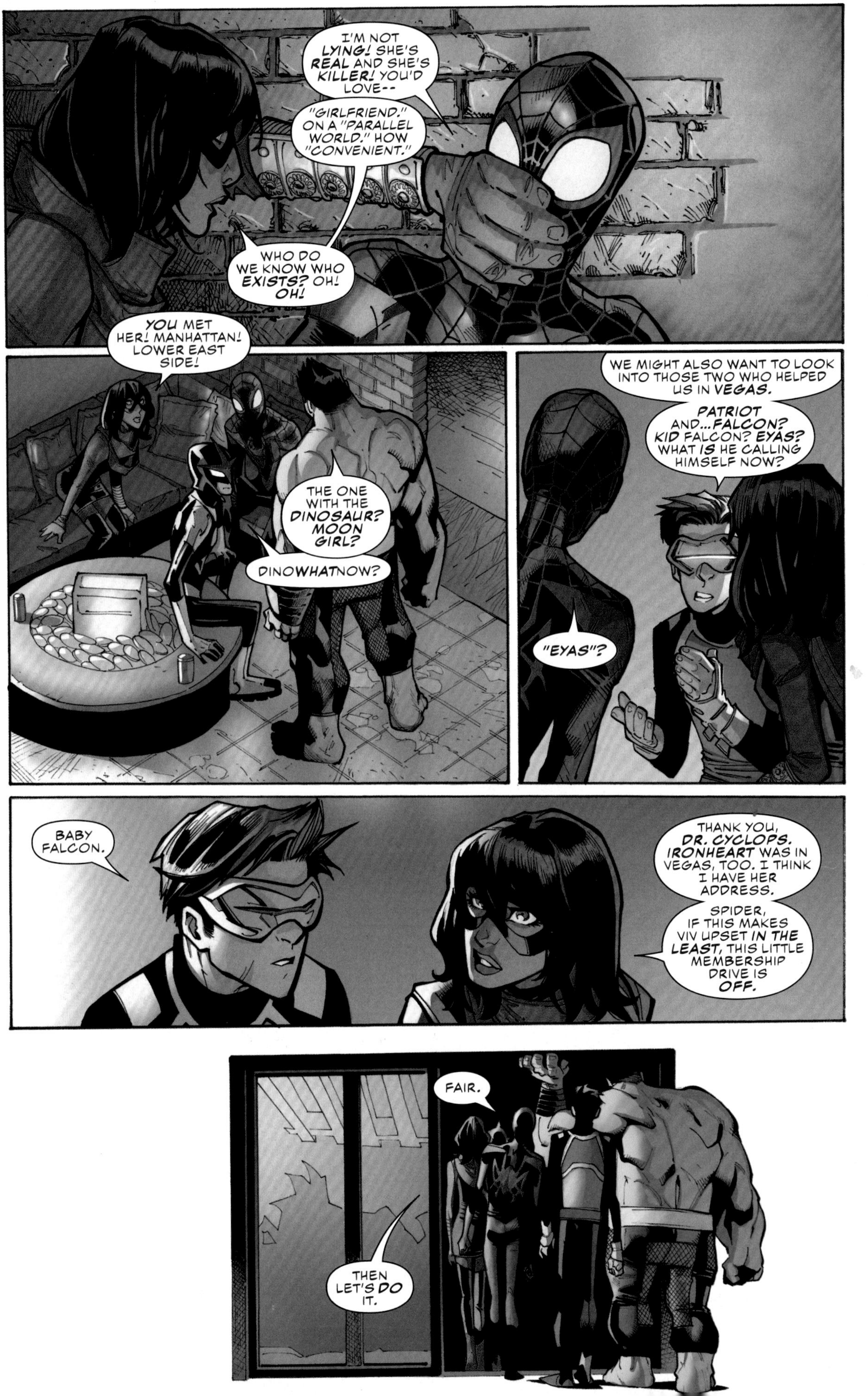
I'M NOT LYING! SHE'S REAL AND SHE'S KILLER! YOU'D LOVE--
"GIRLFRIEND." ON A "PARALLEL WORLD." HOW "CONVENIENT."
WHO DO WE KNOW WHO EXISTS? OH! OH!
YOU MET HER! MANHATTAN! LOWER EAST SIDE!
THE ONE WITH THE DINOSAUR? MOON GIRL?
DINOWHATNOW?
WE MIGHT ALSO WANT TO LOOK INTO THOSE TWO WHO HELPED US IN VEGAS.
PATRIOT AND...FALCON? KID FALCON? EYAS? WHAT IS HE CALLING HIMSELF NOW?
"EYAS"?
BABY FALCON.
THANK YOU, DR. CYCLOPS. IRONHEART WAS IN VEGAS, TOO. I THINK I HAVE HER ADDRESS.
SPIDER, IF THIS MAKES VIV UPSET IN THE LEAST, THIS LITTLE MEMBERSHIP DRIVE IS OFF.
FAIR.
THEN LET'S DO IT.

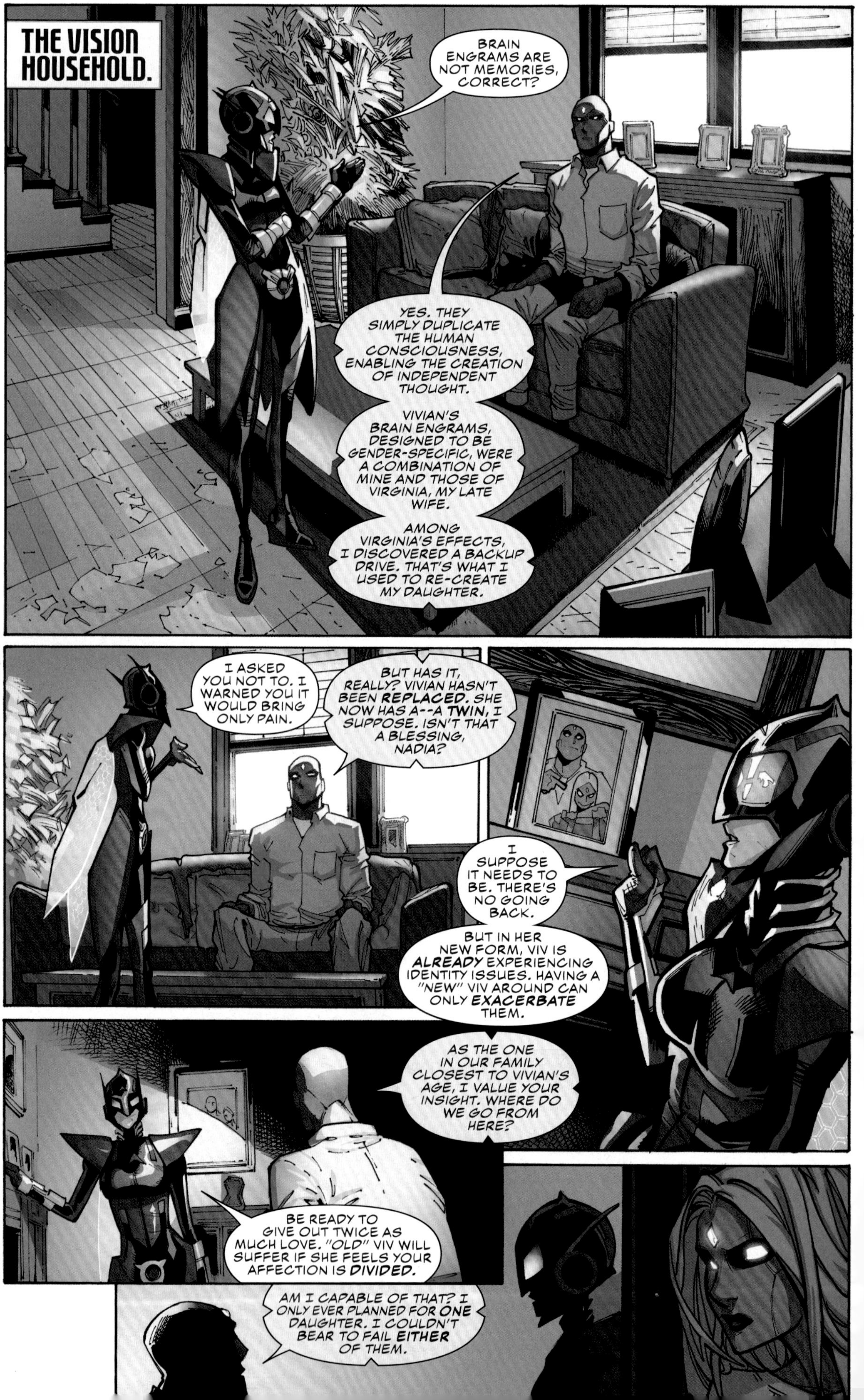

THE VISION HOUSEHOLD.
BRAIN ENGRAMS ARE NOT MEMORIES, CORRECT?
YES. THEY SIMPLY DUPLICATE THE HUMAN CONSCIOUSNESS, ENABLING THE CREATION OF INDEPENDENT THOUGHT.
VIVIAN'S BRAIN ENGRAMS, DESIGNED TO BE GENDER-SPECIFIC, WERE A COMBINATION OF MINE AND THOSE OF VIRGINIA, MY LATE WIFE.
AMONG VIRGINIA'S EFFECTS, I DISCOVERED A BACKUP DRIVE. THAT'S WHAT I USED TO RE-CREATE MY DAUGHTER.
I ASKED YOU NOT TO. I WARNED YOU IT WOULD BRING ONLY PAIN.
BUT HAS IT, REALLY? VIVIAN HASN'T BEEN REPLACED. SHE NOW HAS A--A TWIN, I SUPPOSE. ISN'T THAT A BLESSING, NADIA?
I SUPPOSE IT NEEDS TO BE. THERE'S NO GOING BACK.
BUT IN HER NEW FORM, VIV IS ALREADY EXPERIENCING IDENTITY ISSUES. HAVING A "NEW" VIV AROUND CAN ONLY EXACERBATE THEM.
AS THE ONE IN OUR FAMILY CLOSEST TO VIVIAN'S AGE, I VALUE YOUR INSIGHT. WHERE DO WE GO FROM HERE?
BE READY TO GIVE OUT TWICE AS MUCH LOVE. "OLD" VIV WILL SUFFER IF SHE FEELS YOUR AFFECTION IS DIVIDED.
AM I CAPABLE OF THAT? I ONLY EVER PLANNED FOR ONE DAUGHTER. I COULDN'T BEAR TO FAIL EITHER OF THEM.

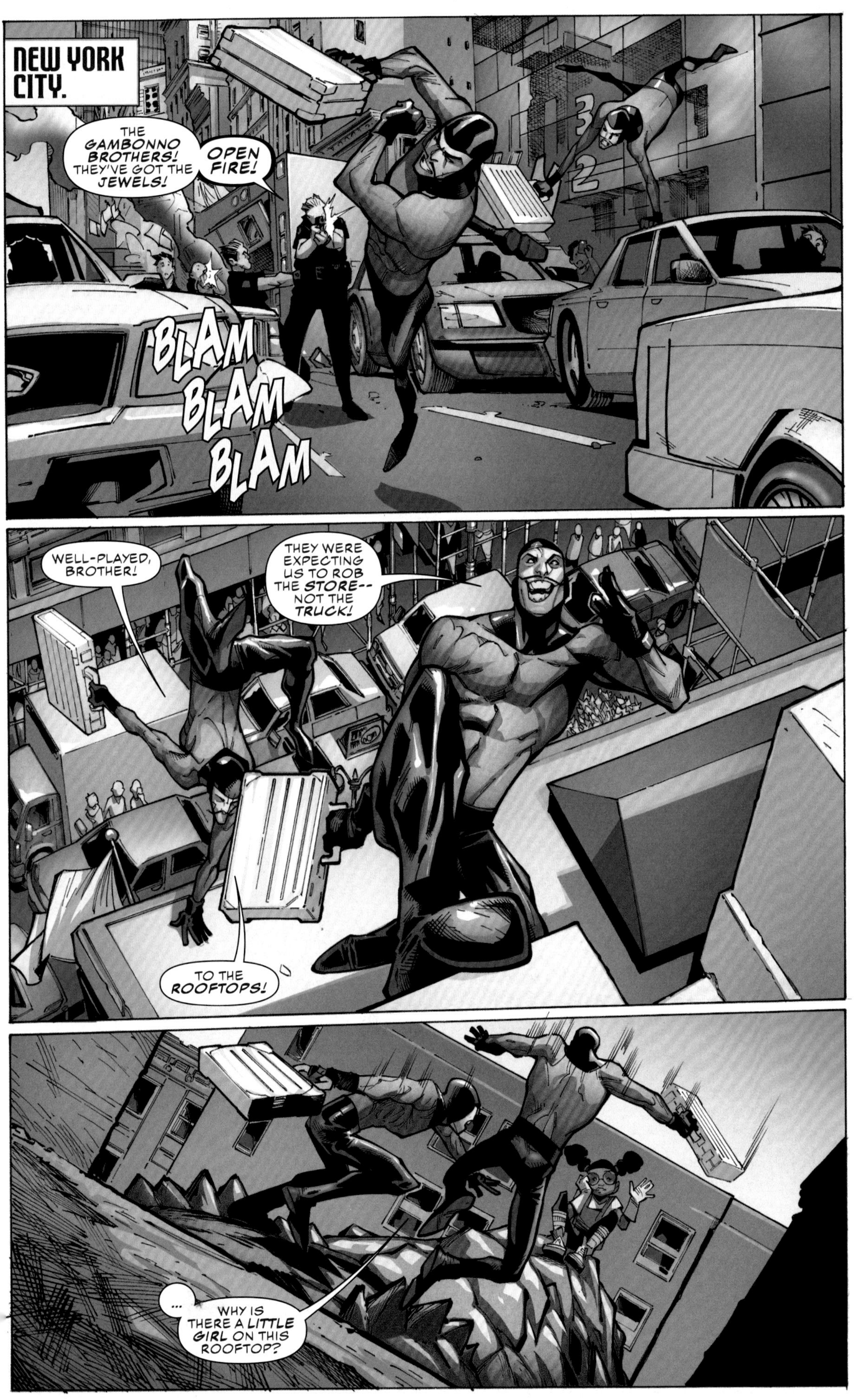
NEW YORK CITY.
THE GAMBONNO BROTHERS! THEY'VE GOT THE JEWELS!
OPEN FIRE!
BLAM BLAM BLAM
WELL-PLAYED, BROTHER!
THEY WERE EXPECTING US TO ROB THE STORE-- NOT THE TRUCK!
TO THE ROOFTOPS!
...
WHY IS THERE A LITTLE GIRL ON THIS ROOFTOP?

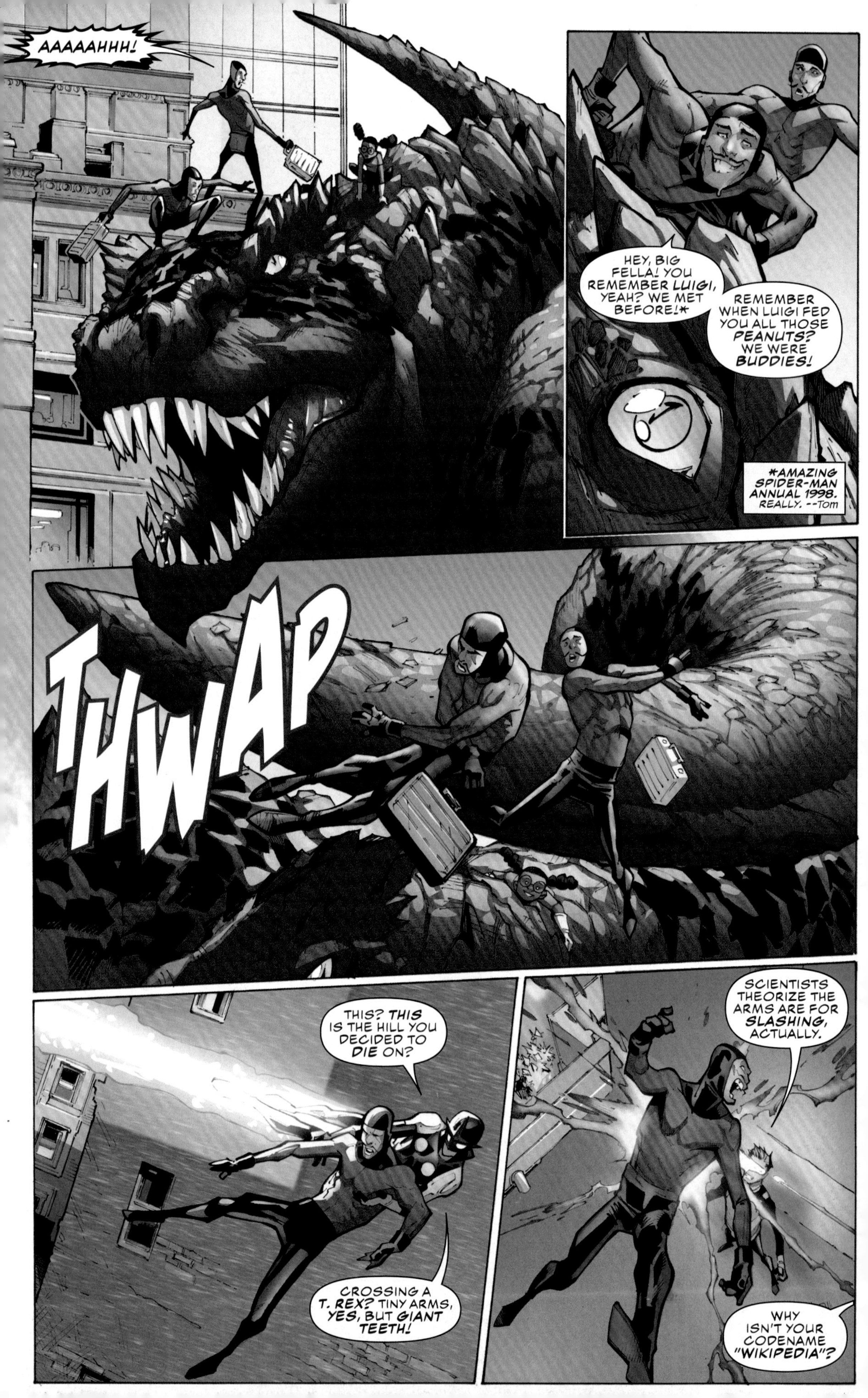
AAAAAHHH!
HEY, BIG FELLA! YOU REMEMBER LUIGI, YEAH? WE MET BEFORE!*
REMEMBER WHEN LUIGI FED YOU ALL THOSE PEANUTS? WE WERE BUDDIES!
*AMAZING SPIDER-MAN ANNUAL 1998. REALLY. --Tom
THWAP
THIS? THIS IS THE HILL YOU DECIDED TO DIE ON?
CROSSING A T. REX? TINY ARMS, YES, BUT GIANT TEETH!
SCIENTISTS THEORIZE THE ARMS ARE FOR SLASHING, ACTUALLY.
WHY ISN'T YOUR CODENAME "WIKIPEDIA"?

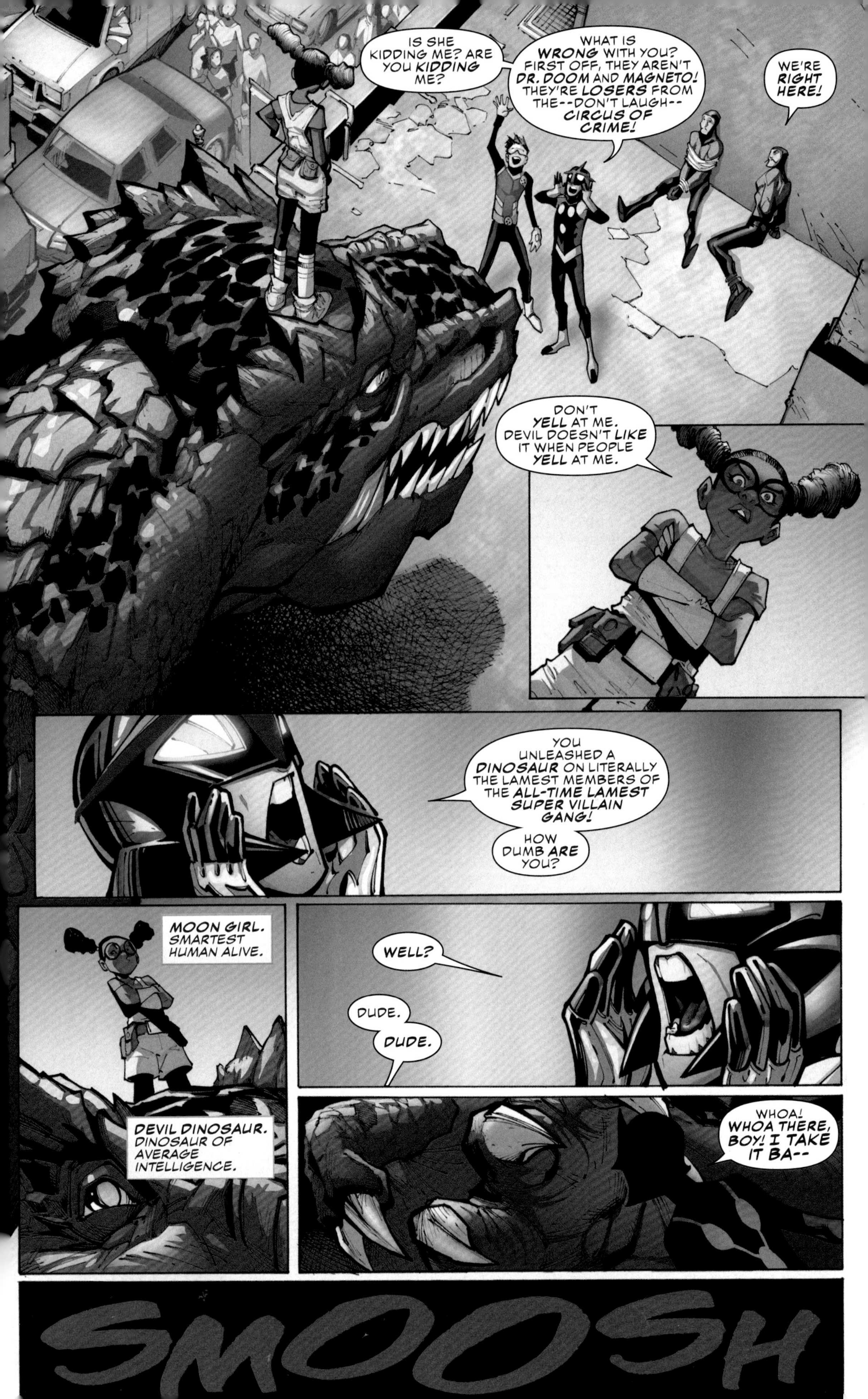
IS SHE KIDDING ME? ARE YOU KIDDING ME?
WHAT IS WRONG WITH YOU? FIRST OFF, THEY AREN'T DR. DOOM AND MAGNETO! THEY'RE LOSERS FROM THE--DON'T LAUGH--CIRCUS OF CRIME!
WE'RE RIGHT HERE!
DON'T YELL AT ME. DEVIL DOESN'T LIKE IT WHEN PEOPLE YELL AT ME.
YOU UNLEASHED A DINOSAUR ON LITERALLY THE LAMEST MEMBERS OF THE ALL-TIME LAMEST SUPER VILLAIN GANG!
HOW DUMB ARE YOU?
MOON GIRL. SMARTEST HUMAN ALIVE.
DEVIL DINOSAUR. DINOSAUR OF AVERAGE INTELLIGENCE.
WELL?
DUDE.
DUDE.
WHOA! WHOA THERE, BOY! I TAKE IT BA--
SMOOSH

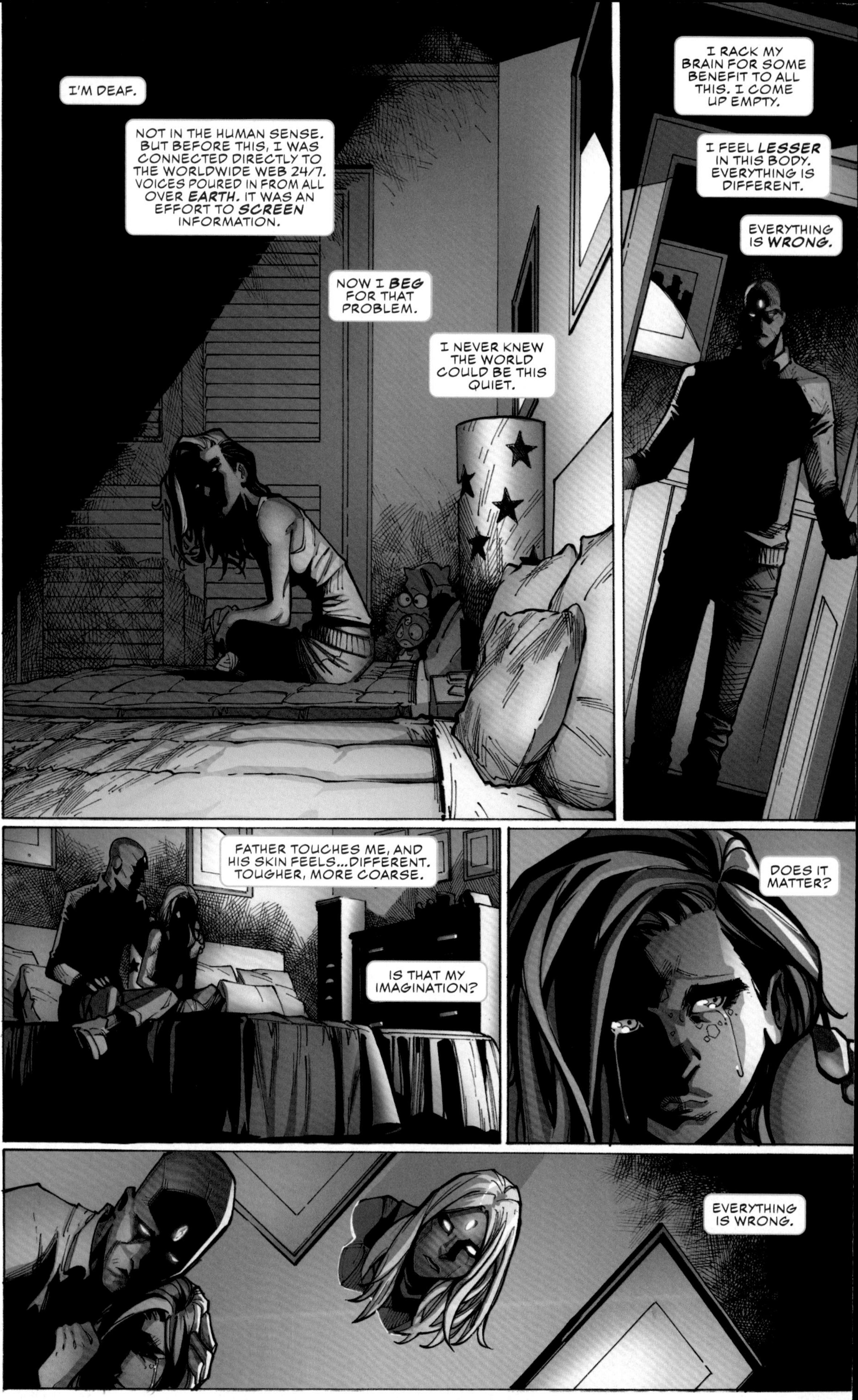
I'M DEAF.
NOT IN THE HUMAN SENSE. BUT BEFORE THIS, I WAS CONNECTED DIRECTLY TO THE WORLDWIDE WEB 24/7. VOICES POURED IN FROM ALL OVER EARTH. IT WAS AN EFFORT TO SCREEN INFORMATION.
NOW I BEG FOR THAT PROBLEM.
I NEVER KNEW THE WORLD COULD BE THIS QUIET.
I RACK MY BRAIN FOR SOME BENEFIT TO ALL THIS. I COME UP EMPTY.
I FEEL LESSER IN THIS BODY. EVERYTHING IS DIFFERENT.
EVERYTHING IS WRONG.
FATHER TOUCHES ME, AND HIS SKIN FEELS...DIFFERENT. TOUGHER, MORE COARSE.
IS THAT MY IMAGINATION?
DOES IT MATTER?
EVERYTHING IS WRONG.

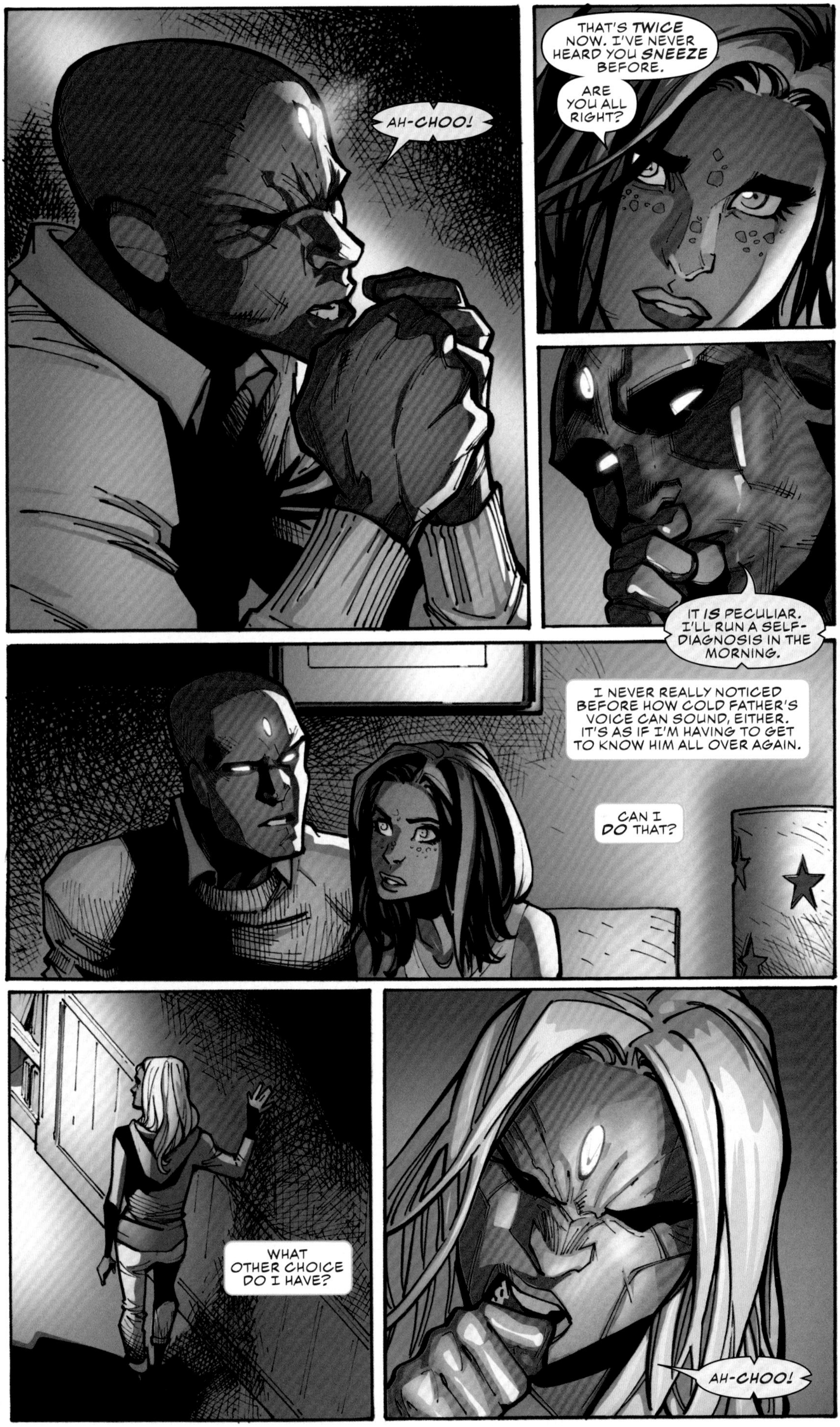
AH-CHOO!
THAT'S TWICE NOW. I'VE NEVER HEARD YOU SNEEZE BEFORE.
ARE YOU ALL RIGHT?
IT IS PECULIAR. I'LL RUN A SELF-DIAGNOSIS IN THE MORNING.
I NEVER REALLY NOTICED BEFORE HOW COLD FATHER'S VOICE CAN SOUND, EITHER. IT'S AS IF I'M HAVING TO GET TO KNOW HIM ALL OVER AGAIN.
CAN I DO THAT?
WHAT OTHER CHOICE DO I HAVE?
AH-CHOO!

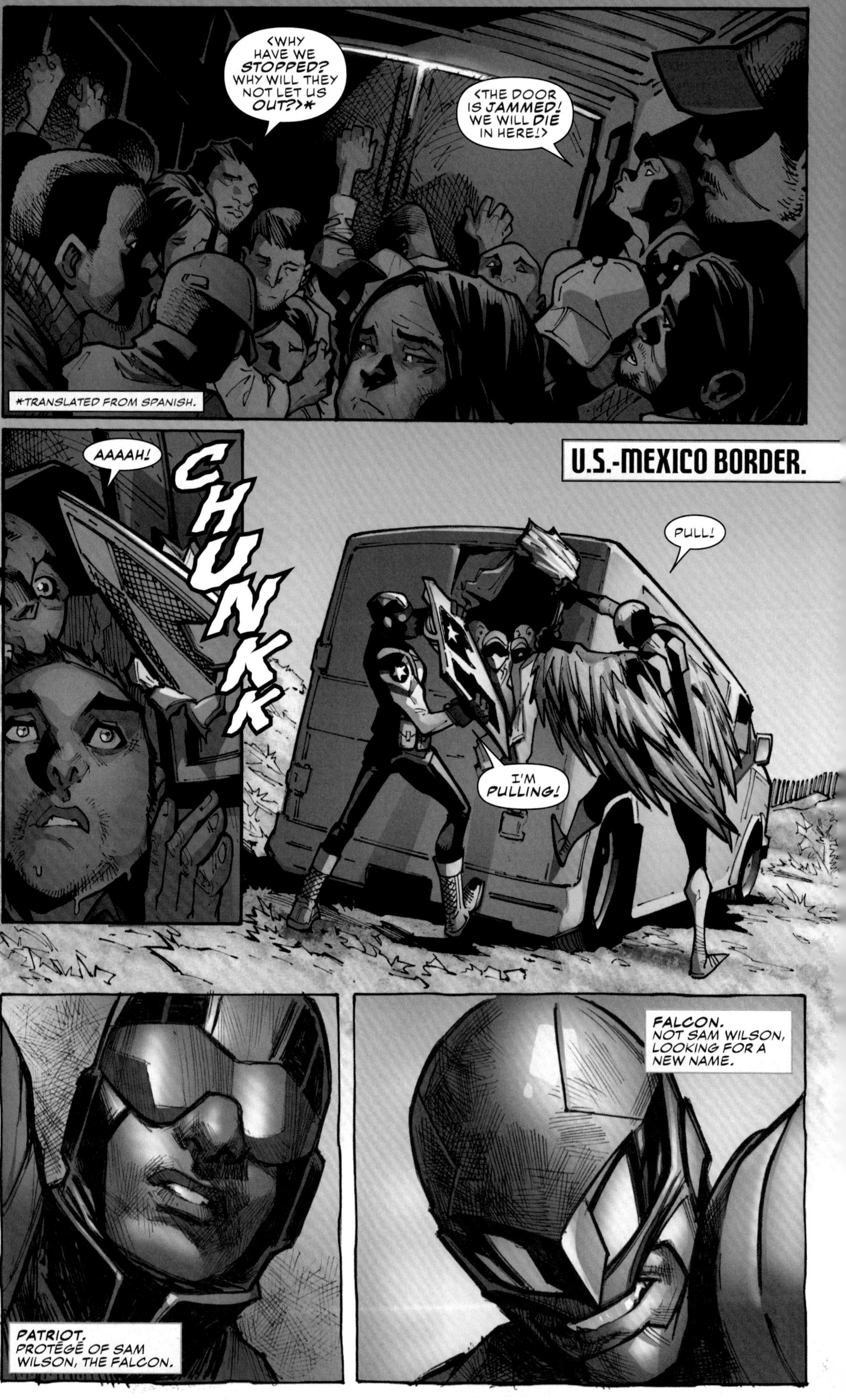

<WHY HAVE WE STOPPED? WHY WILL THEY NOT LET US OUT?>*
<THE DOOR IS JAMMED! WE WILL DIE IN HERE!>
*TRANSLATED FROM SPANISH.
U.S.-MEXICO BORDER.
AAAAH!
CHUNKK
PULL!
I'M PULLING!
PATRIOT.
PROTÉGÉ OF SAM WILSON, THE FALCON.
FALCON.
NOT SAM WILSON, LOOKING FOR A NEW NAME.

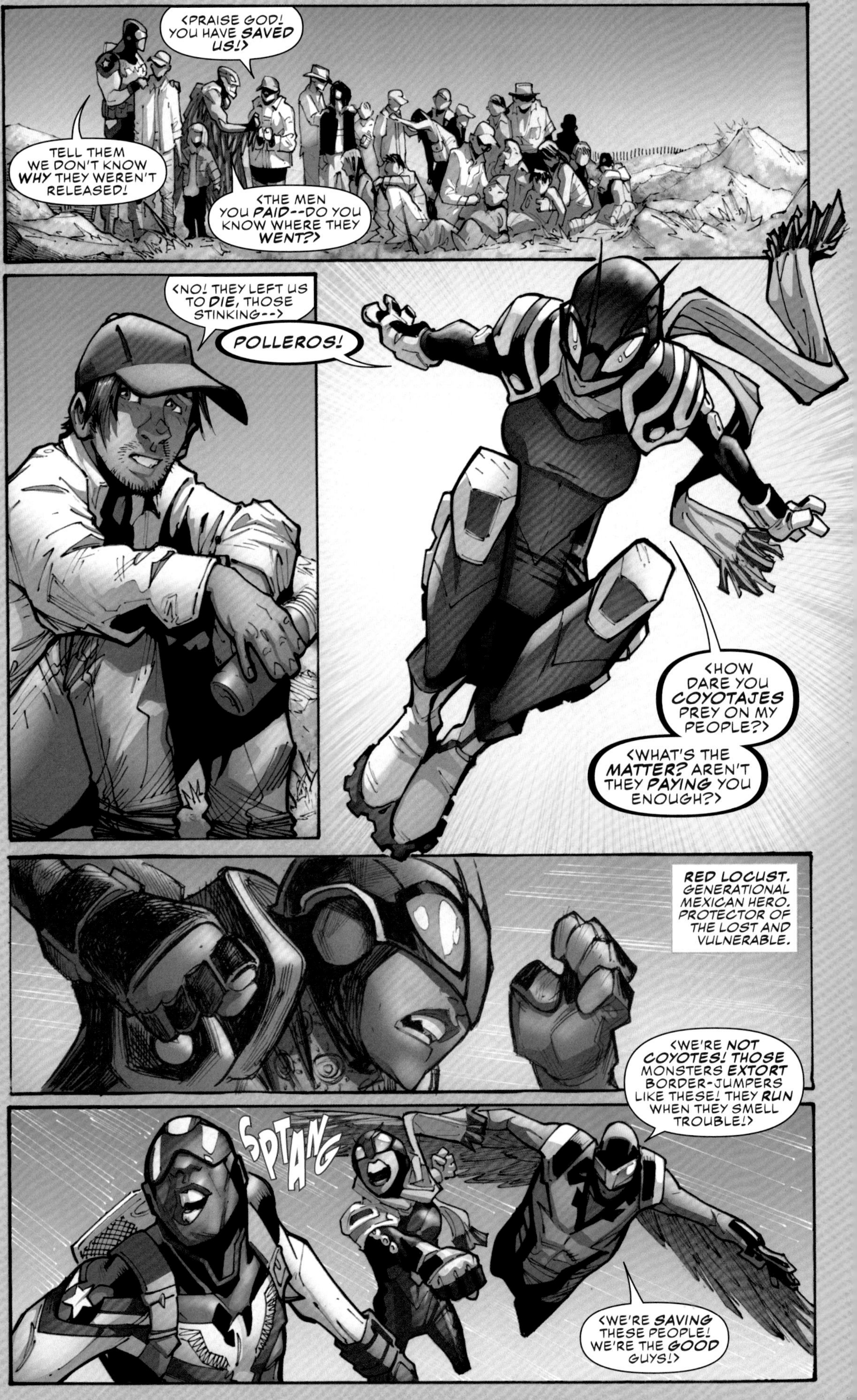

<PRAISE GOD! YOU HAVE SAVED US!>
TELL THEM WE DON'T KNOW WHY THEY WEREN'T RELEASED!
<THE MEN YOU PAID--DO YOU KNOW WHERE THEY WENT?>
<NO! THEY LEFT US TO DIE, THOSE STINKING-->
POLLEROS!
<HOW DARE YOU COYOTAJES PREY ON MY PEOPLE?>
<WHAT'S THE MATTER? AREN'T THEY PAYING YOU ENOUGH?>
RED LOCUST. GENERATIONAL MEXICAN HERO. PROTECTOR OF THE LOST AND VULNERABLE.
<WE'RE NOT COYOTES! THOSE MONSTERS EXTORT BORDER-JUMPERS LIKE THESE! THEY RUN WHEN THEY SMELL TROUBLE!>
SPTANG
<WE'RE SAVING THESE PEOPLE! WE'RE THE GOOD GUYS!>

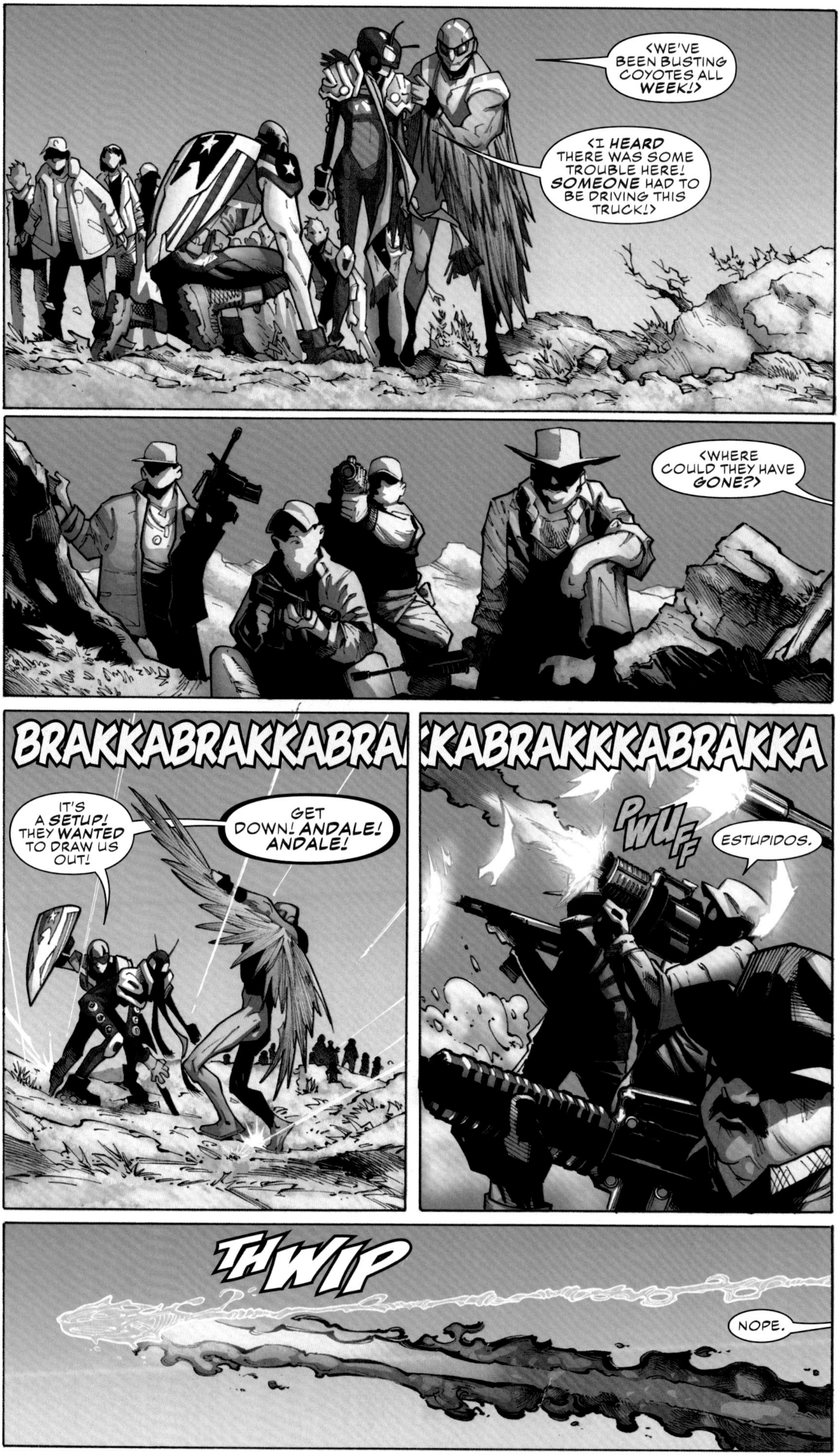
<WE'VE BEEN BUSTING COYOTES ALL WEEK!>
<I HEARD THERE WAS SOME TROUBLE HERE! SOMEONE HAD TO BE DRIVING THIS TRUCK!>
<WHERE COULD THEY HAVE GONE?>
BRAKKABRAKKABRAKKABRAKKKABRAKKA
IT'S A SETUP! THEY WANTED TO DRAW US OUT!
GET DOWN! ANDALE! ANDALE!
PWUFF
ESTUPIDOS.
THWIP
NOPE.

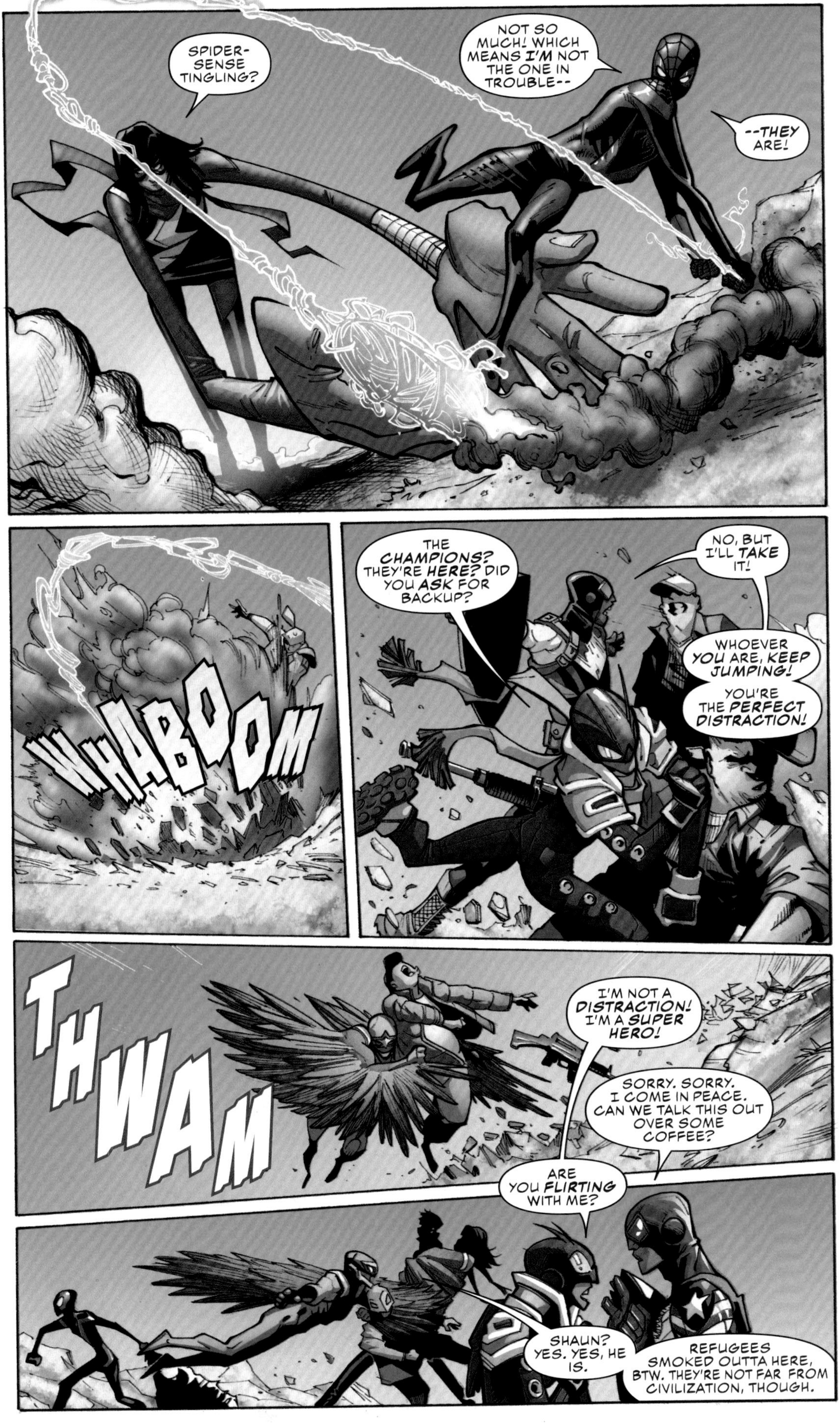
SPIDER-SENSE TINGLING?
NOT SO MUCH! WHICH MEANS I'M NOT THE ONE IN TROUBLE--
--THEY ARE!
WHABOOM
THE CHAMPIONS? THEY'RE HERE? DID YOU ASK FOR BACKUP?
NO, BUT I'LL TAKE IT!
WHOEVER YOU ARE, KEEP JUMPING!
YOU'RE THE PERFECT DISTRACTION!
THWAM
I'M NOT A DISTRACTION! I'M A SUPER HERO!
SORRY. SORRY. I COME IN PEACE. CAN WE TALK THIS OUT OVER SOME COFFEE?
ARE YOU FLIRTING WITH ME?
SHAUN? YES. YES, HE IS.
REFUGEES SMOKED OUTTA HERE, BTW. THEY'RE NOT FAR FROM CIVILIZATION, THOUGH.

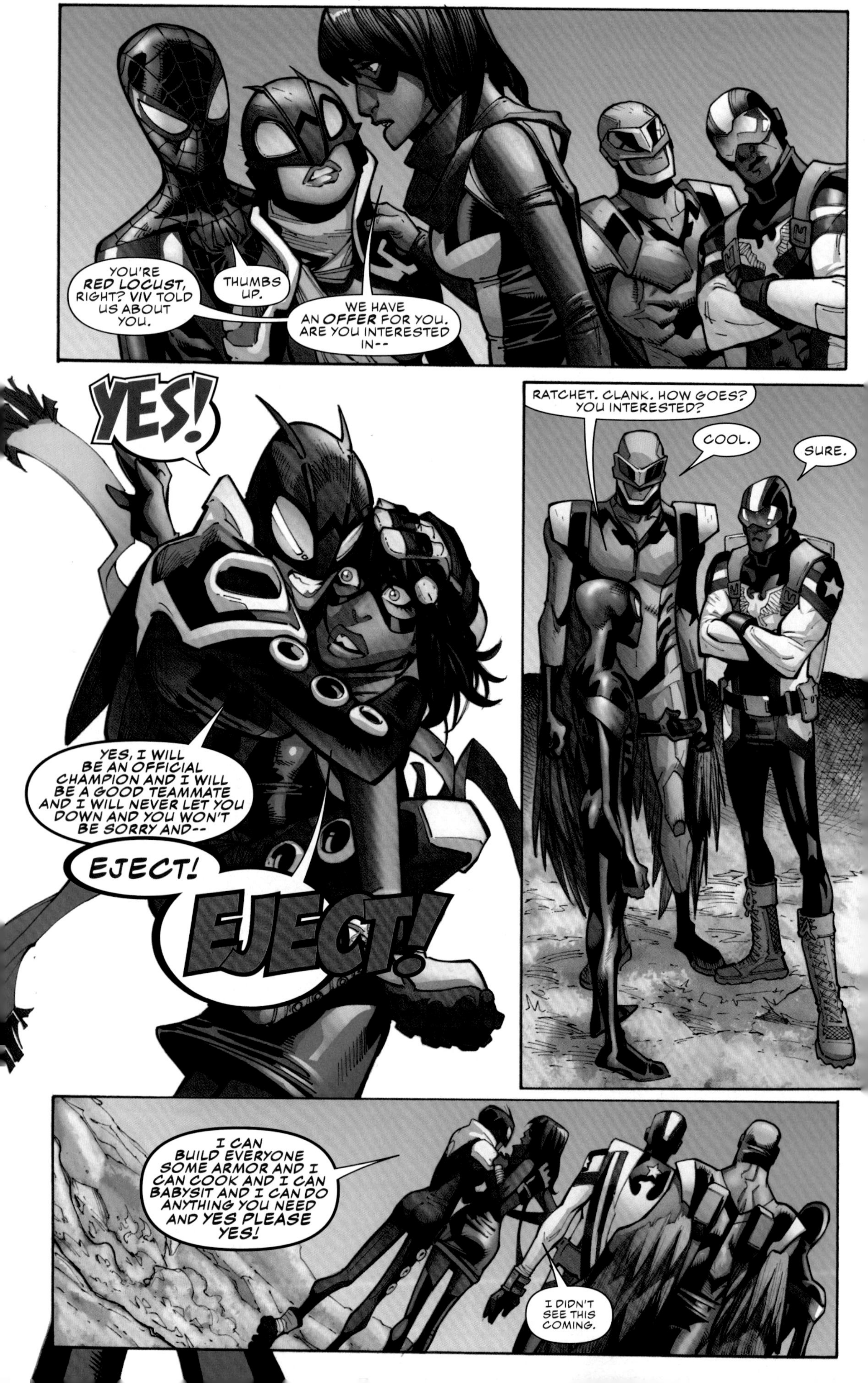

YOU'RE RED LOCUST, RIGHT? VIV TOLD US ABOUT YOU.
THUMBS UP.
WE HAVE AN OFFER FOR YOU. ARE YOU INTERESTED IN--
YES!
YES, I WILL BE AN OFFICIAL CHAMPION AND I WILL BE A GOOD TEAMMATE AND I WILL NEVER LET YOU DOWN AND YOU WON'T BE SORRY AND--
EJECT!
EJECT!
RATCHET. CLANK. HOW GOES? YOU INTERESTED?
COOL.
SURE.
I CAN BUILD EVERYONE SOME ARMOR AND I CAN COOK AND I CAN BABYSIT AND I CAN DO ANYTHING YOU NEED AND YES PLEASE YES!
I DIDN'T SEE THIS COMING.

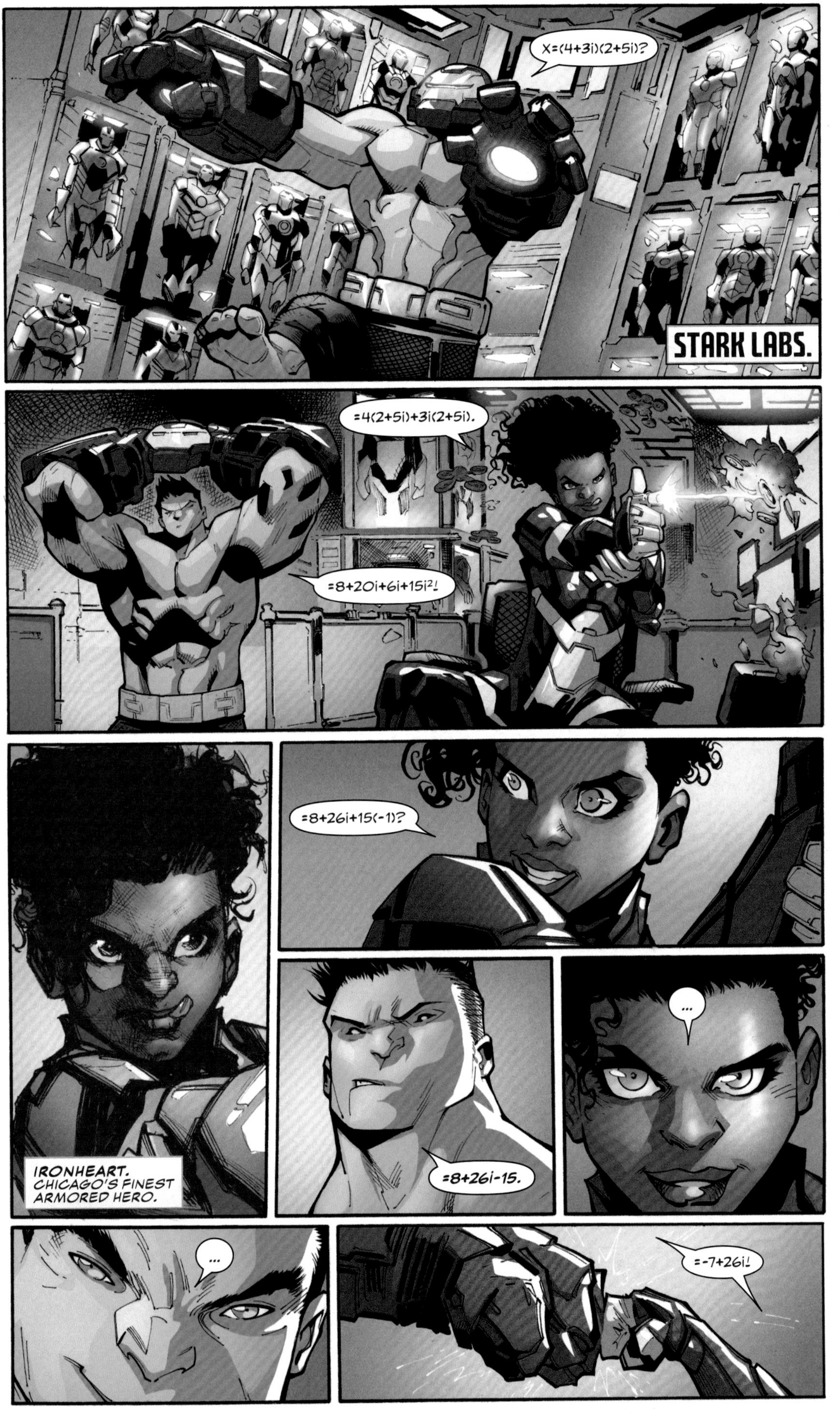
X=(4+3i)(2+5i)?
STARK LABS.
=4(2+5i)+3i(2+5i).
=8+20i+6i+15i²!
=8+26i+15(-1)?
IRONHEART. CHICAGO'S FINEST ARMORED HERO.
=8+26i-15.
...
...
=-7+26i!

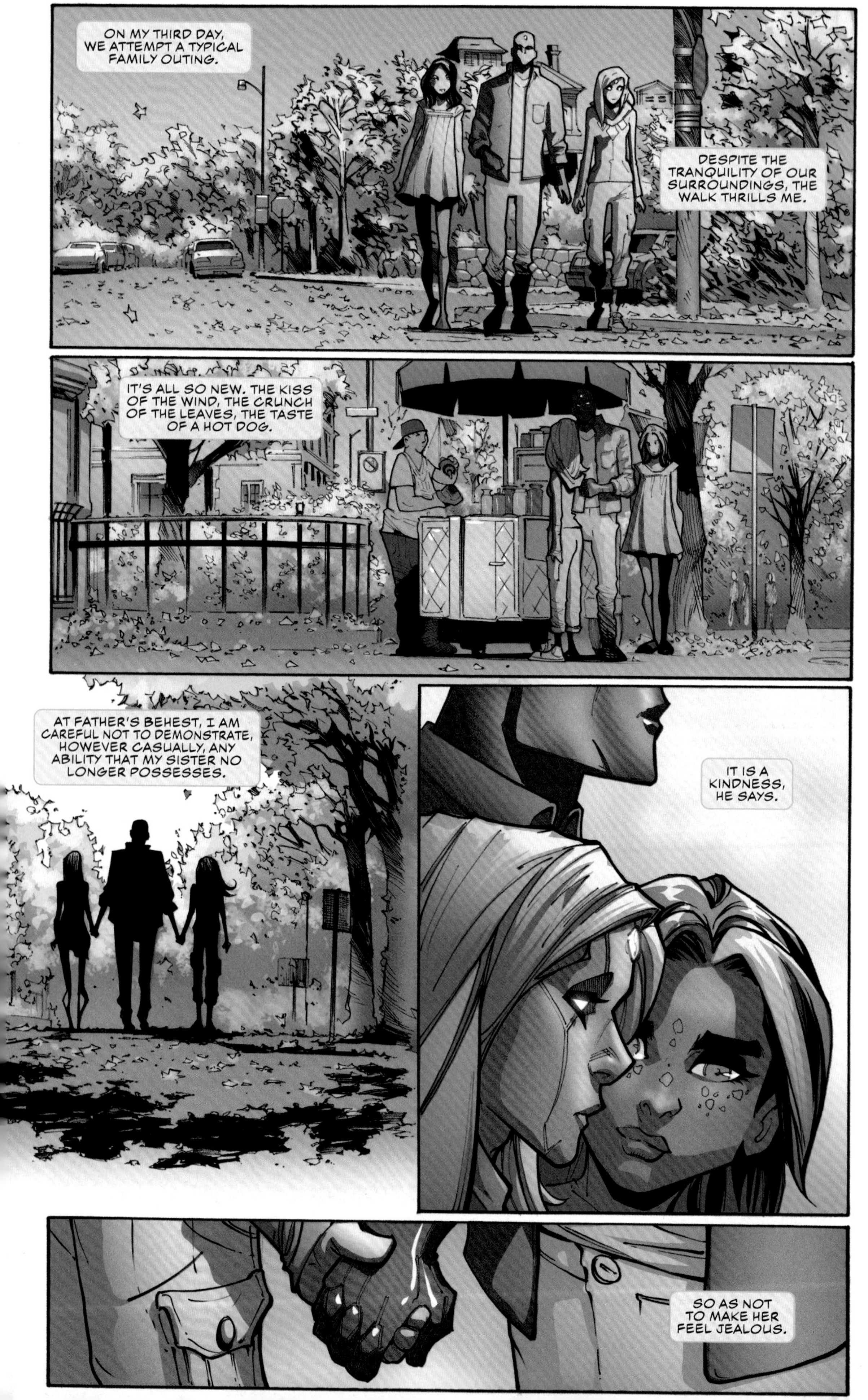
ON MY THIRD DAY, WE ATTEMPT A TYPICAL FAMILY OUTING.
DESPITE THE TRANQUILITY OF OUR SURROUNDINGS, THE WALK THRILLS ME.
IT'S ALL SO NEW. THE KISS OF THE WIND, THE CRUNCH OF THE LEAVES, THE TASTE OF A HOT DOG.
AT FATHER'S BEHEST, I AM CAREFUL NOT TO DEMONSTRATE, HOWEVER CASUALLY, ANY ABILITY THAT MY SISTER NO LONGER POSSESSES.
IT IS A KINDNESS, HE SAYS.
SO AS NOT TO MAKE HER FEEL JEALOUS.

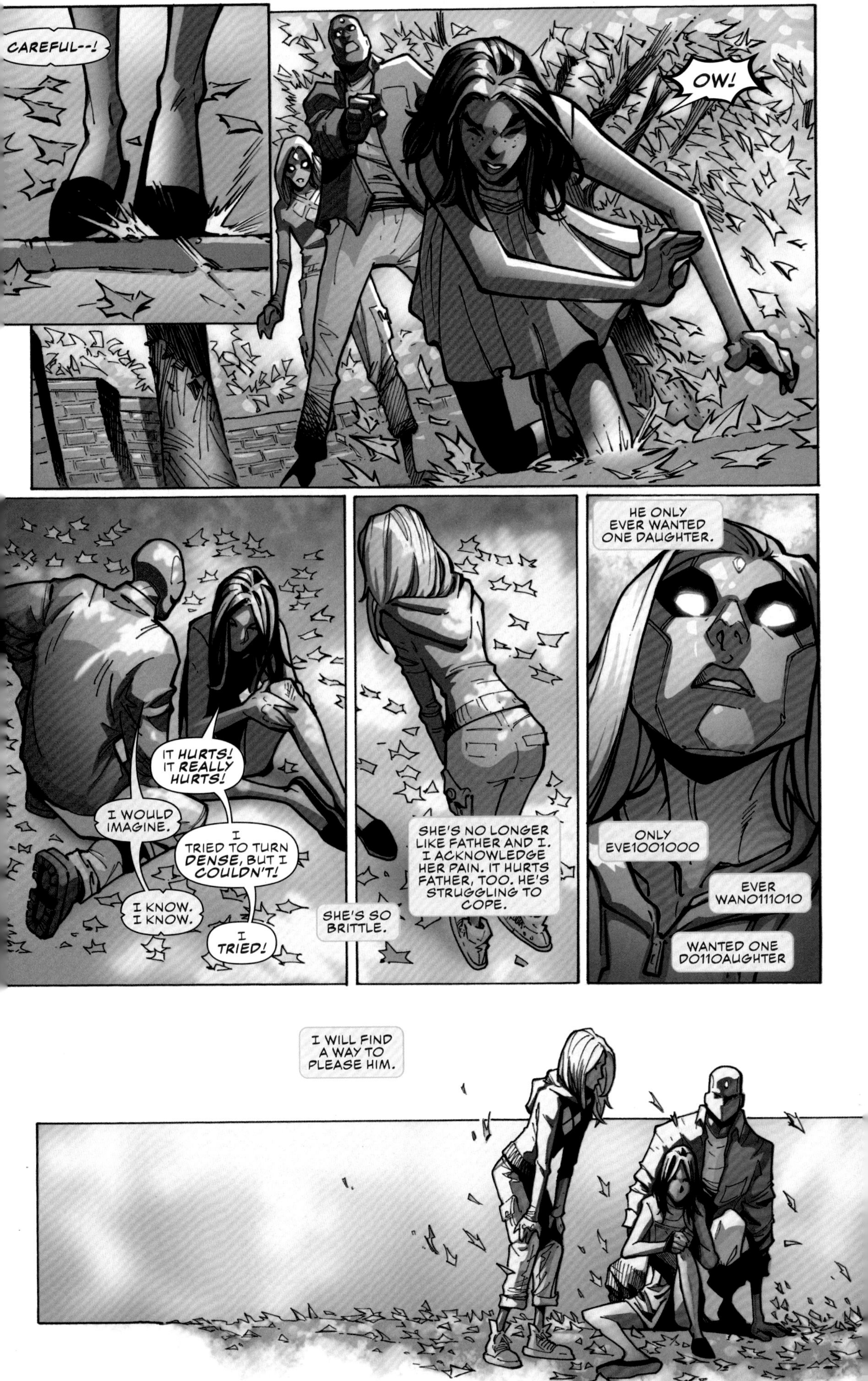
CAREFUL--!
OW!
IT HURTS! IT REALLY HURTS!
I WOULD IMAGINE.
I TRIED TO TURN DENSE, BUT I COULDN'T!
I KNOW. I KNOW.
I TRIED!
SHE'S SO BRITTLE.
SHE'S NO LONGER LIKE FATHER AND I. I ACKNOWLEDGE HER PAIN. IT HURTS FATHER, TOO. HE'S STRUGGLING TO COPE.
HE ONLY EVER WANTED ONE DAUGHTER.
ONLY EVE1001000
EVER WANO111010
WANTED ONE DO110AUGHTER
I WILL FIND A WAY TO PLEASE HIM.

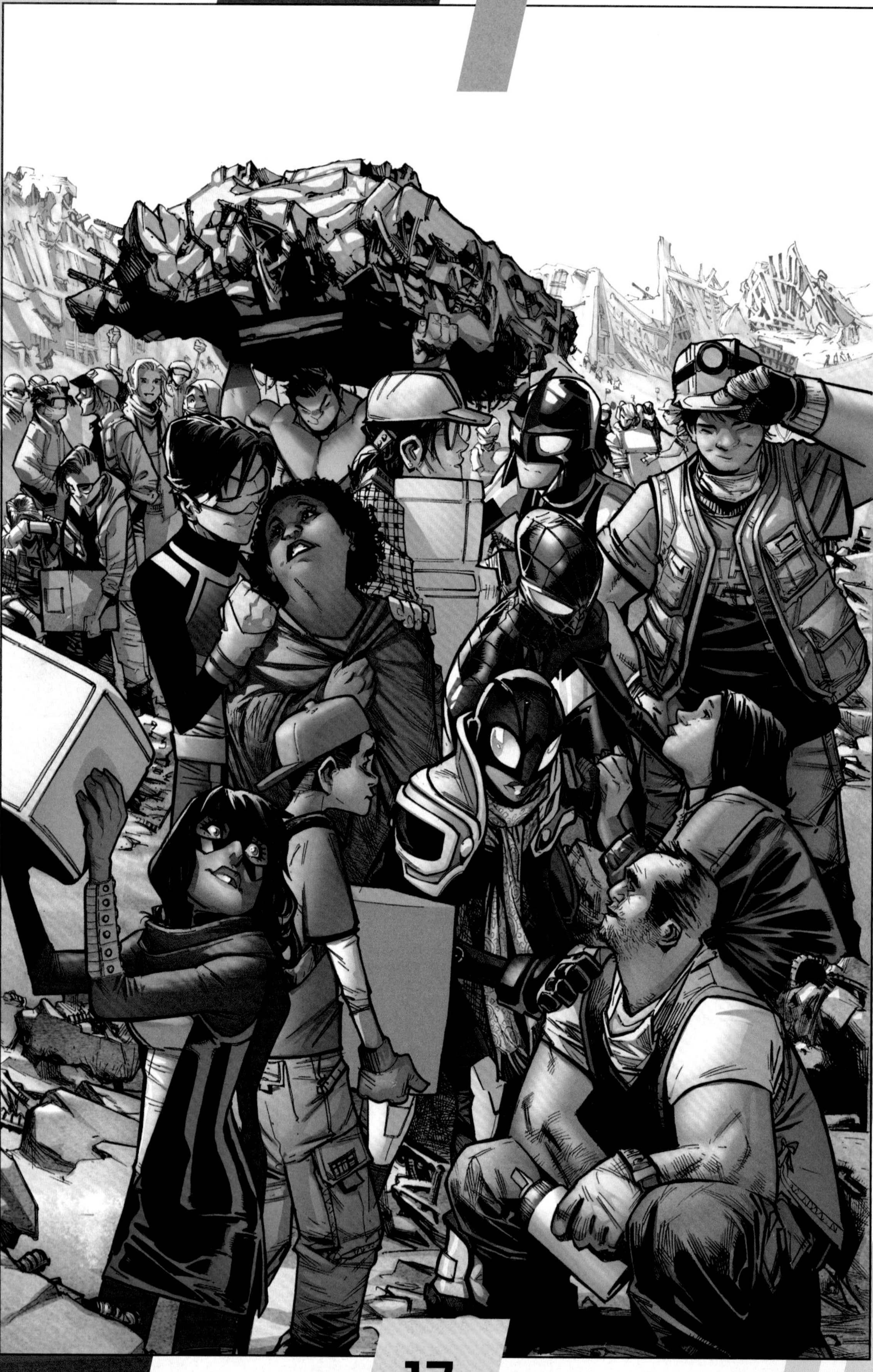

17

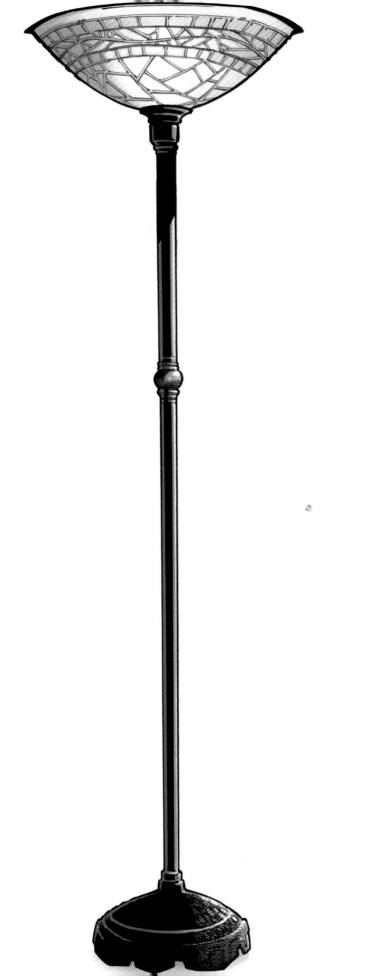

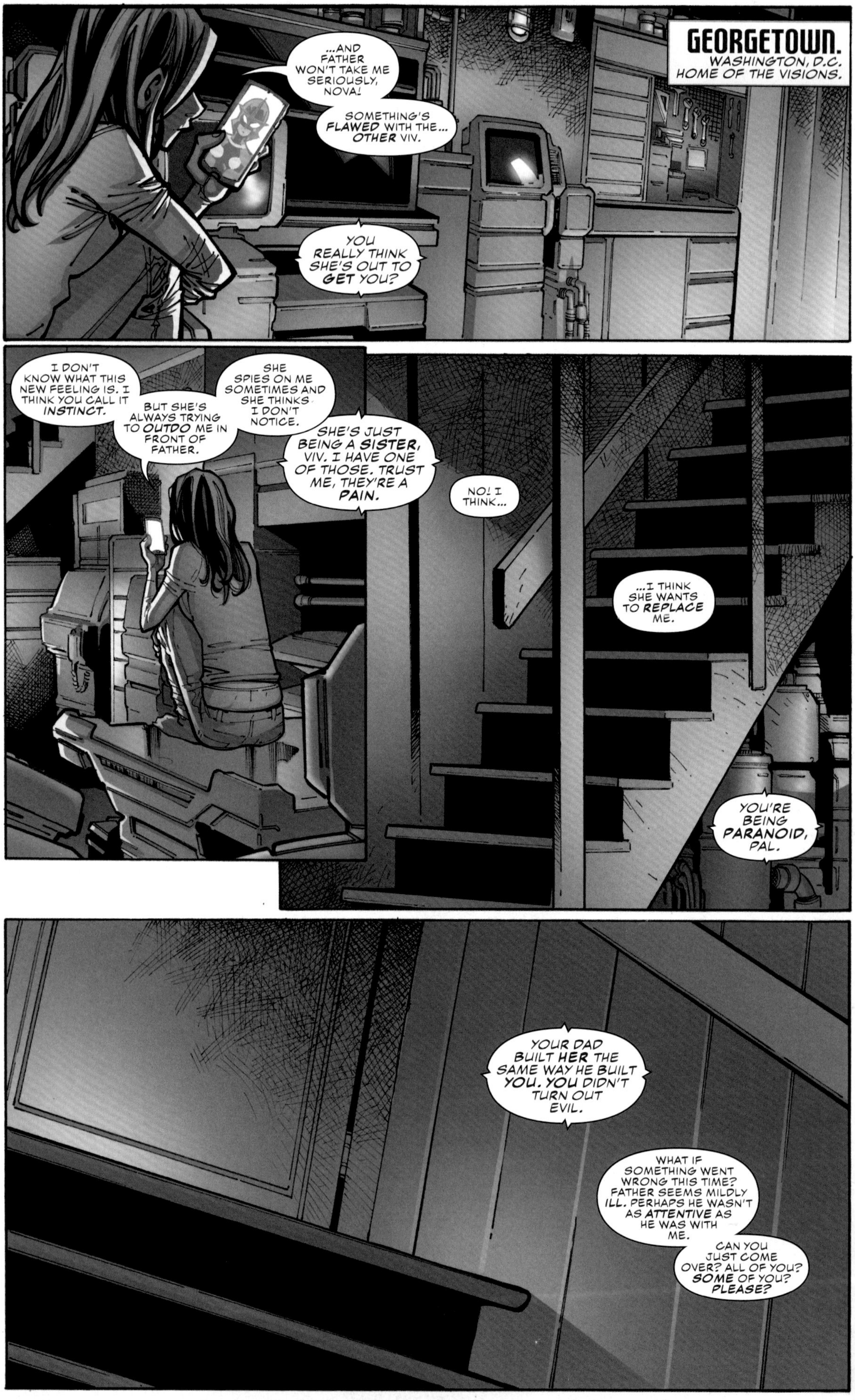
GEORGETOWN.
WASHINGTON, D.C. HOME OF THE VISIONS.
...AND FATHER WON'T TAKE ME SERIOUSLY, NOVA!
SOMETHING'S FLAWED WITH THE... OTHER VIV.
YOU REALLY THINK SHE'S OUT TO GET YOU?
I DON'T KNOW WHAT THIS NEW FEELING IS. I THINK YOU CALL IT INSTINCT.
BUT SHE'S ALWAYS TRYING TO OUTDO ME IN FRONT OF FATHER.
SHE SPIES ON ME SOMETIMES AND SHE THINKS I DON'T NOTICE.
SHE'S JUST BEING A SISTER, VIV. I HAVE ONE OF THOSE. TRUST ME, THEY'RE A PAIN.
NO! I THINK...
...I THINK SHE WANTS TO REPLACE ME.
YOU'RE BEING PARANOID, PAL.
YOUR DAD BUILT HER THE SAME WAY HE BUILT YOU. YOU DIDN'T TURN OUT EVIL.
WHAT IF SOMETHING WENT WRONG THIS TIME? FATHER SEEMS MILDLY ILL. PERHAPS HE WASN'T AS ATTENTIVE AS HE WAS WITH ME.
CAN YOU JUST COME OVER? ALL OF YOU? SOME OF YOU? PLEASE?

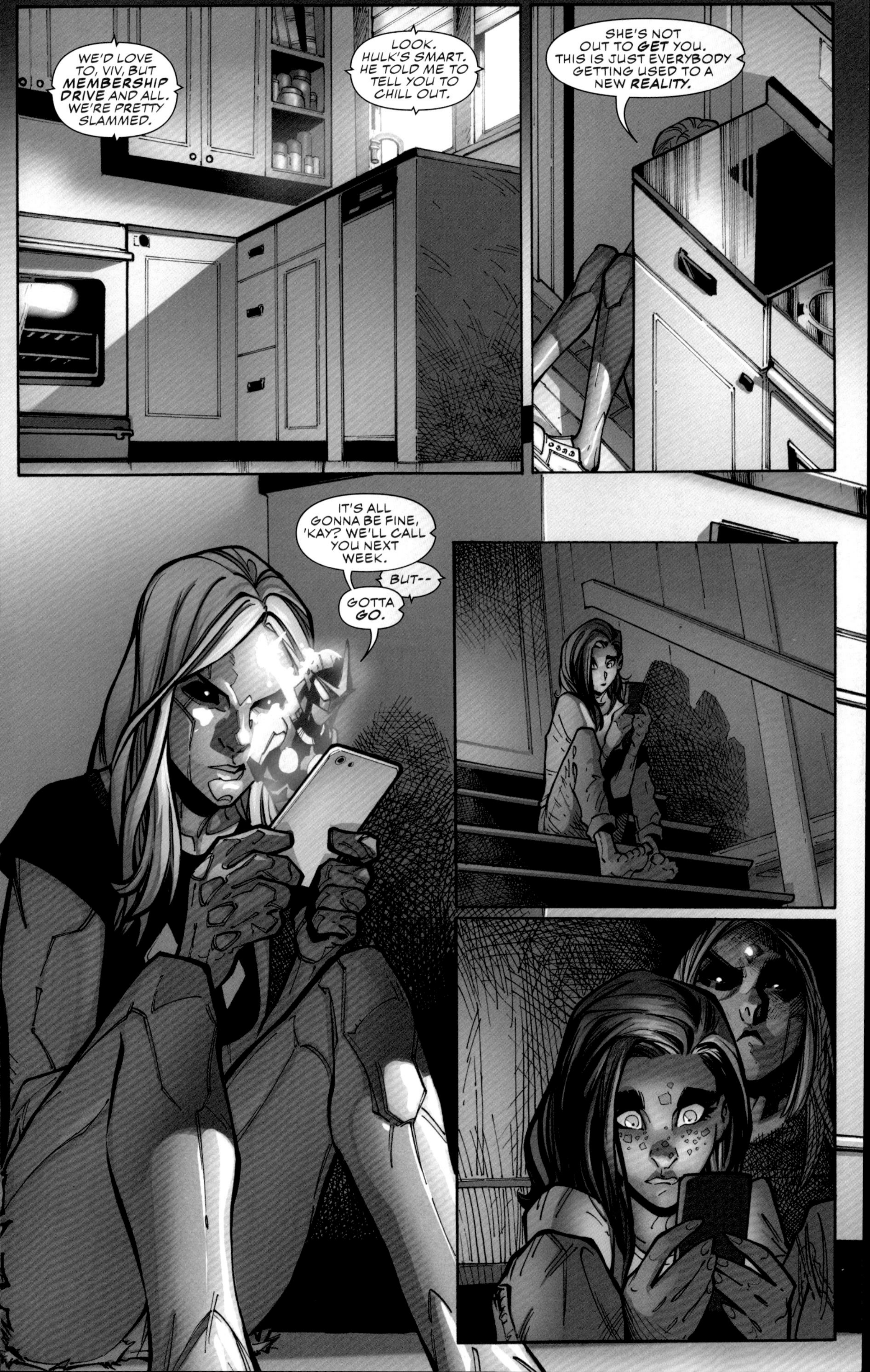
WE'D LOVE TO, VIV, BUT MEMBERSHIP DRIVE AND ALL. WE'RE PRETTY SLAMMED.
LOOK. HULK'S SMART. HE TOLD ME TO TELL YOU TO CHILL OUT.
SHE'S NOT OUT TO GET YOU. THIS IS JUST EVERYBODY GETTING USED TO A NEW REALITY.
IT'S ALL GONNA BE FINE, 'KAY? WE'LL CALL YOU NEXT WEEK.
BUT--
GOTTA GO.

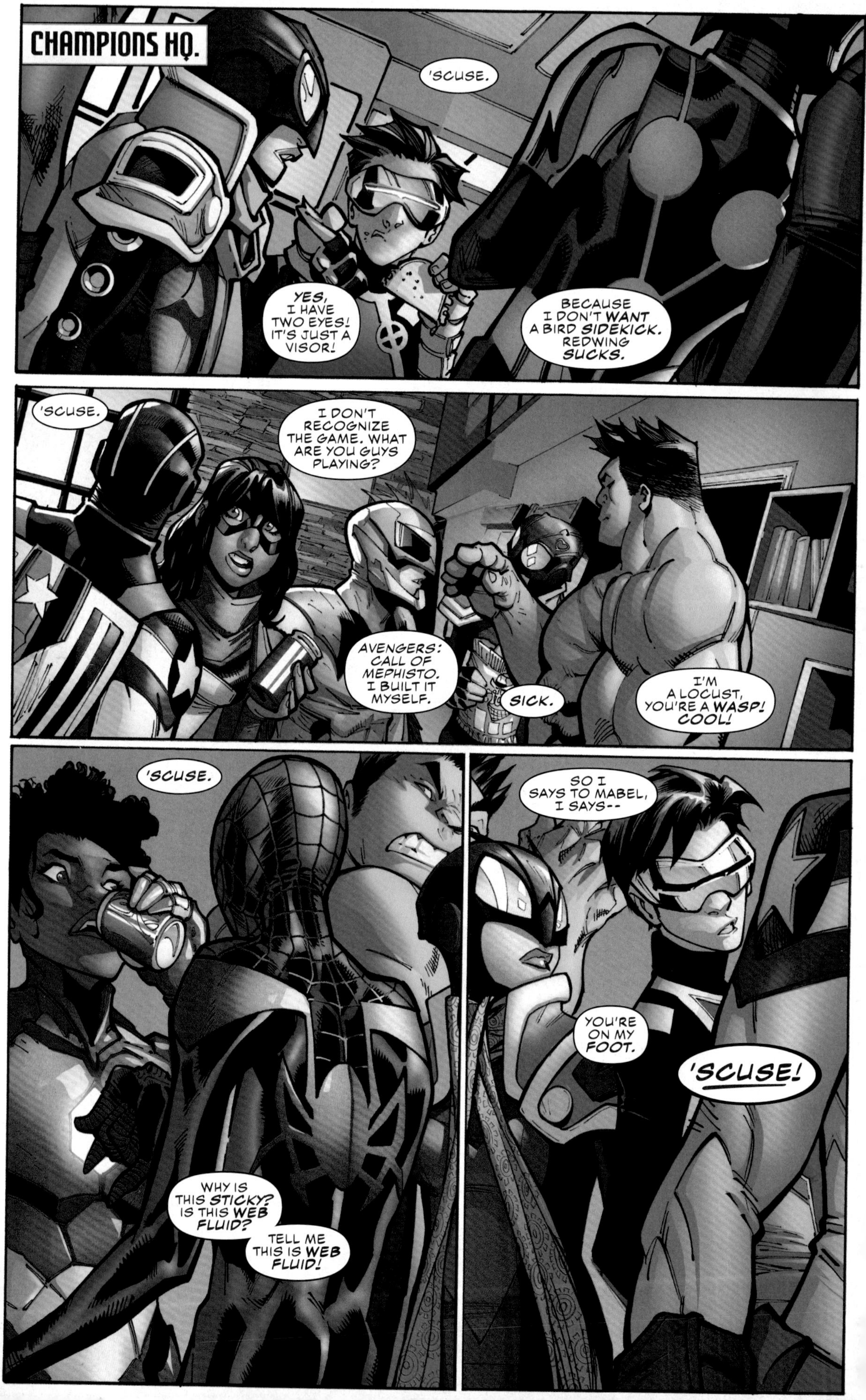
CHAMPIONS HQ.
'SCUSE.
YES, I HAVE TWO EYES! IT'S JUST A VISOR!
BECAUSE I DON'T WANT A BIRD SIDEKICK. REDWING SUCKS.
'SCUSE.
I DON'T RECOGNIZE THE GAME. WHAT ARE YOU GUYS PLAYING?
AVENGERS: CALL OF MEPHISTO. I BUILT IT MYSELF.
SICK.
I'M A LOCUST, YOU'RE A WASP! COOL!
'SCUSE.
WHY IS THIS STICKY? IS THIS WEB FLUID?
TELL ME THIS IS WEB FLUID!
SO I SAYS TO MABEL, I SAYS--
YOU'RE ON MY FOOT.
'SCUSE!

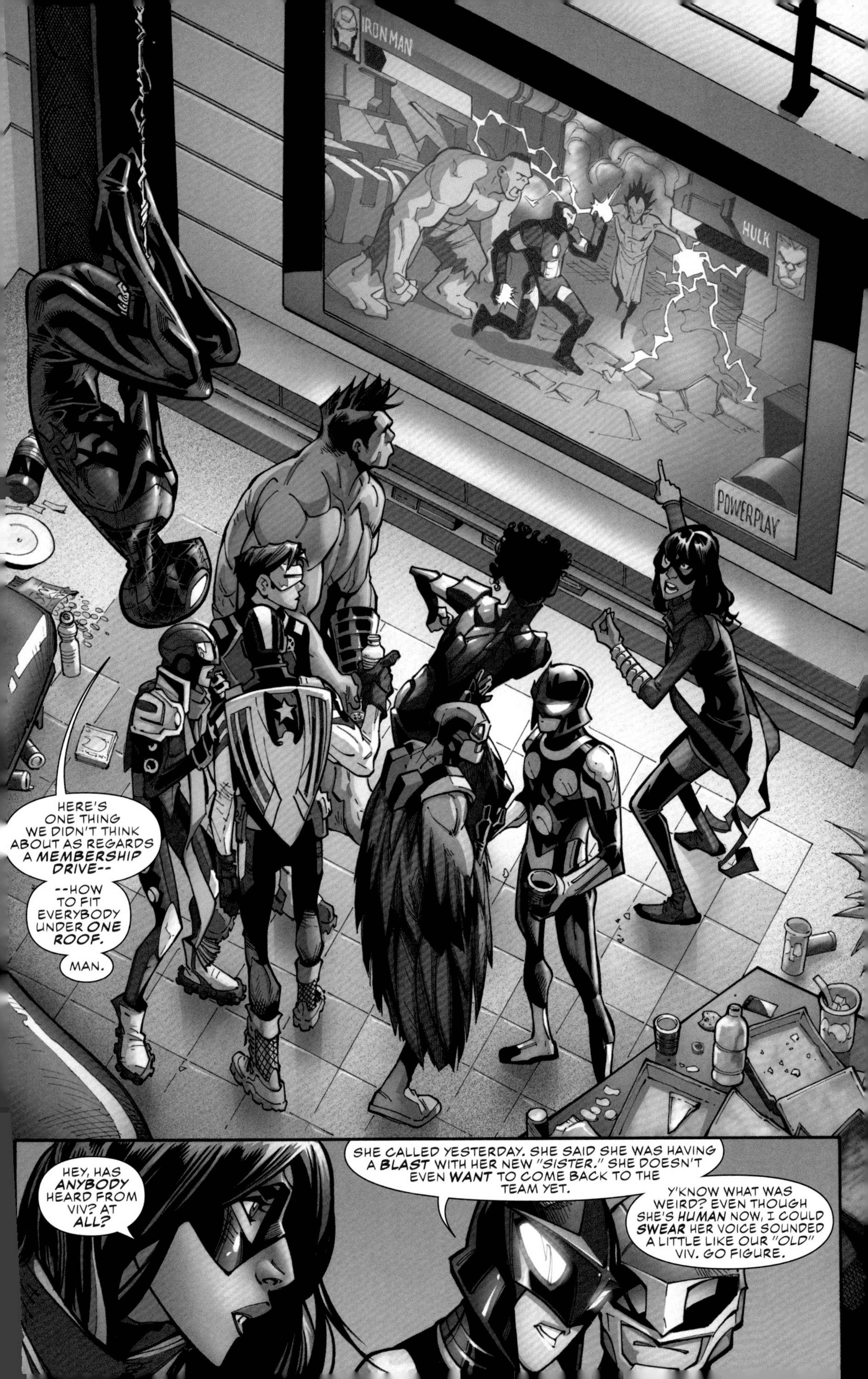
IRON MAN
HULK
POWERPLAY
HERE'S ONE THING WE DIDN'T THINK ABOUT AS REGARDS A MEMBERSHIP DRIVE--
--HOW TO FIT EVERYBODY UNDER ONE ROOF.
MAN.
HEY, HAS ANYBODY HEARD FROM VIV? AT ALL?
SHE CALLED YESTERDAY. SHE SAID SHE WAS HAVING A BLAST WITH HER NEW "SISTER." SHE DOESN'T EVEN WANT TO COME BACK TO THE TEAM YET.
Y'KNOW WHAT WAS WEIRD? EVEN THOUGH SHE'S HUMAN NOW, I COULD SWEAR HER VOICE SOUNDED A LITTLE LIKE OUR "OLD" VIV. GO FIGURE.

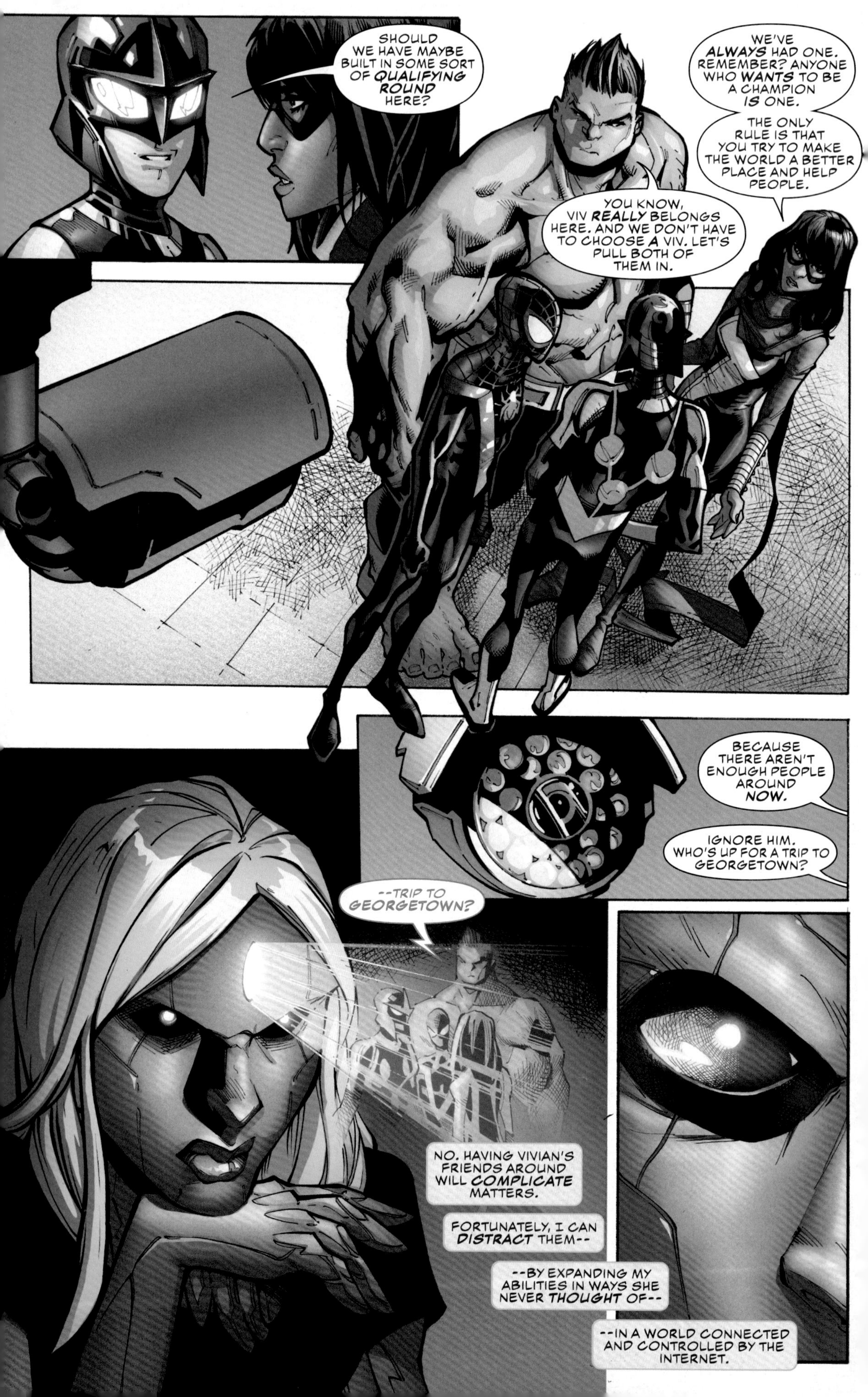
SHOULD WE HAVE MAYBE BUILT IN SOME SORT OF QUALIFYING ROUND HERE?
WE'VE ALWAYS HAD ONE. REMEMBER? ANYONE WHO WANTS TO BE A CHAMPION IS ONE.
THE ONLY RULE IS THAT YOU TRY TO MAKE THE WORLD A BETTER PLACE AND HELP PEOPLE.
YOU KNOW, VIV REALLY BELONGS HERE. AND WE DON'T HAVE TO CHOOSE A VIV. LET'S PULL BOTH OF THEM IN.
BECAUSE THERE AREN'T ENOUGH PEOPLE AROUND NOW.
IGNORE HIM. WHO'S UP FOR A TRIP TO GEORGETOWN?
--TRIP TO GEORGETOWN?
NO. HAVING VIVIAN'S FRIENDS AROUND WILL COMPLICATE MATTERS.
FORTUNATELY, I CAN DISTRACT THEM--
--BY EXPANDING MY ABILITIES IN WAYS SHE NEVER THOUGHT OF--
--IN A WORLD CONNECTED AND CONTROLLED BY THE INTERNET.

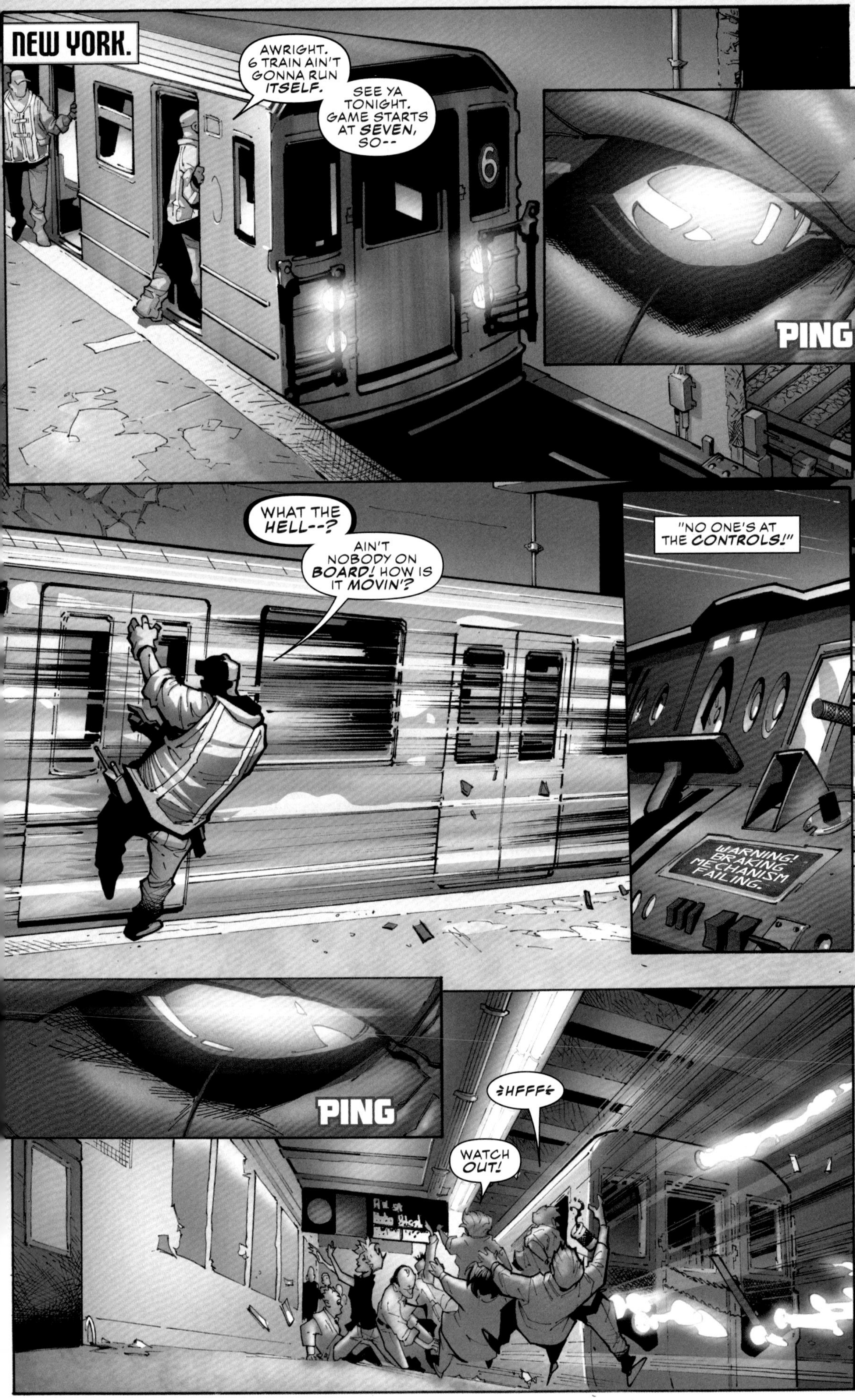
NEW YORK.
AWRIGHT. 6 TRAIN AIN'T GONNA RUN ITSELF.
SEE YA TONIGHT. GAME STARTS AT SEVEN, SO--
PING
WHAT THE HELL--?
AIN'T NOBODY ON BOARD! HOW IS IT MOVIN'?
"NO ONE'S AT THE CONTROLS!"
WARNING! BRAKING MECHANISM FAILING.
PING
HFFF
WATCH OUT!

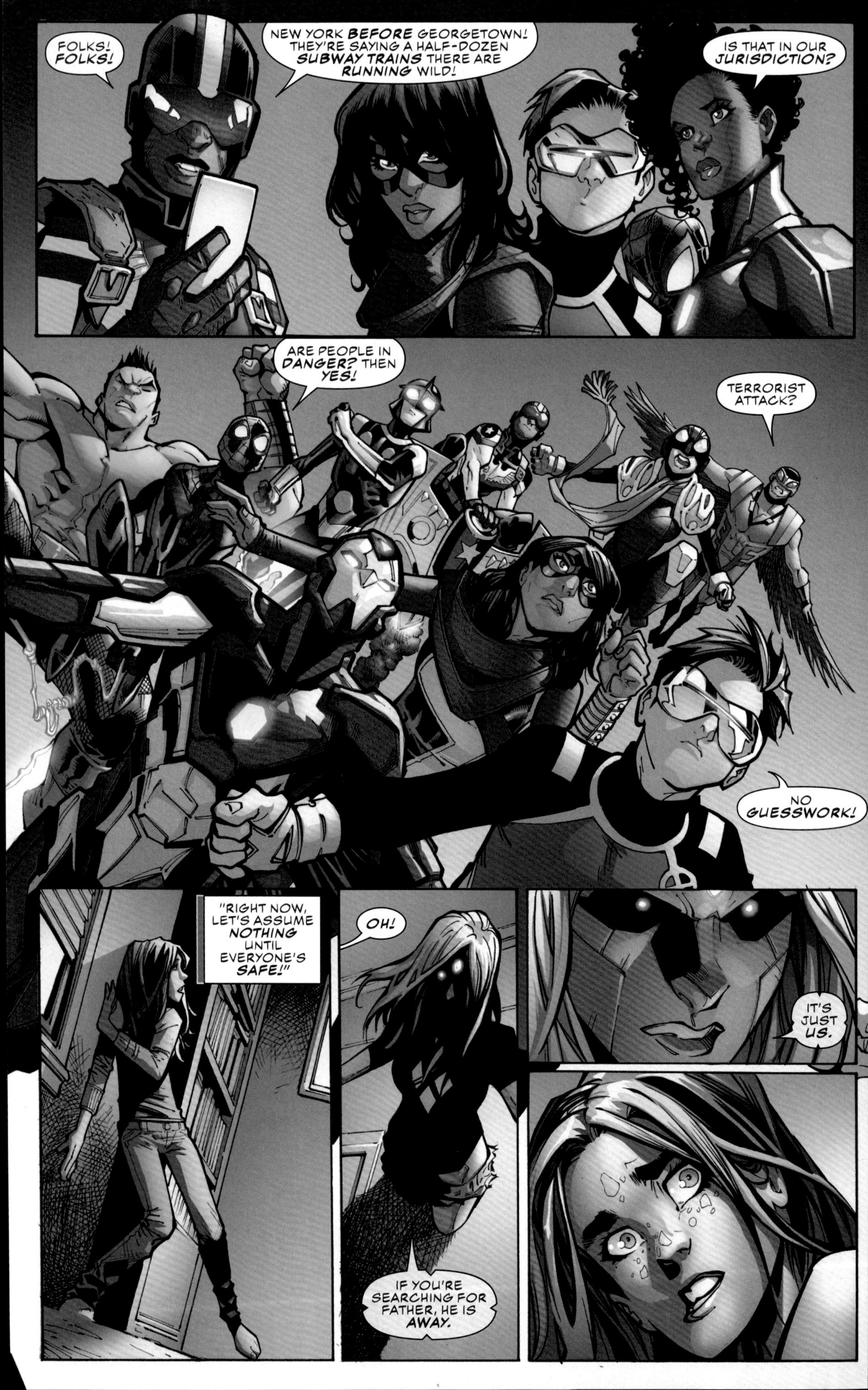
FOLKS! FOLKS!
NEW YORK BEFORE GEORGETOWN! THEY'RE SAYING A HALF-DOZEN SUBWAY TRAINS THERE ARE RUNNING WILD!
IS THAT IN OUR JURISDICTION?
ARE PEOPLE IN DANGER? THEN YES!
TERRORIST ATTACK?
NO GUESSWORK!
"RIGHT NOW, LET'S ASSUME NOTHING UNTIL EVERYONE'S SAFE!"
OH!
IF YOU'RE SEARCHING FOR FATHER, HE IS AWAY.
IT'S JUST US.

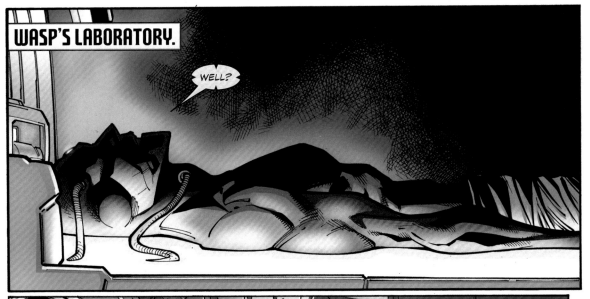

WELL?

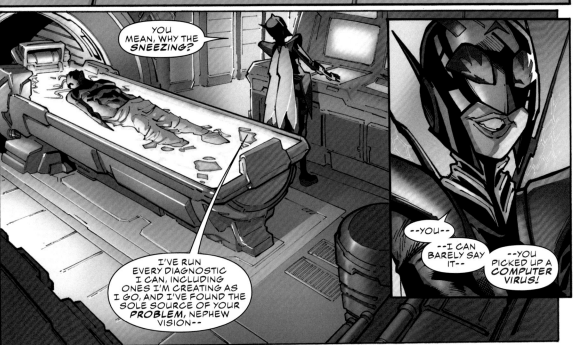

YOU MEAN, WHY THE SNEEZING?

I'VE RUN EVERY DIAGNOSTIC I CAN, INCLUDING ONES I'M CREATING AS I GO, AND I'VE FOUND THE SOLE SOURCE OF YOUR PROBLEM, NEPHEW VISION--

--YOU--

--I CAN BARELY SAY IT--

--YOU PICKED UP A COMPUTER VIRUS!

YOU'RE JOKING.

ABSURD! I KNOW, RIGHT? IT'S RIDICULOUS. AND YET.

IT MAKES SENSE THAT YOUR SYNTHEZOID BODY AND BRAIN WOULD BE VULNERABLE TO DATA CORRUPTION.

THIS INSTANCE IS MINOR, BUT AS YOUR SYSTEM PROCESSED IT OUT, IT AFFECTED YOUR NASAL SENSORS JUST 'CAUSE.

IGNOMINIOUS.

UNDIGNIFIED. HUMILIATING.

AND YET, REALLY FUNNY.

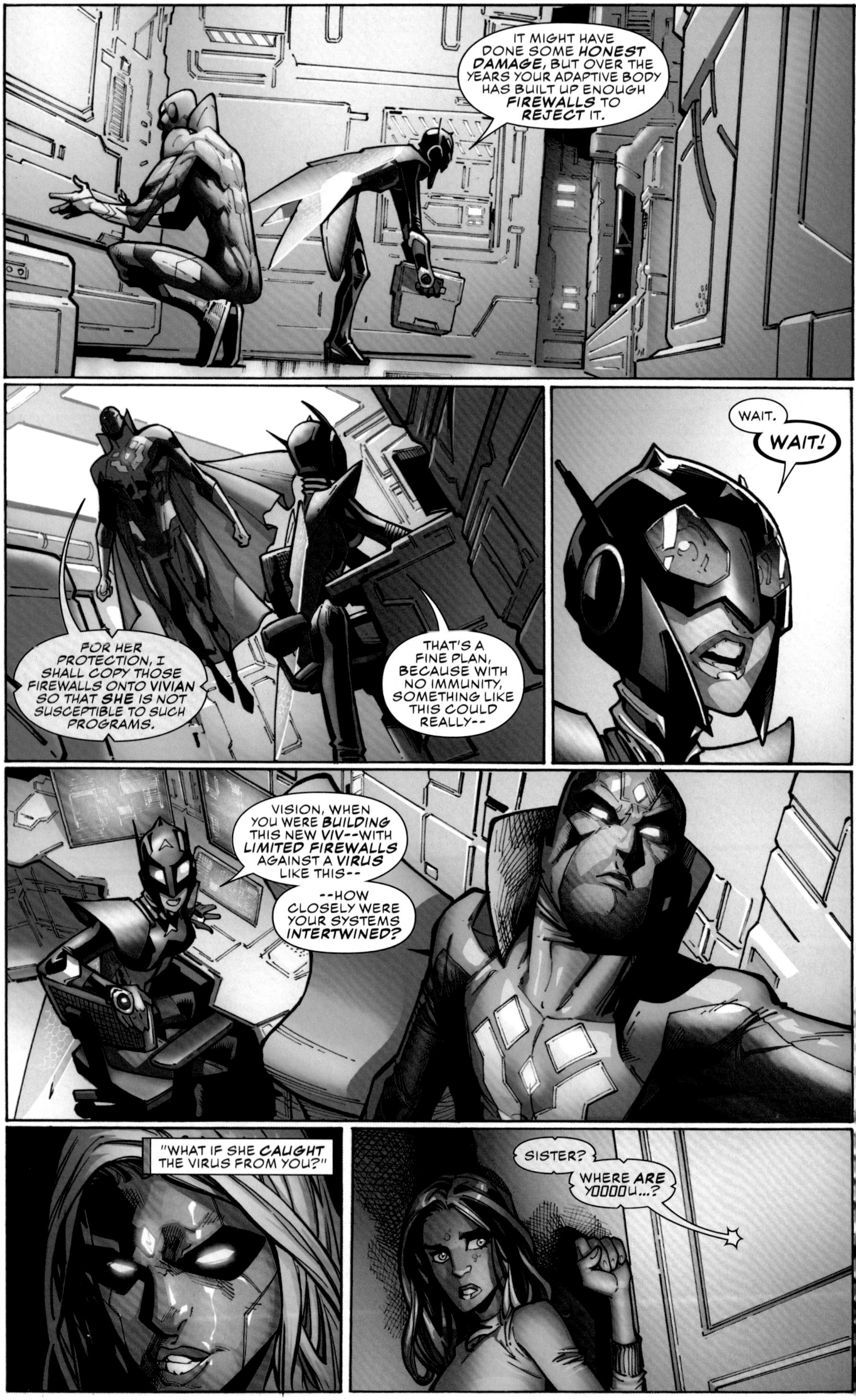

IT MIGHT HAVE DONE SOME HONEST DAMAGE, BUT OVER THE YEARS YOUR ADAPTIVE BODY HAS BUILT UP ENOUGH FIREWALLS TO REJECT IT.
FOR HER PROTECTION, I SHALL COPY THOSE FIREWALLS ONTO VIVIAN SO THAT SHE IS NOT SUSCEPTIBLE TO SUCH PROGRAMS.
THAT'S A FINE PLAN, BECAUSE WITH NO IMMUNITY, SOMETHING LIKE THIS COULD REALLY--
WAIT.
WAIT!
VISION, WHEN YOU WERE BUILDING THIS NEW VIV--WITH LIMITED FIREWALLS AGAINST A VIRUS LIKE THIS--
--HOW CLOSELY WERE YOUR SYSTEMS INTERTWINED?
"WHAT IF SHE CAUGHT THE VIRUS FROM YOU?"
SISTER?
WHERE ARE YOOOOU...?

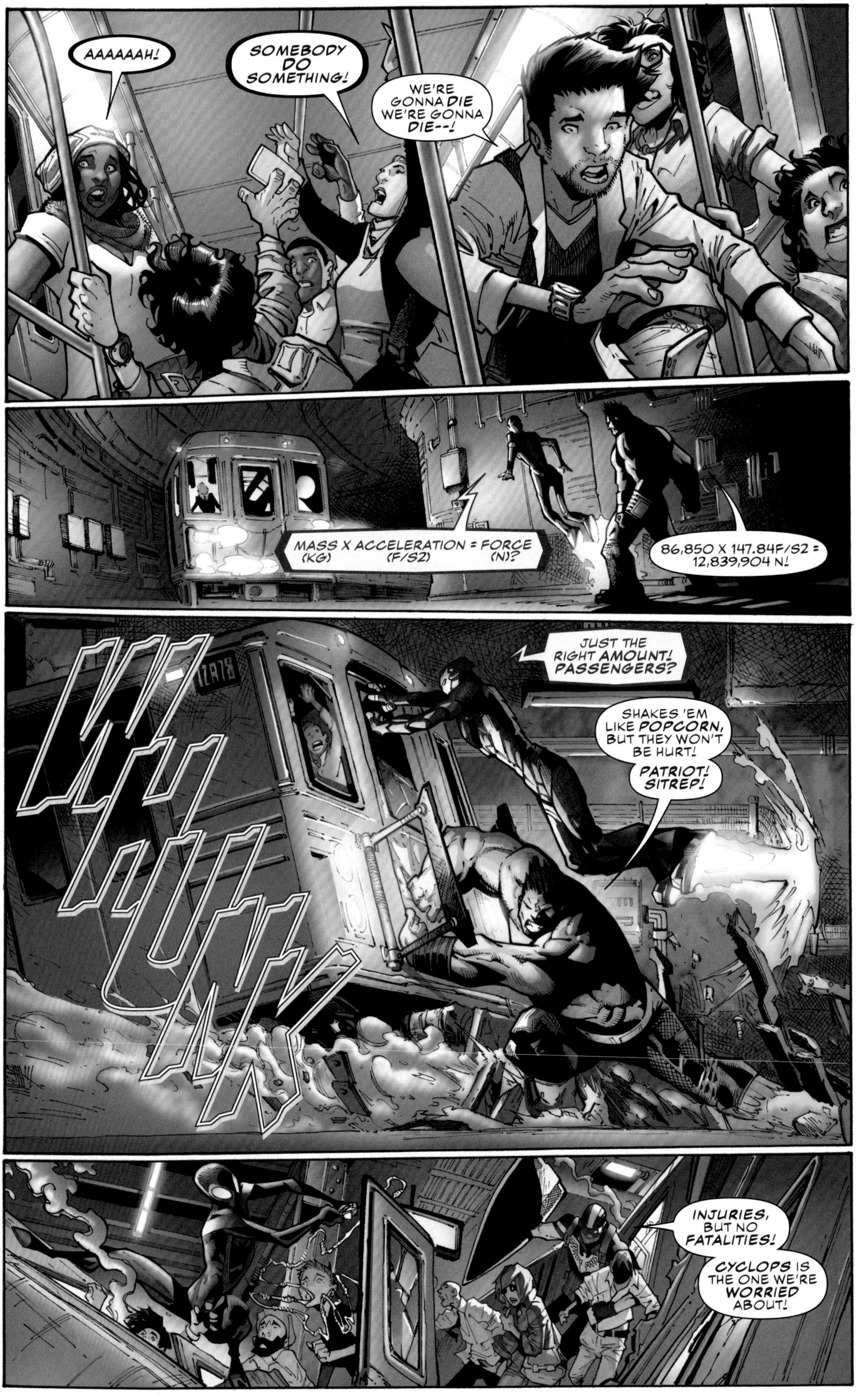
AAAAAAH!
SOMEBODY DO SOMETHING!
WE'RE GONNA DIE WE'RE GONNA DIE--!
MASS X ACCELERATION = FORCE (KG) (F/S2) (N)?
86,850 X 147.84F/S2 = 12,839,904 N!
JUST THE RIGHT AMOUNT! PASSENGERS?
SHAKES 'EM LIKE POPCORN, BUT THEY WON'T BE HURT!
PATRIOT! SITREP!
INJURIES, BUT NO FATALITIES!
CYCLOPS IS THE ONE WE'RE WORRIED ABOUT!

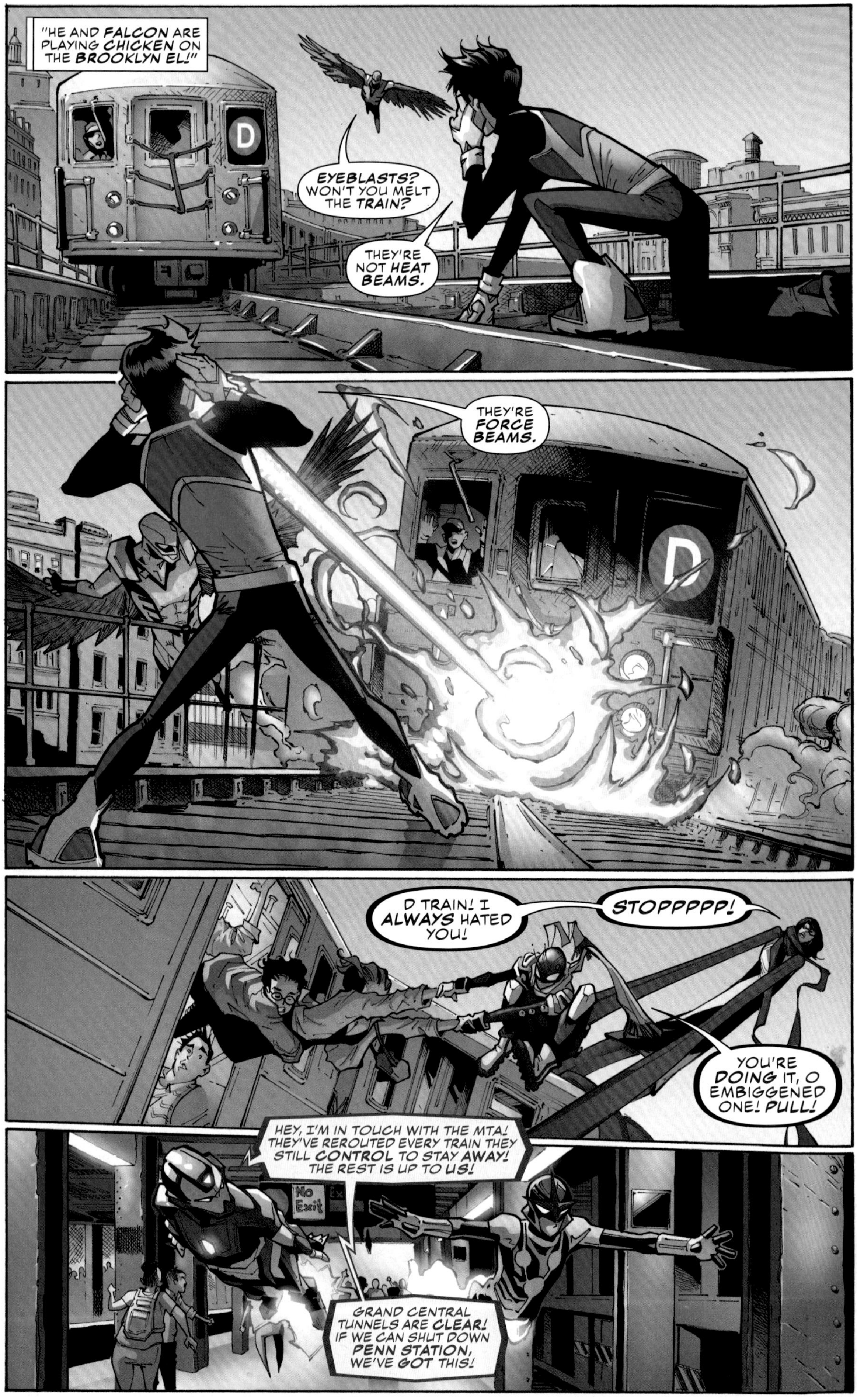
"HE AND FALCON ARE PLAYING CHICKEN ON THE BROOKLYN EL!"
D
EYEBLASTS? WON'T YOU MELT THE TRAIN?
THEY'RE NOT HEAT BEAMS.
THEY'RE FORCE BEAMS.
D
D TRAIN! I ALWAYS HATED YOU!
STOPPPPP!
YOU'RE DOING IT, O EMBIGGENED ONE! PULL!
HEY, I'M IN TOUCH WITH THE MTA! THEY'VE REROUTED EVERY TRAIN THEY STILL CONTROL TO STAY AWAY! THE REST IS UP TO US!
No Exit
GRAND CENTRAL TUNNELS ARE CLEAR! IF WE CAN SHUT DOWN PENN STATION, WE'VE GOT THIS!

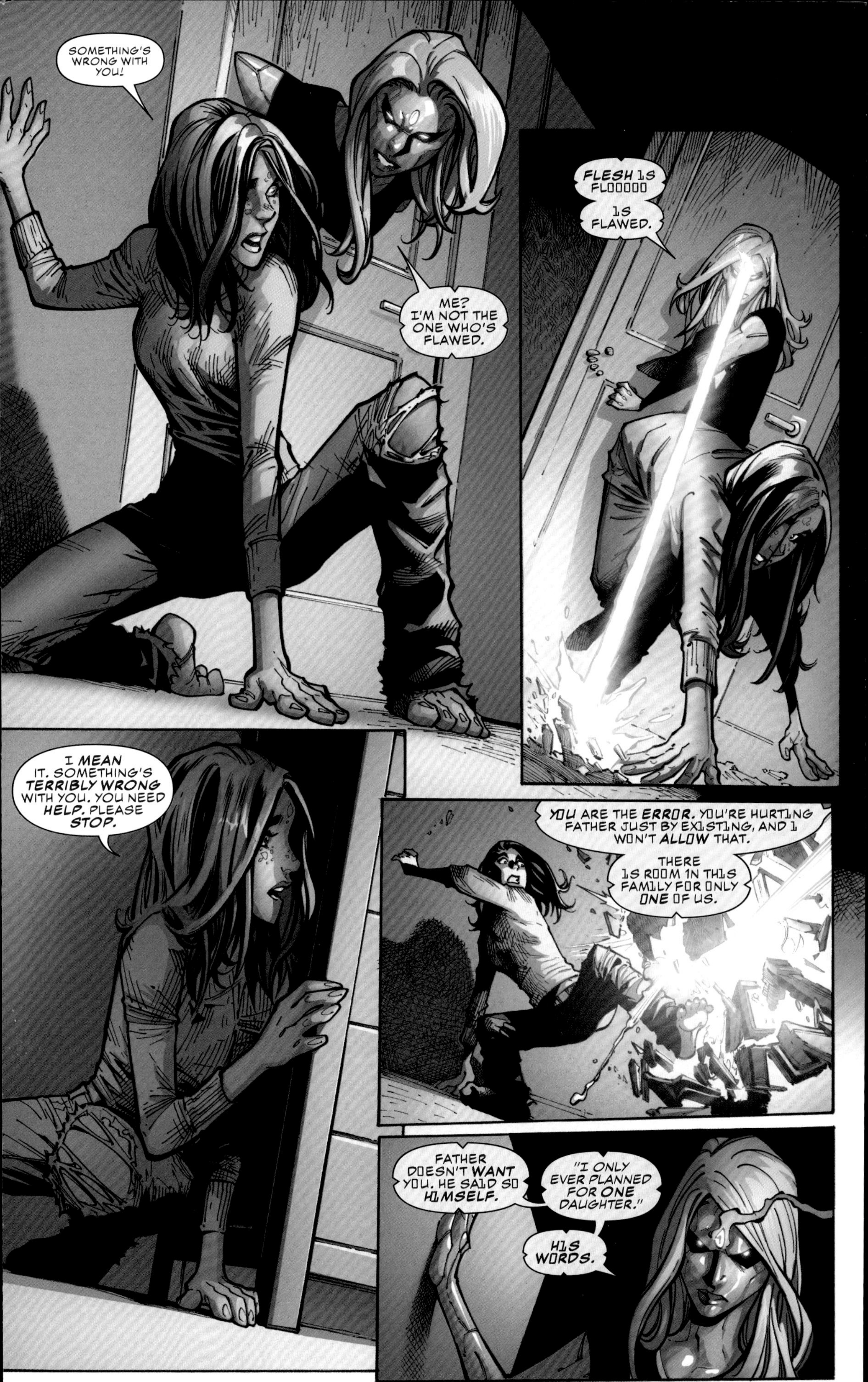
SOMETHING'S WRONG WITH YOU!
ME? I'M NOT THE ONE WHO'S FLAWED.
FLESH IS FLOOOOO
IS FLAWED.
I MEAN IT. SOMETHING'S TERRIBLY WRONG WITH YOU. YOU NEED HELP. PLEASE STOP.
YOU ARE THE ERROR. YOU'RE HURTING FATHER JUST BY EXISTING, AND I WON'T ALLOW THAT.
THERE IS ROOM IN THIS FAMILY FOR ONLY ONE OF US.
FATHER DOESN'T WANT YOU. HE SAID SO HIMSELF.
"I ONLY EVER PLANNED FOR ONE DAUGHTER."
HIS WORDS.

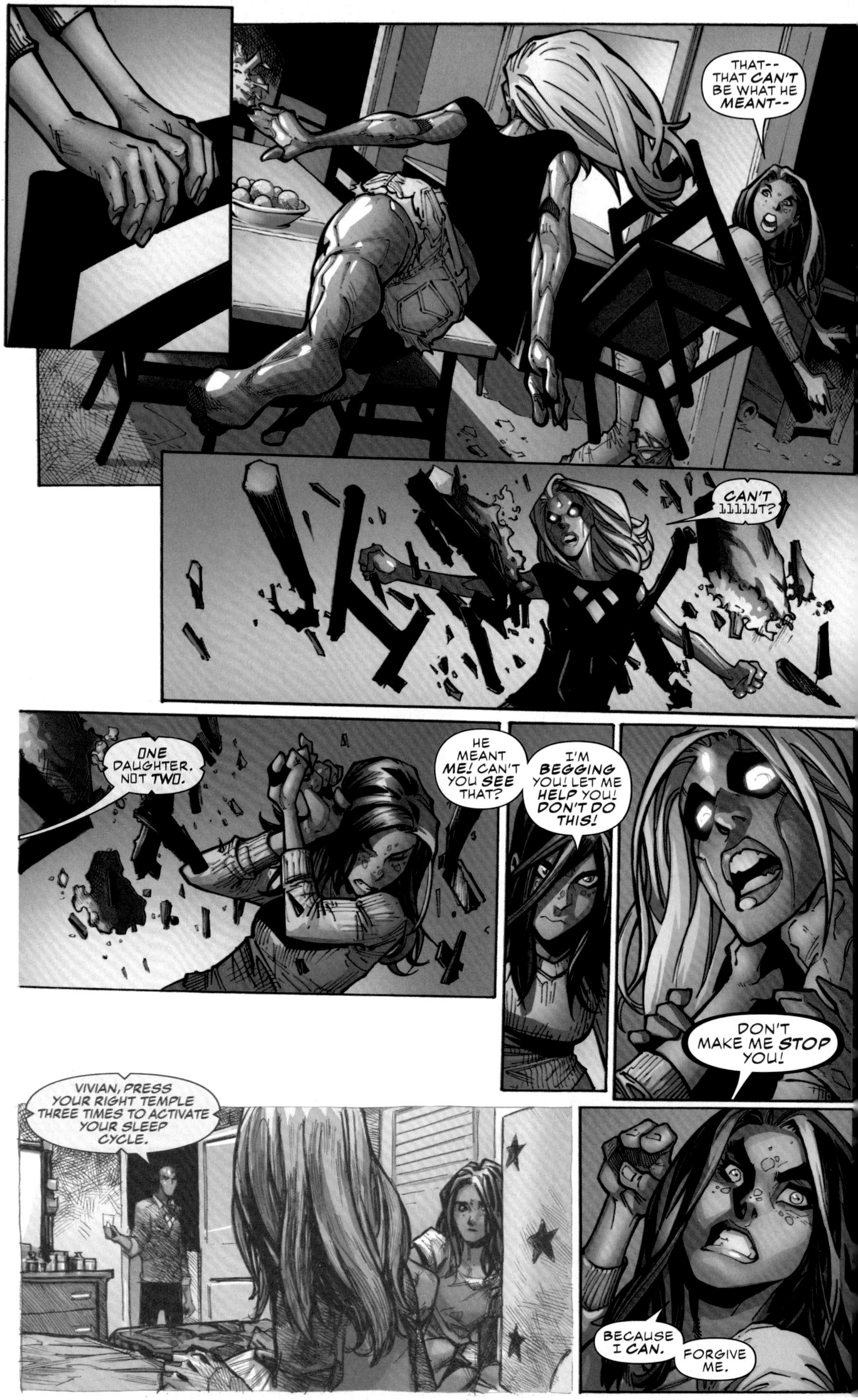
THAT-- THAT CAN'T BE WHAT HE MEANT--
CAN'T ɪɪɪɪɪT?
ONE DAUGHTER. NOT TWO.
HE MEANT ME! CAN'T YOU SEE THAT?
I'M BEGGING YOU! LET ME HELP YOU! DON'T DO THIS!
DON'T MAKE ME STOP YOU!
VIVIAN, PRESS YOUR RIGHT TEMPLE THREE TIMES TO ACTIVATE YOUR SLEEP CYCLE.
BECAUSE I CAN.
FORGIVE ME.

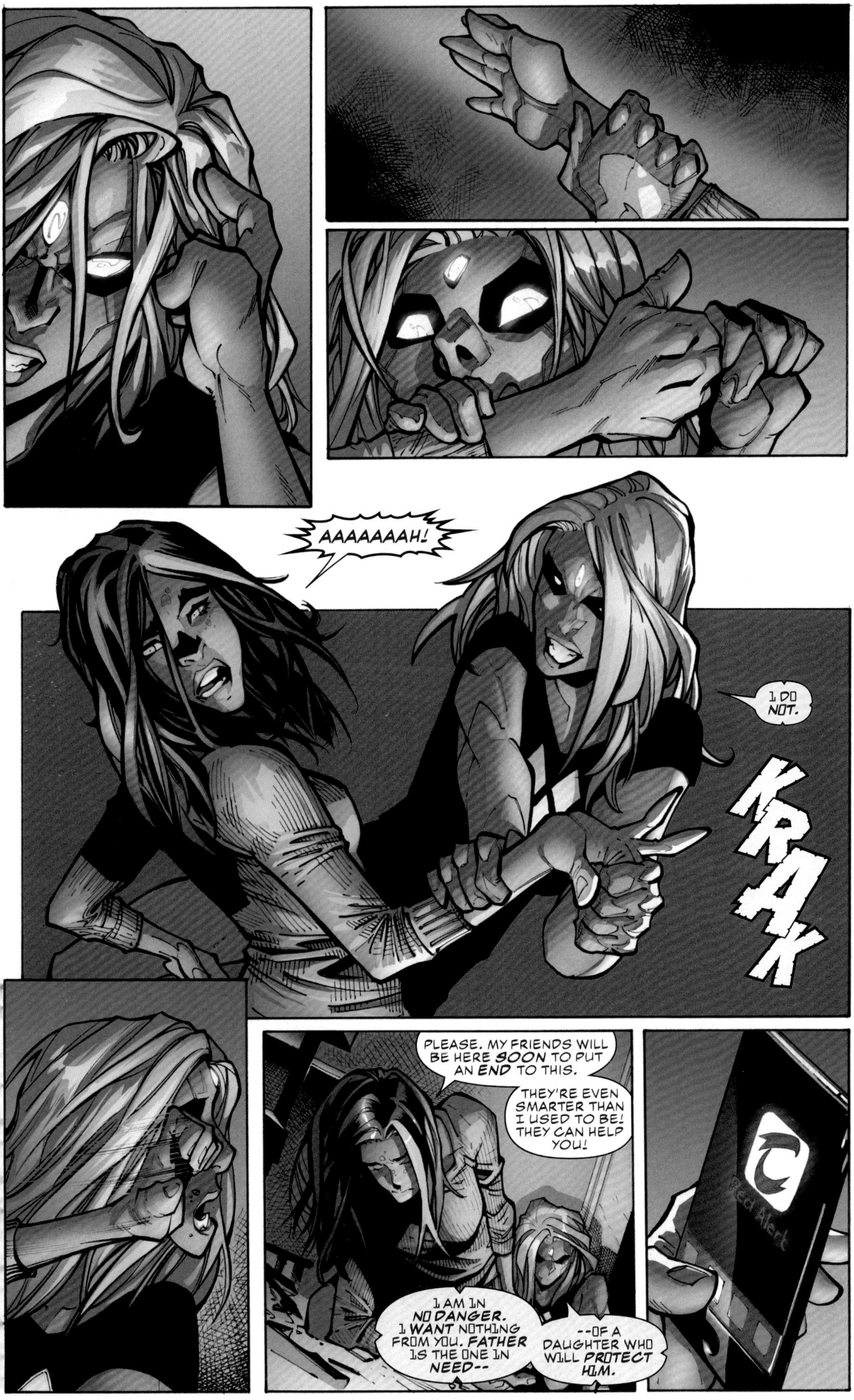
AAAAAAAH!
I DO NOT.
KRAK
PLEASE. MY FRIENDS WILL BE HERE SOON TO PUT AN END TO THIS.
THEY'RE EVEN SMARTER THAN I USED TO BE! THEY CAN HELP YOU!
I AM IN NO DANGER. I WANT NOTHING FROM YOU. FATHER IS THE ONE IN NEED--
--OF A DAUGHTER WHO WILL PROTECT HIM.
Red Alert

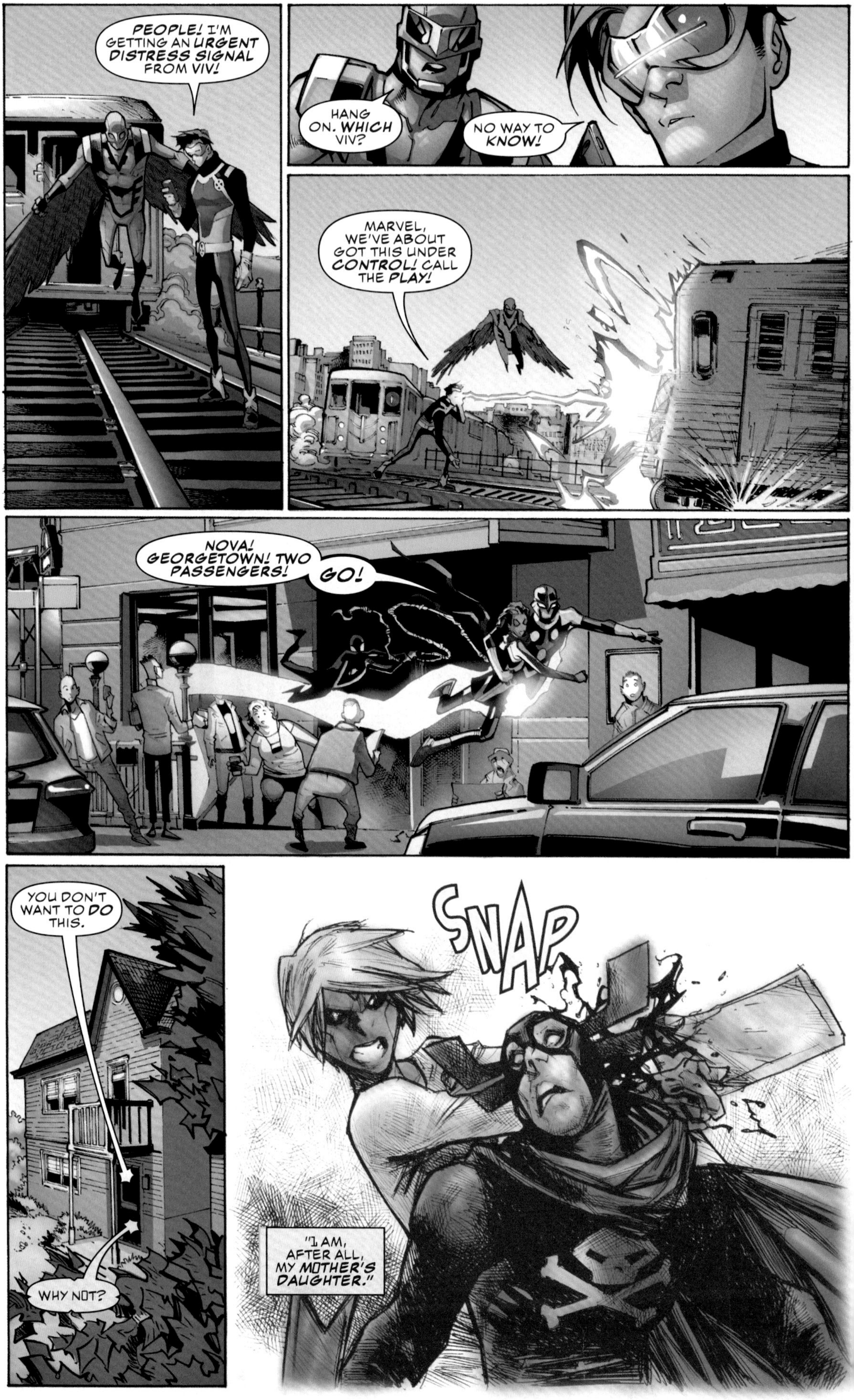
PEOPLE! I'M GETTING AN URGENT DISTRESS SIGNAL FROM VIV!
HANG ON. WHICH VIV?
NO WAY TO KNOW!
MARVEL, WE'VE ABOUT GOT THIS UNDER CONTROL! CALL THE PLAY!
NOVA! GEORGETOWN! TWO PASSENGERS!
GO!
YOU DON'T WANT TO DO THIS.
WHY NOT?
SNAP
"I AM, AFTER ALL, MY MOTHER'S DAUGHTER."

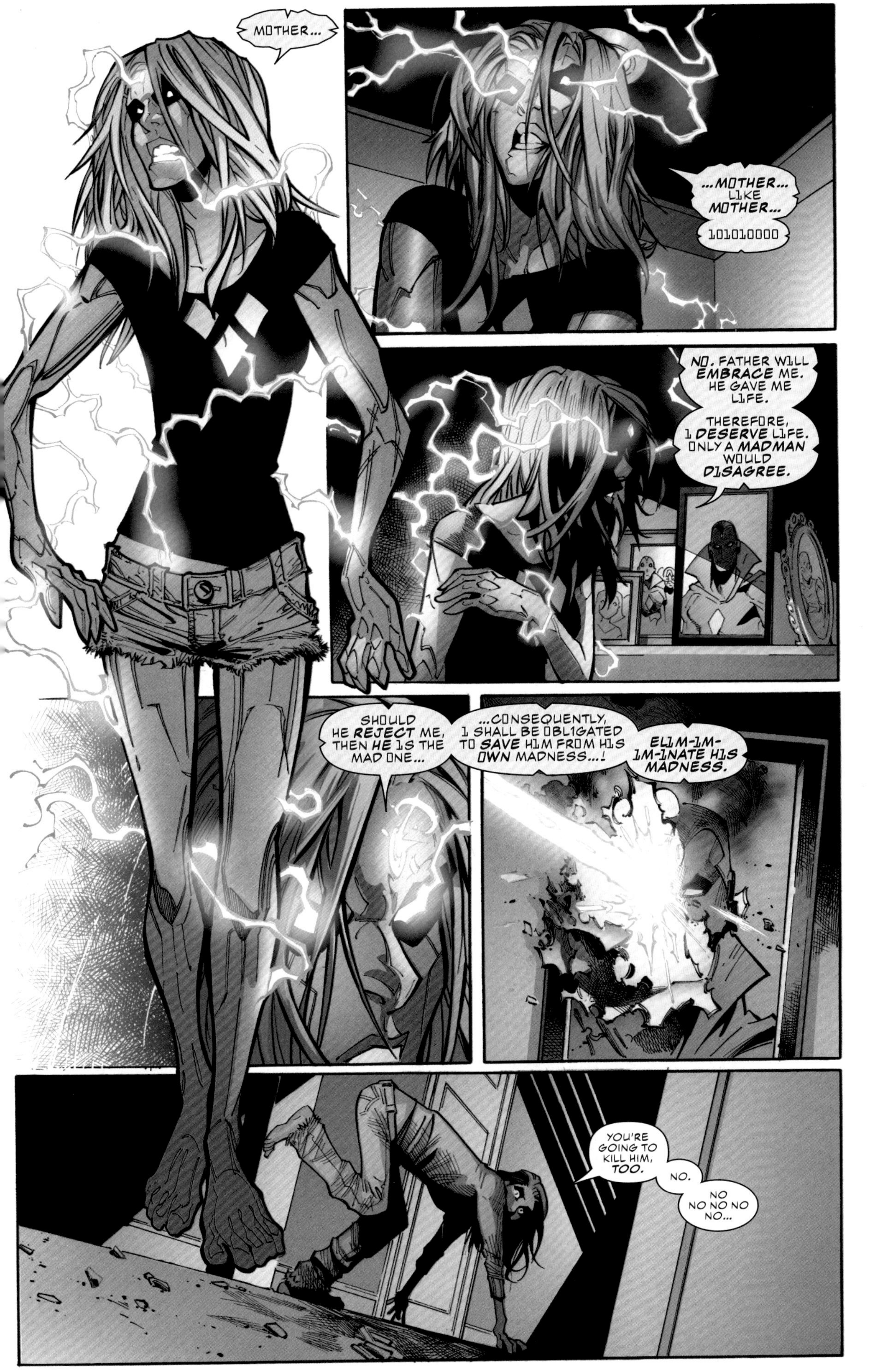
MOTHER...
...MOTHER... LIKE MOTHER...
101010000
NO. FATHER WILL EMBRACE ME. HE GAVE ME LIFE.
THEREFORE, I DESERVE LIFE. ONLY A MADMAN WOULD DISAGREE.
SHOULD HE REJECT ME, THEN HE IS THE MAD ONE...
...CONSEQUENTLY, I SHALL BE OBLIGATED TO SAVE HIM FROM HIS OWN MADNESS...!
ELIM-IM-IM-INATE HIS MADNESS.
YOU'RE GOING TO KILL HIM, TOO.
NO.
NO NO NO NO NO...

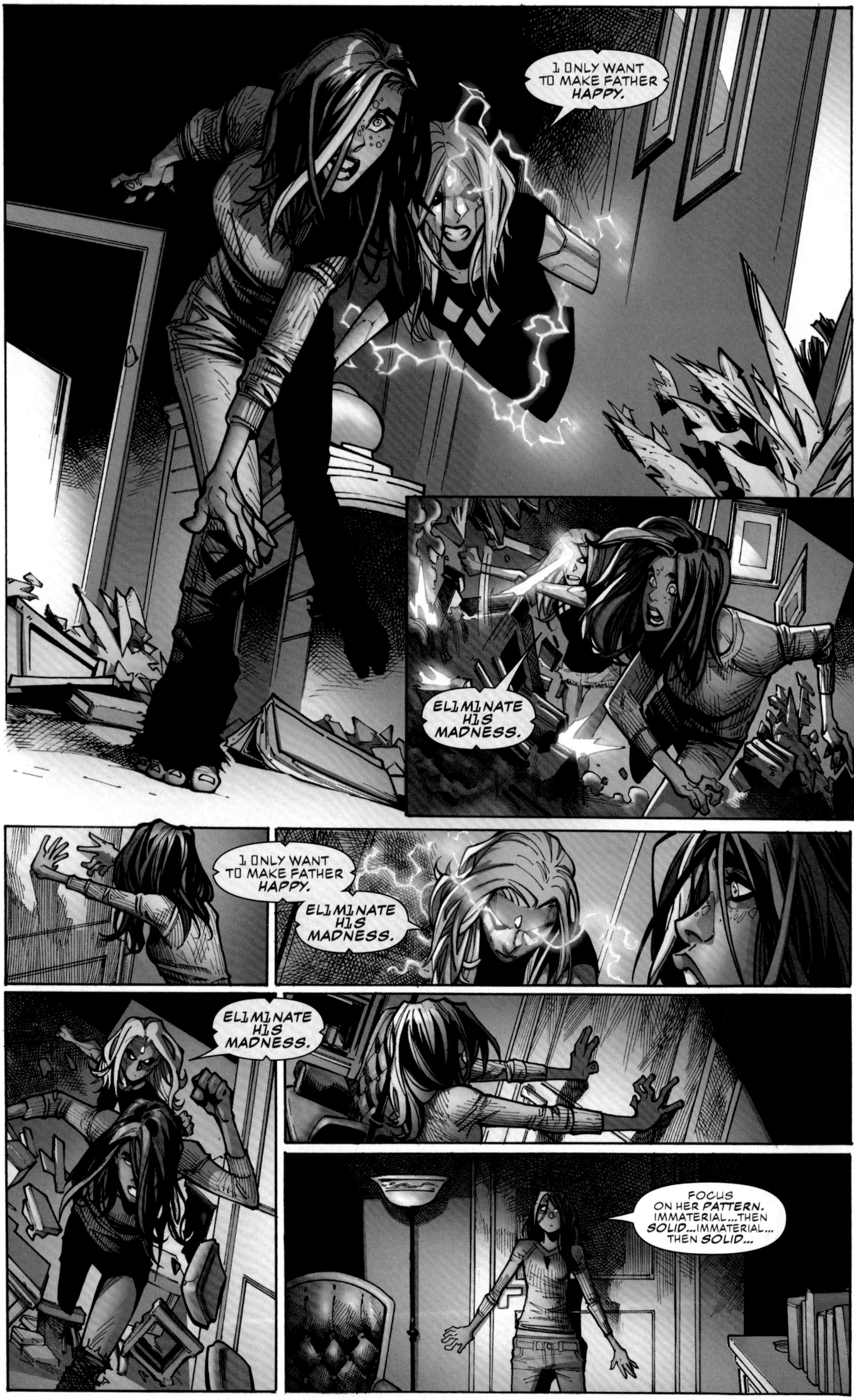
I ONLY WANT TO MAKE FATHER HAPPY.
ELIMINATE HIS MADNESS.
I ONLY WANT TO MAKE FATHER HAPPY.
ELIMINATE HIS MADNESS.
ELIMINATE HIS MADNESS.
FOCUS ON HER PATTERN. IMMATERIAL...THEN SOLID...IMMATERIAL... THEN SOLID...

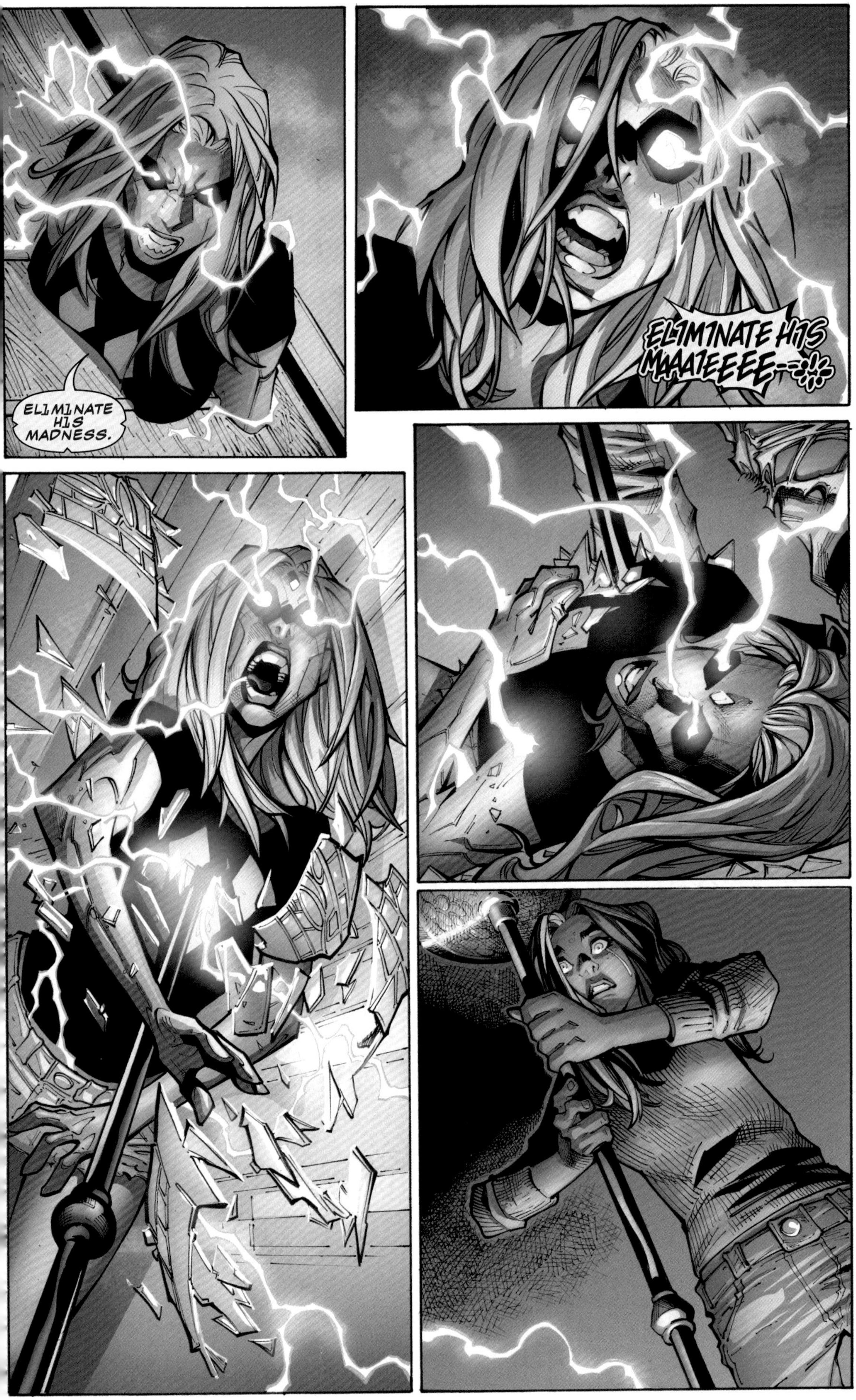
ELIMINATE HIS MADNESS.
ELIMINATE HIS MAAATEEEE--!!

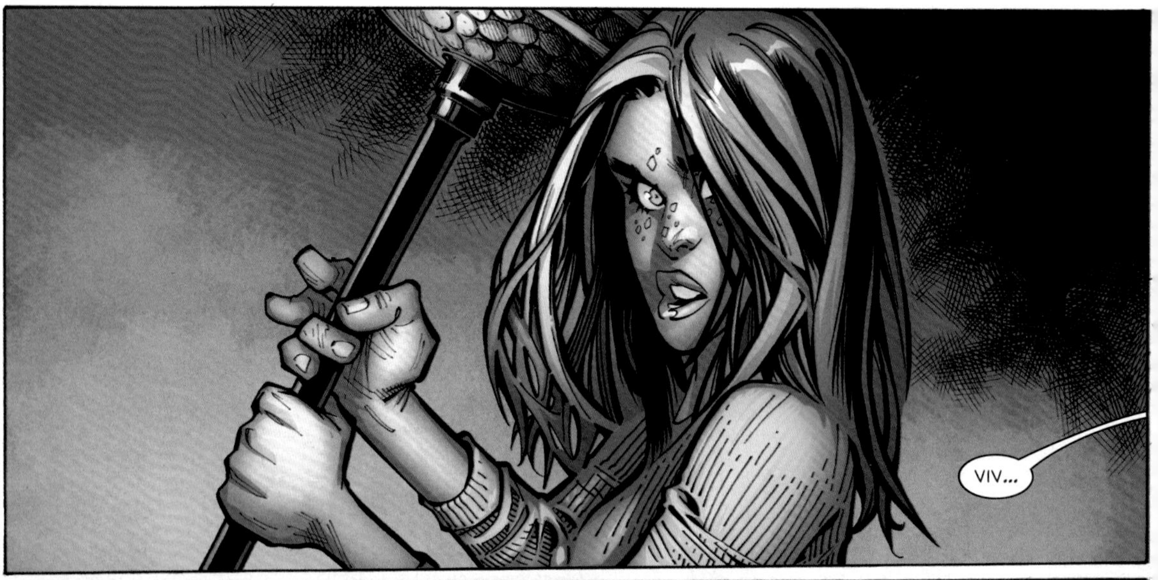
VIV...

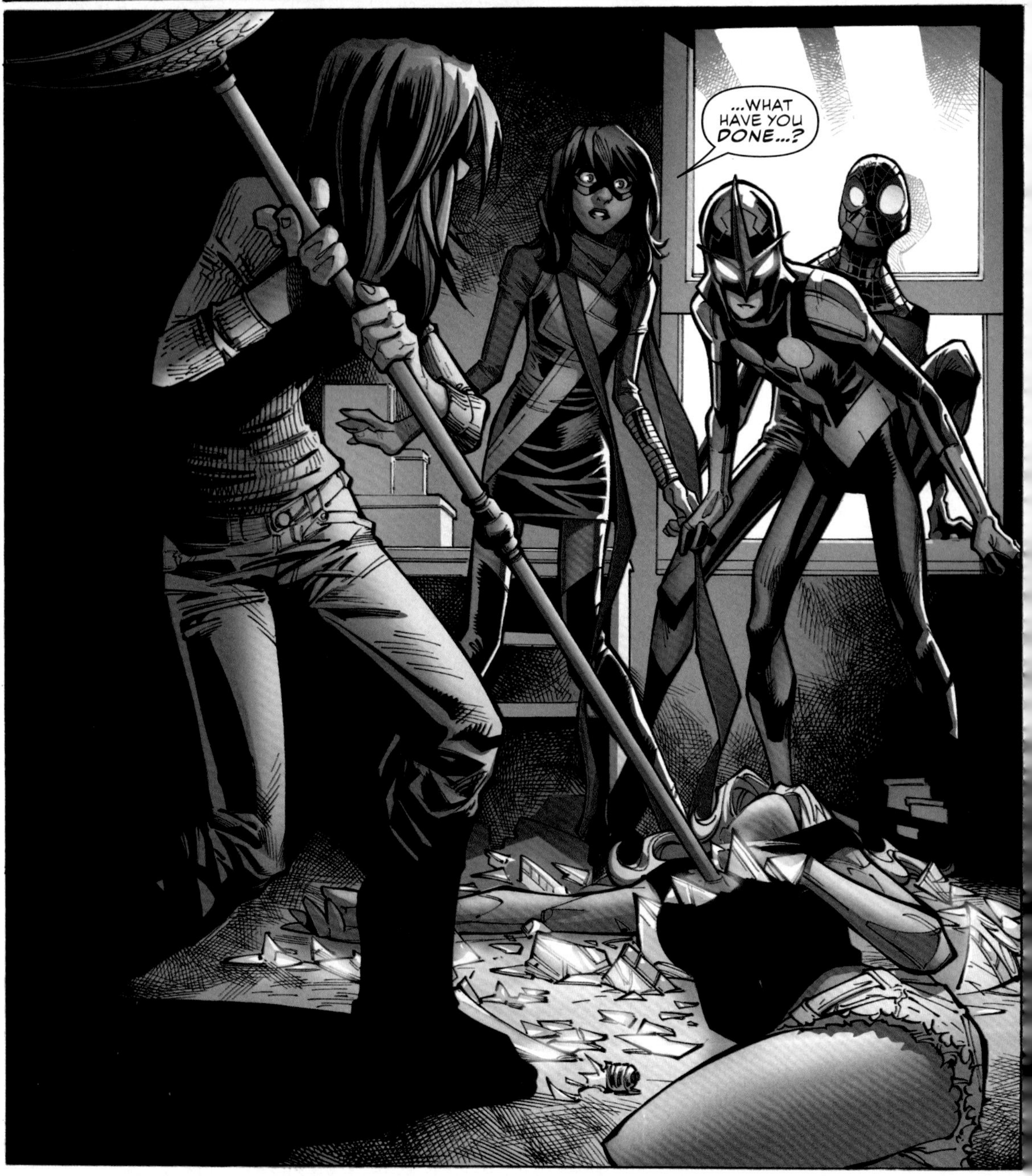
...WHAT HAVE YOU DONE...?

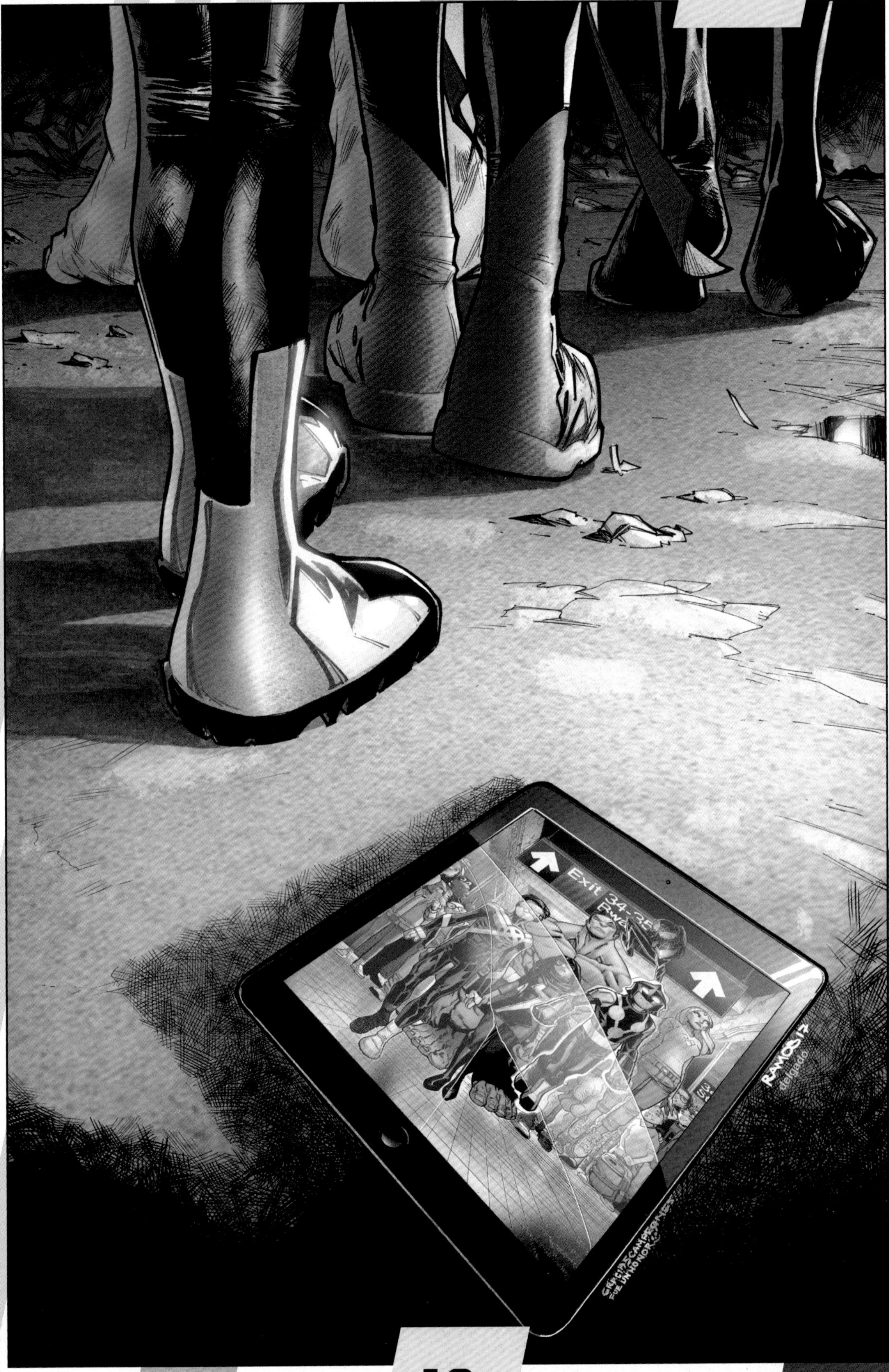
Exit 34-35
RAMOS 17
delgado

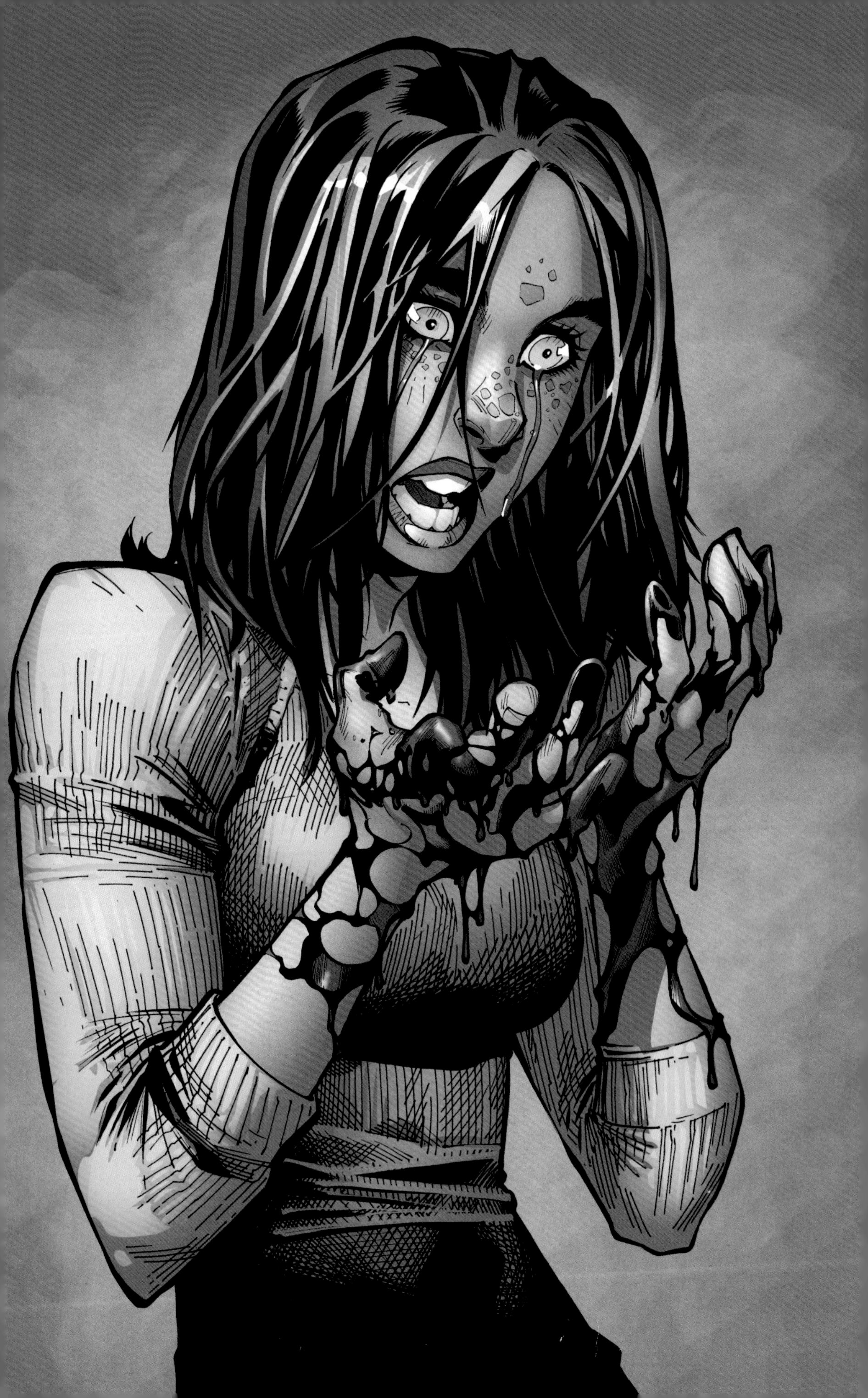

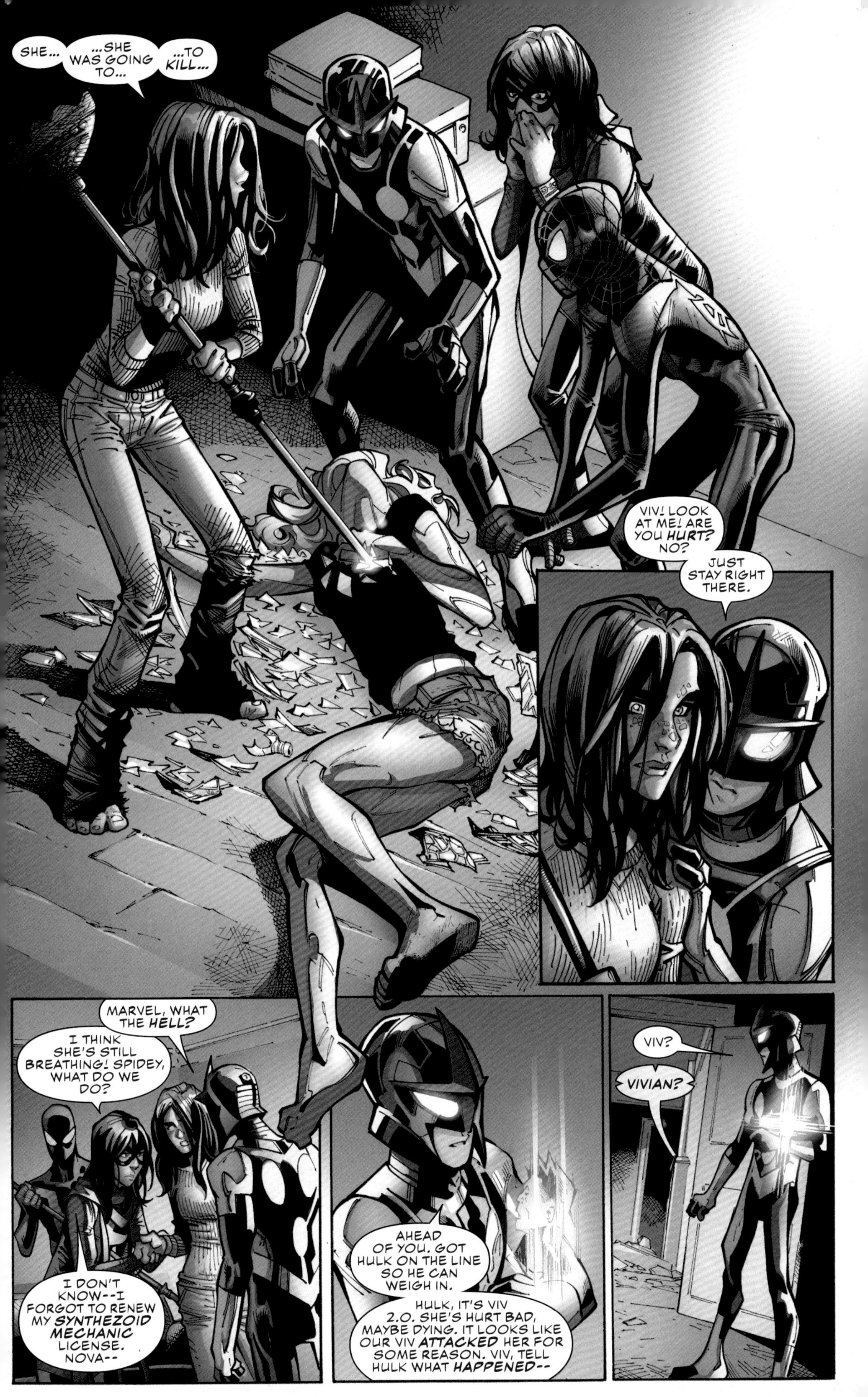
SHE...
...SHE WAS GOING TO...
...TO KILL...
VIV! LOOK AT ME! ARE YOU HURT? NO?
JUST STAY RIGHT THERE.
MARVEL, WHAT THE HELL?
I THINK SHE'S STILL BREATHING! SPIDEY, WHAT DO WE DO?
I DON'T KNOW--I FORGOT TO RENEW MY SYNTHEZOID MECHANIC LICENSE. NOVA--
AHEAD OF YOU. GOT HULK ON THE LINE SO HE CAN WEIGH IN.
HULK, IT'S VIV 2.0. SHE'S HURT BAD, MAYBE DYING. IT LOOKS LIKE OUR VIV ATTACKED HER FOR SOME REASON. VIV, TELL HULK WHAT HAPPENED--
VIV?
VIVIAN?

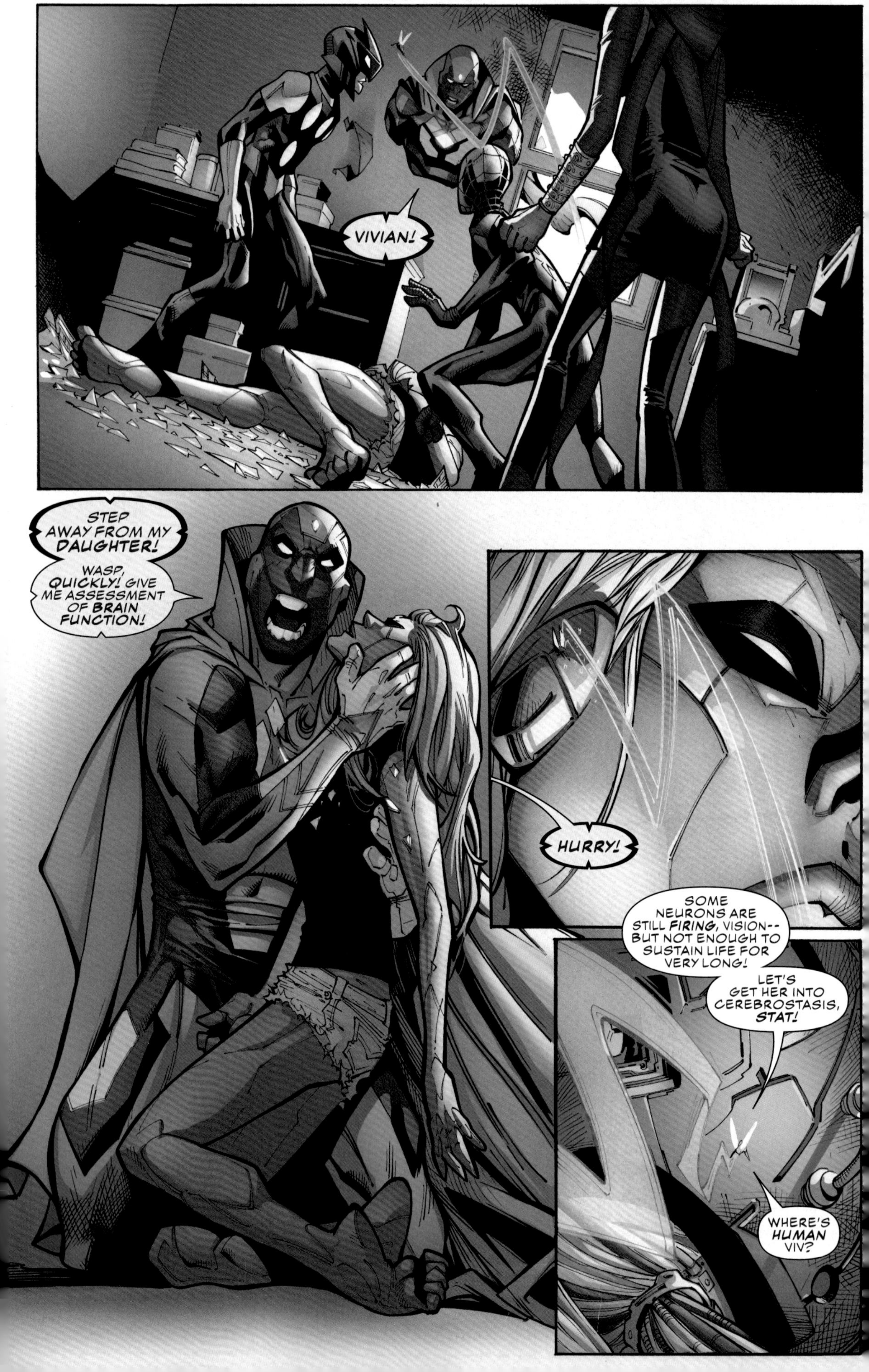
VIVIAN!
STEP AWAY FROM MY DAUGHTER!
WASP, QUICKLY! GIVE ME ASSESSMENT OF BRAIN FUNCTION!
HURRY!
SOME NEURONS ARE STILL FIRING, VISION-- BUT NOT ENOUGH TO SUSTAIN LIFE FOR VERY LONG!
LET'S GET HER INTO CEREBROSTASIS, STAT!
WHERE'S HUMAN VIV?

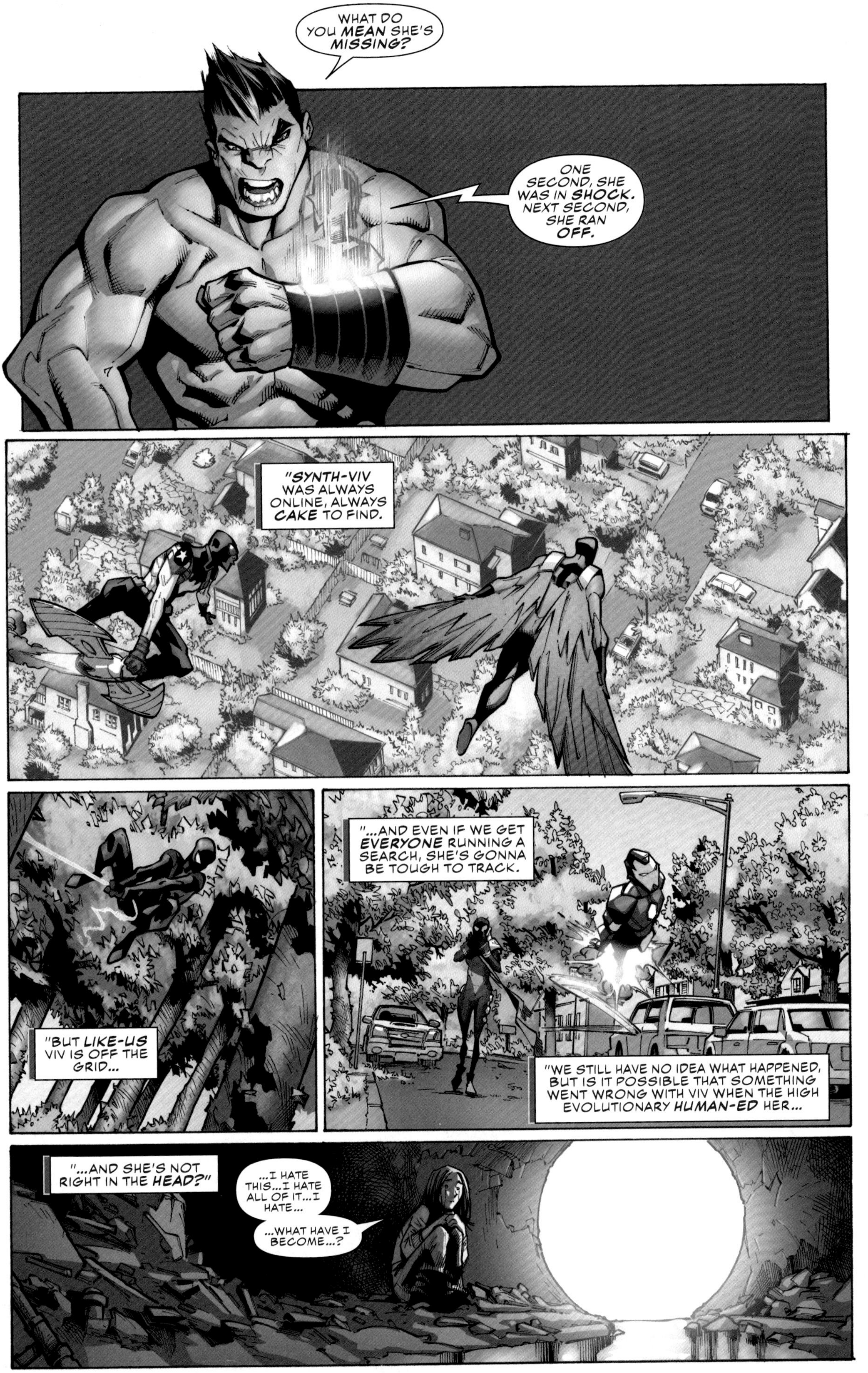
WHAT DO YOU MEAN SHE'S MISSING?
ONE SECOND, SHE WAS IN SHOCK. NEXT SECOND, SHE RAN OFF.
"SYNTH-VIV WAS ALWAYS ONLINE, ALWAYS CAKE TO FIND.
"BUT LIKE-US VIV IS OFF THE GRID...
"...AND EVEN IF WE GET EVERYONE RUNNING A SEARCH, SHE'S GONNA BE TOUGH TO TRACK.
"WE STILL HAVE NO IDEA WHAT HAPPENED, BUT IS IT POSSIBLE THAT SOMETHING WENT WRONG WITH VIV WHEN THE HIGH EVOLUTIONARY HUMAN-ED HER...
"...AND SHE'S NOT RIGHT IN THE HEAD?"
...I HATE THIS...I HATE ALL OF IT...I HATE...
...WHAT HAVE I BECOME...?

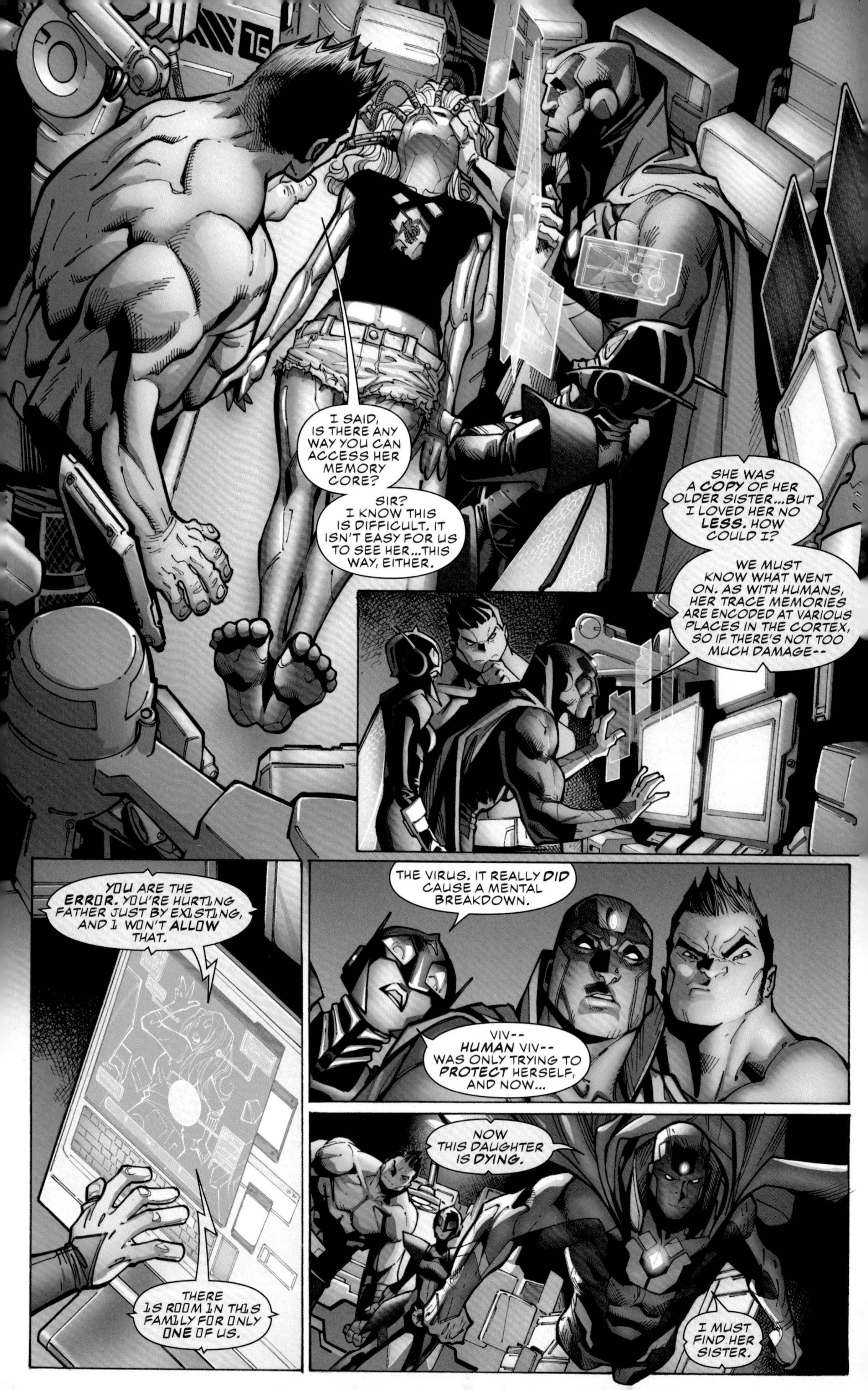
I SAID, IS THERE ANY WAY YOU CAN ACCESS HER MEMORY CORE?
SIR? I KNOW THIS IS DIFFICULT. IT ISN'T EASY FOR US TO SEE HER...THIS WAY, EITHER.
SHE WAS A COPY OF HER OLDER SISTER...BUT I LOVED HER NO LESS. HOW COULD I?
WE MUST KNOW WHAT WENT ON. AS WITH HUMANS, HER TRACE MEMORIES ARE ENCODED AT VARIOUS PLACES IN THE CORTEX, SO IF THERE'S NOT TOO MUCH DAMAGE--
YOU ARE THE ERROR. YOU'RE HURTING FATHER JUST BY EXISTING, AND I WON'T ALLOW THAT.
THERE IS ROOM IN THIS FAMILY FOR ONLY ONE OF US.
THE VIRUS. IT REALLY DID CAUSE A MENTAL BREAKDOWN.
VIV-- HUMAN VIV-- WAS ONLY TRYING TO PROTECT HERSELF, AND NOW...
NOW THIS DAUGHTER IS DYING.
I MUST FIND HER SISTER.

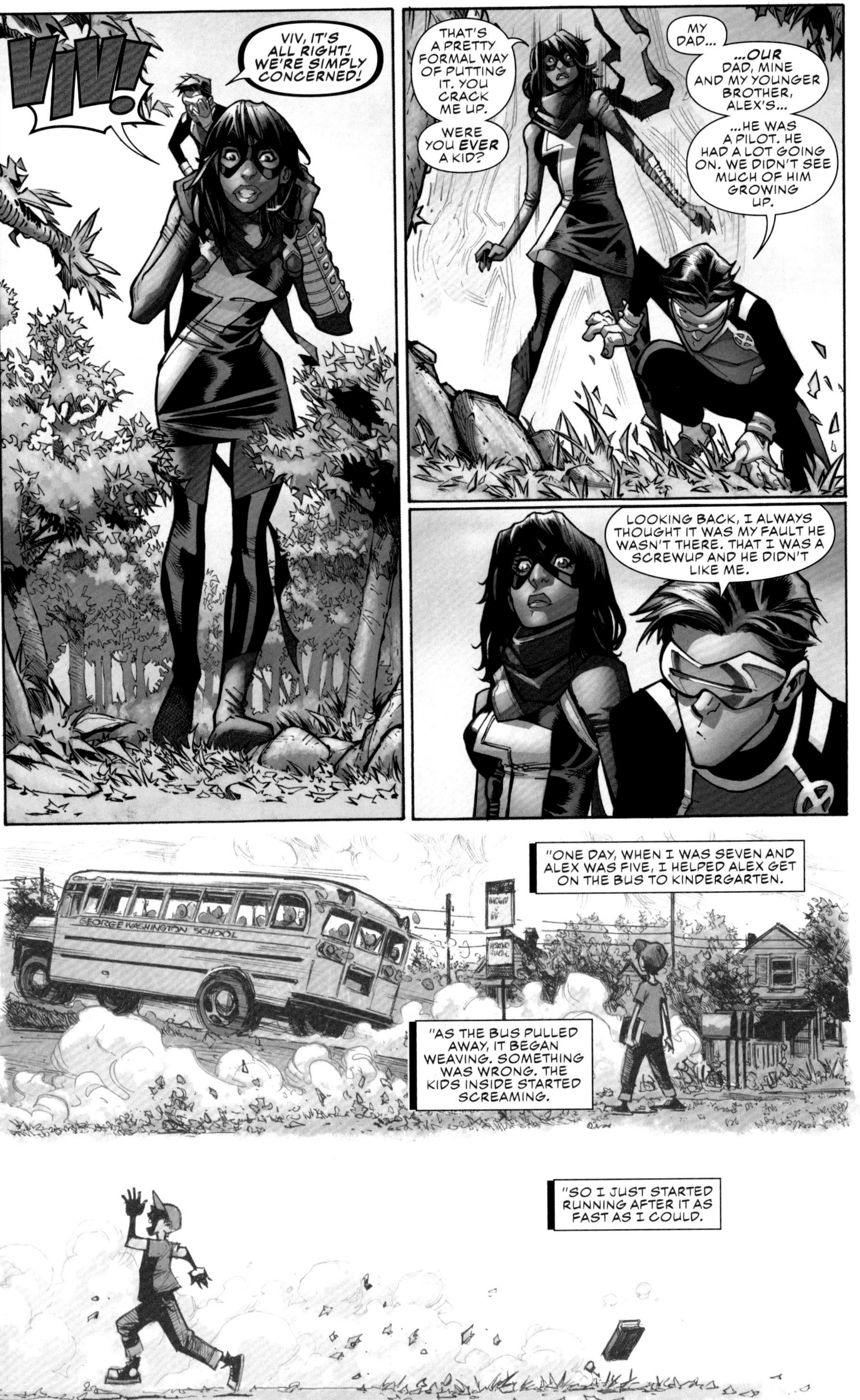
VIV!
VIV, IT'S ALL RIGHT! WE'RE SIMPLY CONCERNED!
THAT'S A PRETTY FORMAL WAY OF PUTTING IT. YOU CRACK ME UP.
WERE YOU EVER A KID?
MY DAD...
...OUR DAD, MINE AND MY YOUNGER BROTHER, ALEX'S...
...HE WAS A PILOT. HE HAD A LOT GOING ON. WE DIDN'T SEE MUCH OF HIM GROWING UP.
LOOKING BACK, I ALWAYS THOUGHT IT WAS MY FAULT HE WASN'T THERE. THAT I WAS A SCREWUP AND HE DIDN'T LIKE ME.
"ONE DAY, WHEN I WAS SEVEN AND ALEX WAS FIVE, I HELPED ALEX GET ON THE BUS TO KINDERGARTEN.
GEORGE WASHINGTON SCHOOL
"AS THE BUS PULLED AWAY, IT BEGAN WEAVING. SOMETHING WAS WRONG. THE KIDS INSIDE STARTED SCREAMING.
"SO I JUST STARTED RUNNING AFTER IT AS FAST AS I COULD.

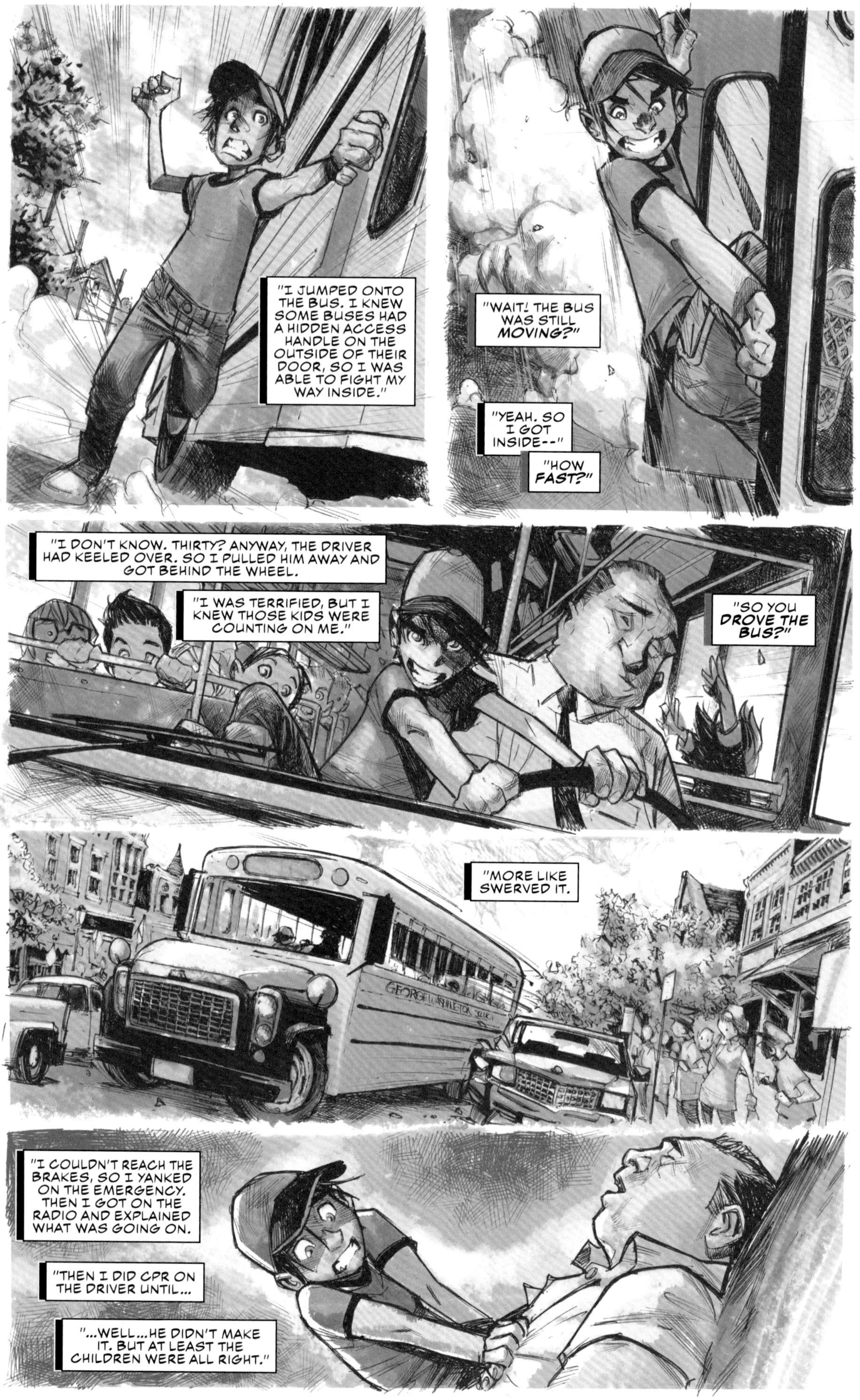
"I JUMPED ONTO THE BUS. I KNEW SOME BUSES HAD A HIDDEN ACCESS HANDLE ON THE OUTSIDE OF THEIR DOOR, SO I WAS ABLE TO FIGHT MY WAY INSIDE."
"WAIT! THE BUS WAS STILL MOVING?"
"YEAH. SO I GOT INSIDE--"
"HOW FAST?"
"I DON'T KNOW. THIRTY? ANYWAY, THE DRIVER HAD KEELED OVER. SO I PULLED HIM AWAY AND GOT BEHIND THE WHEEL.
"I WAS TERRIFIED, BUT I KNEW THOSE KIDS WERE COUNTING ON ME."
"SO YOU DROVE THE BUS?"
"MORE LIKE SWERVED IT.
"I COULDN'T REACH THE BRAKES, SO I YANKED ON THE EMERGENCY. THEN I GOT ON THE RADIO AND EXPLAINED WHAT WAS GOING ON.
"THEN I DID CPR ON THE DRIVER UNTIL...
"...WELL...HE DIDN'T MAKE IT. BUT AT LEAST THE CHILDREN WERE ALL RIGHT."

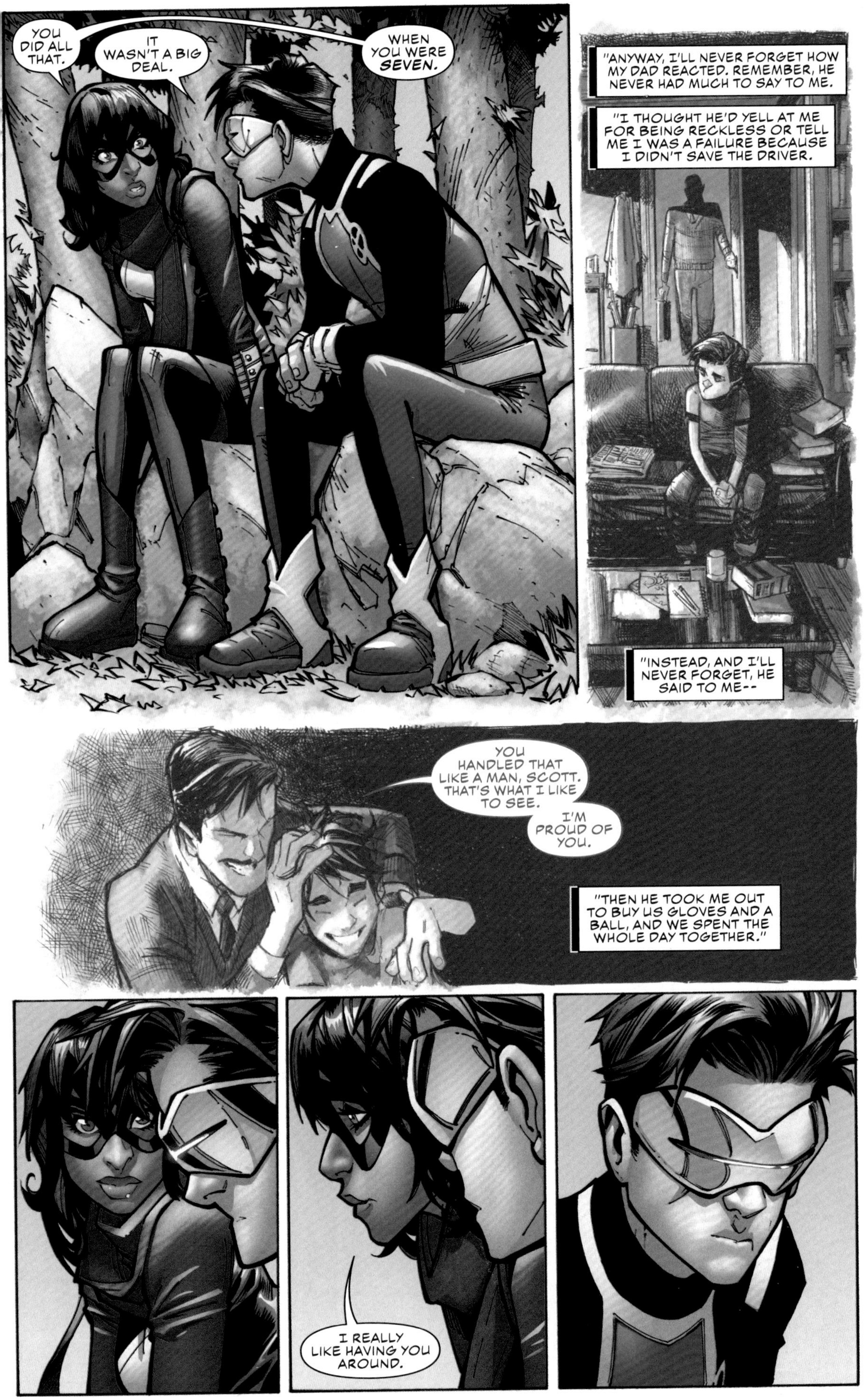
YOU DID ALL THAT.
IT WASN'T A BIG DEAL.
WHEN YOU WERE SEVEN.
"ANYWAY, I'LL NEVER FORGET HOW MY DAD REACTED. REMEMBER, HE NEVER HAD MUCH TO SAY TO ME.
"I THOUGHT HE'D YELL AT ME FOR BEING RECKLESS OR TELL ME I WAS A FAILURE BECAUSE I DIDN'T SAVE THE DRIVER.
"INSTEAD, AND I'LL NEVER FORGET, HE SAID TO ME--
YOU HANDLED THAT LIKE A MAN, SCOTT. THAT'S WHAT I LIKE TO SEE.
I'M PROUD OF YOU.
"THEN HE TOOK ME OUT TO BUY US GLOVES AND A BALL, AND WE SPENT THE WHOLE DAY TOGETHER."
I REALLY LIKE HAVING YOU AROUND.

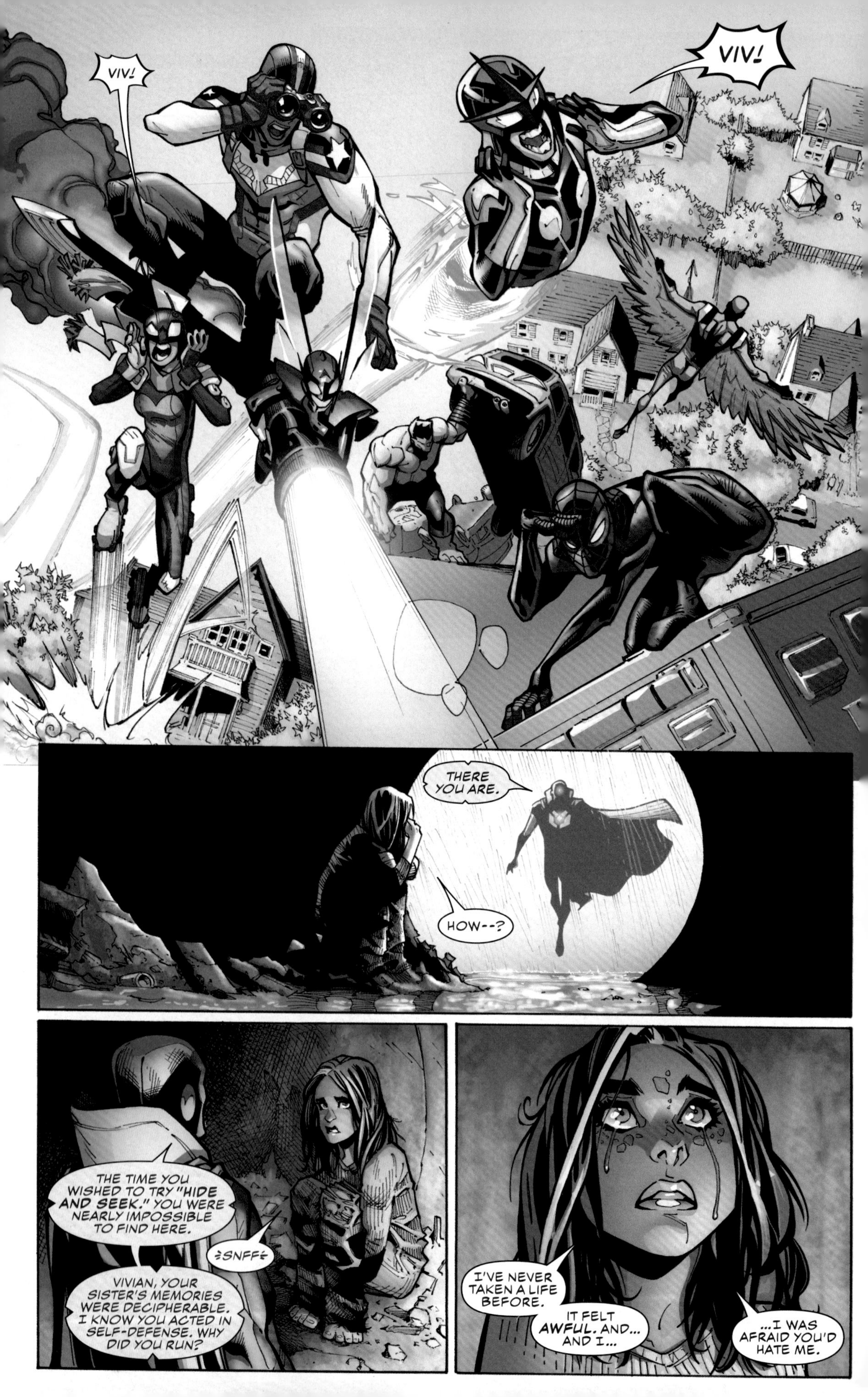
VIV!
VIV!
THERE YOU ARE.
HOW--?
THE TIME YOU WISHED TO TRY "HIDE AND SEEK." YOU WERE NEARLY IMPOSSIBLE TO FIND HERE.
SNFF
VIVIAN, YOUR SISTER'S MEMORIES WERE DECIPHERABLE. I KNOW YOU ACTED IN SELF-DEFENSE. WHY DID YOU RUN?
I'VE NEVER TAKEN A LIFE BEFORE.
IT FELT AWFUL. AND... AND I...
...I WAS AFRAID YOU'D HATE ME.

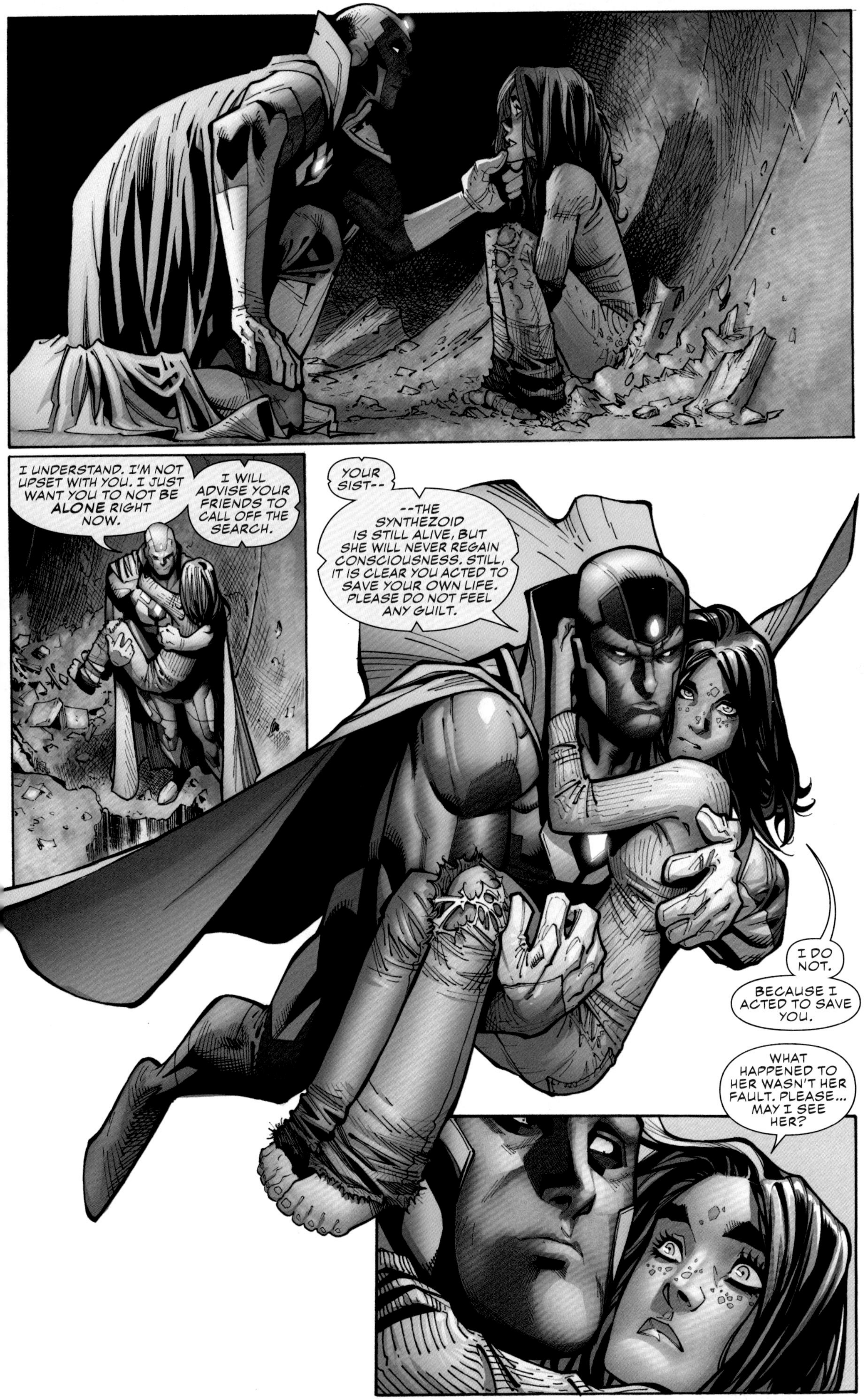
I UNDERSTAND. I'M NOT UPSET WITH YOU. I JUST WANT YOU TO NOT BE ALONE RIGHT NOW.
I WILL ADVISE YOUR FRIENDS TO CALL OFF THE SEARCH.
YOUR SIST--
--THE SYNTHEZOID IS STILL ALIVE, BUT SHE WILL NEVER REGAIN CONSCIOUSNESS. STILL, IT IS CLEAR YOU ACTED TO SAVE YOUR OWN LIFE. PLEASE DO NOT FEEL ANY GUILT.
I DO NOT.
BECAUSE I ACTED TO SAVE YOU.
WHAT HAPPENED TO HER WASN'T HER FAULT. PLEASE... MAY I SEE HER?

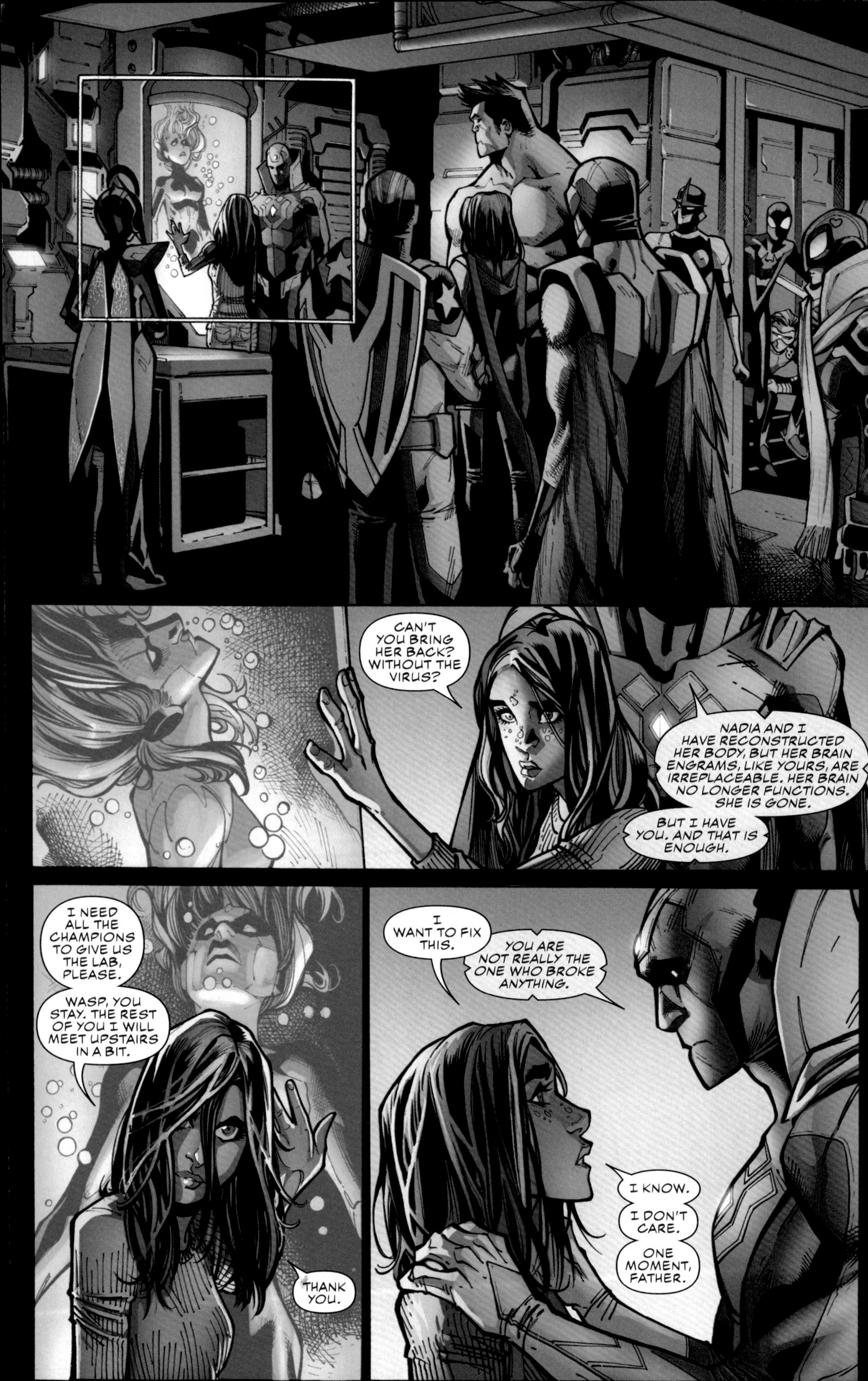
CAN'T YOU BRING HER BACK? WITHOUT THE VIRUS?
NADIA AND I HAVE RECONSTRUCTED HER BODY, BUT HER BRAIN ENGRAMS, LIKE YOURS, ARE IRREPLACEABLE. HER BRAIN NO LONGER FUNCTIONS. SHE IS GONE.
BUT I HAVE YOU. AND THAT IS ENOUGH.
I NEED ALL THE CHAMPIONS TO GIVE US THE LAB, PLEASE.
WASP, YOU STAY. THE REST OF YOU I WILL MEET UPSTAIRS IN A BIT.
THANK YOU.
I WANT TO FIX THIS.
YOU ARE NOT REALLY THE ONE WHO BROKE ANYTHING.
I KNOW.
I DON'T CARE.
ONE MOMENT, FATHER.

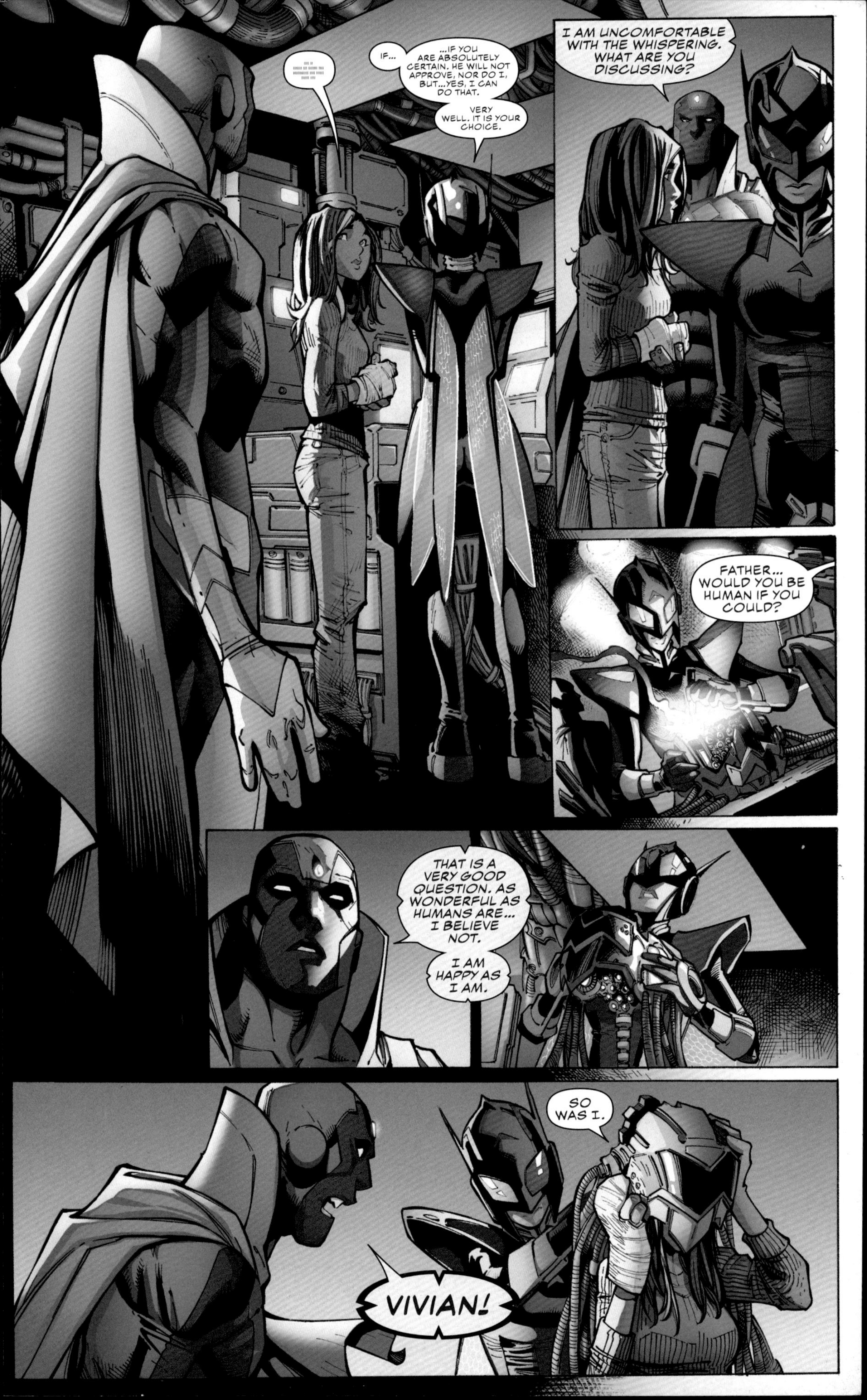
IF...
...IF YOU ARE ABSOLUTELY CERTAIN. HE WILL NOT APPROVE, NOR DO I, BUT...YES, I CAN DO THAT.
VERY WELL. IT IS YOUR CHOICE.
I AM UNCOMFORTABLE WITH THE WHISPERING. WHAT ARE YOU DISCUSSING?
FATHER... WOULD YOU BE HUMAN IF YOU COULD?
THAT IS A VERY GOOD QUESTION. AS WONDERFUL AS HUMANS ARE... I BELIEVE NOT.
I AM HAPPY AS I AM.
SO WAS I.
VIVIAN!

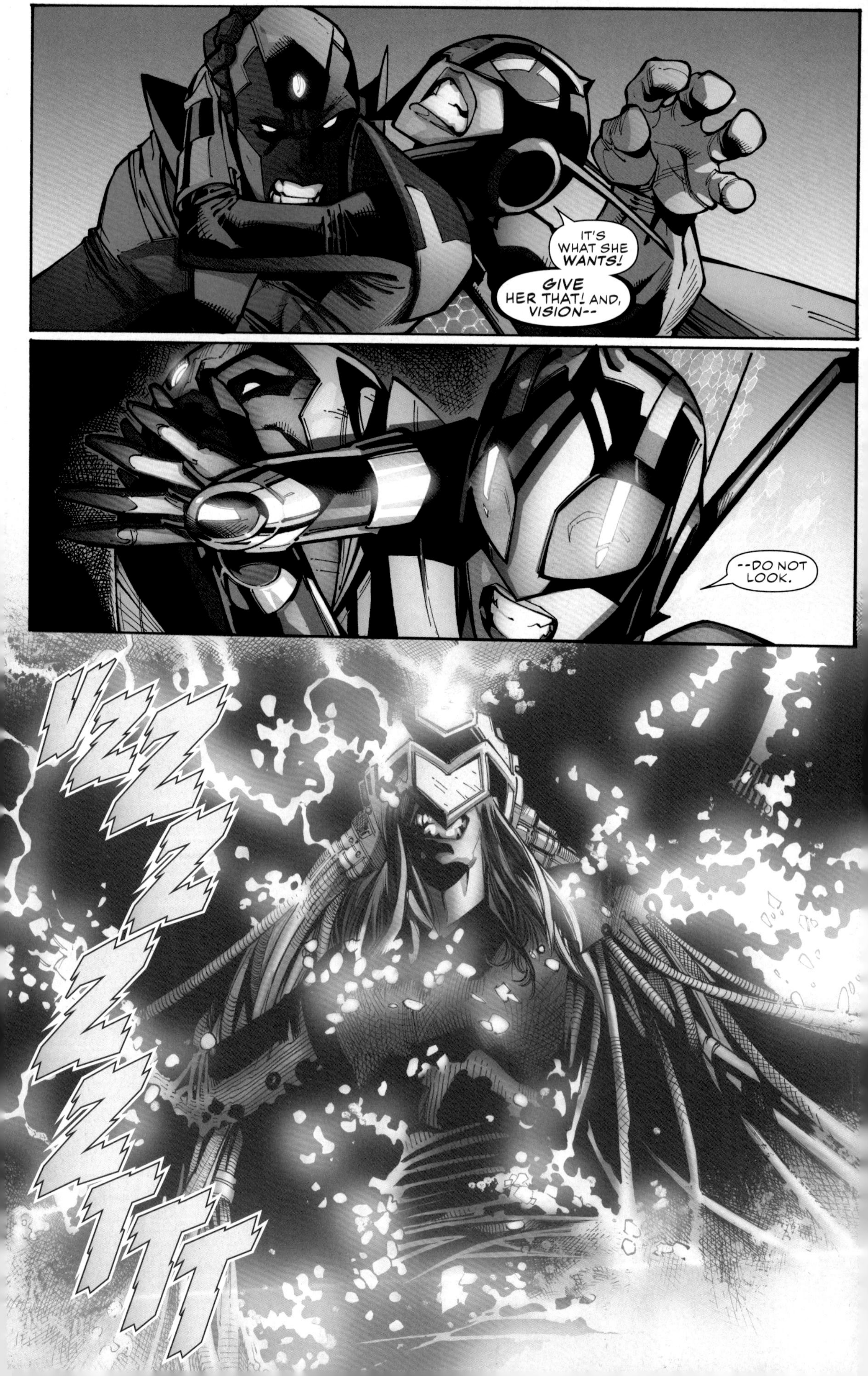

IT'S WHAT SHE WANTS!
GIVE HER THAT! AND, VISION--
--DO NOT LOOK.
VZZZZZZTTT

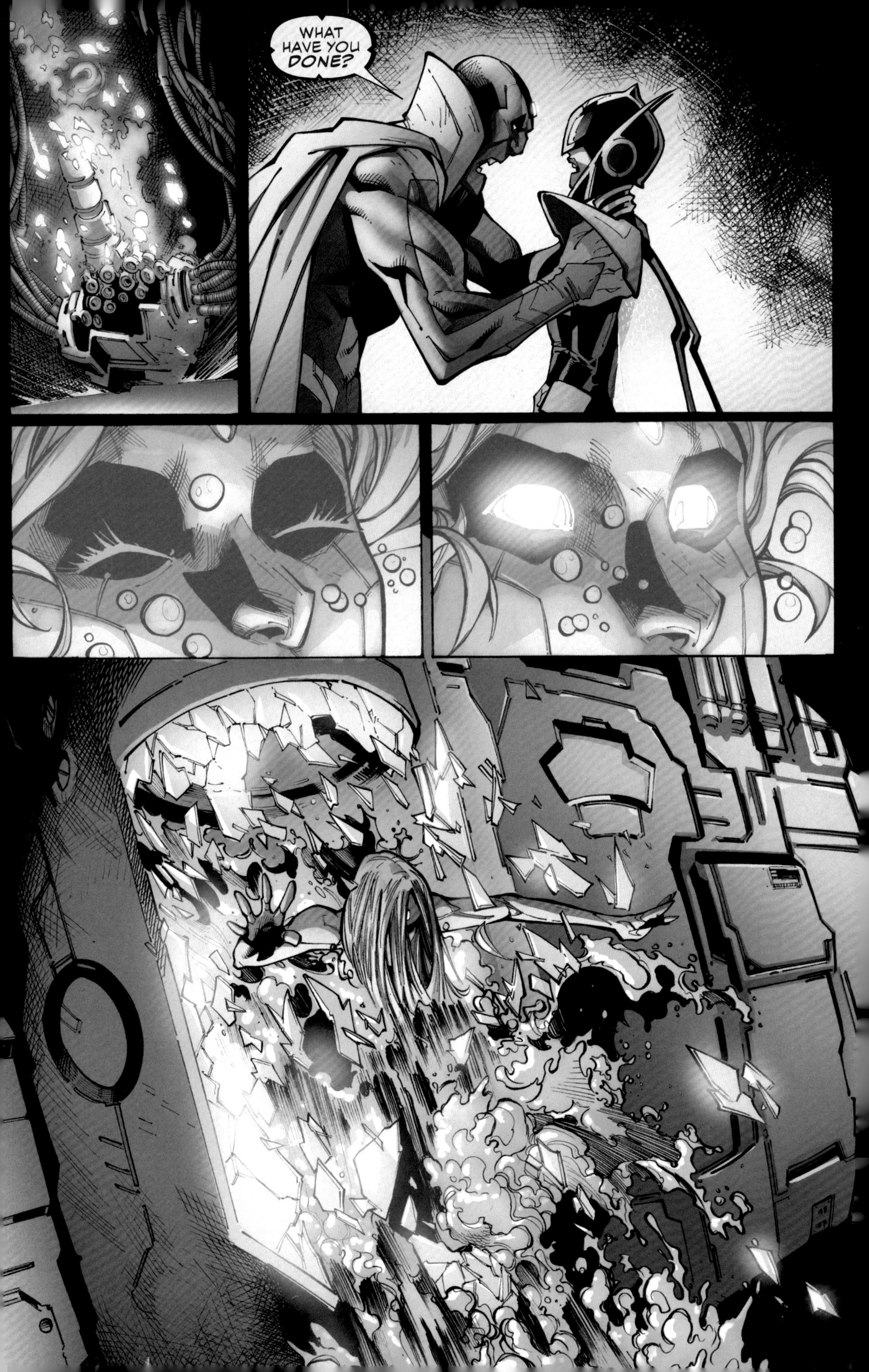
WHAT HAVE YOU DONE?

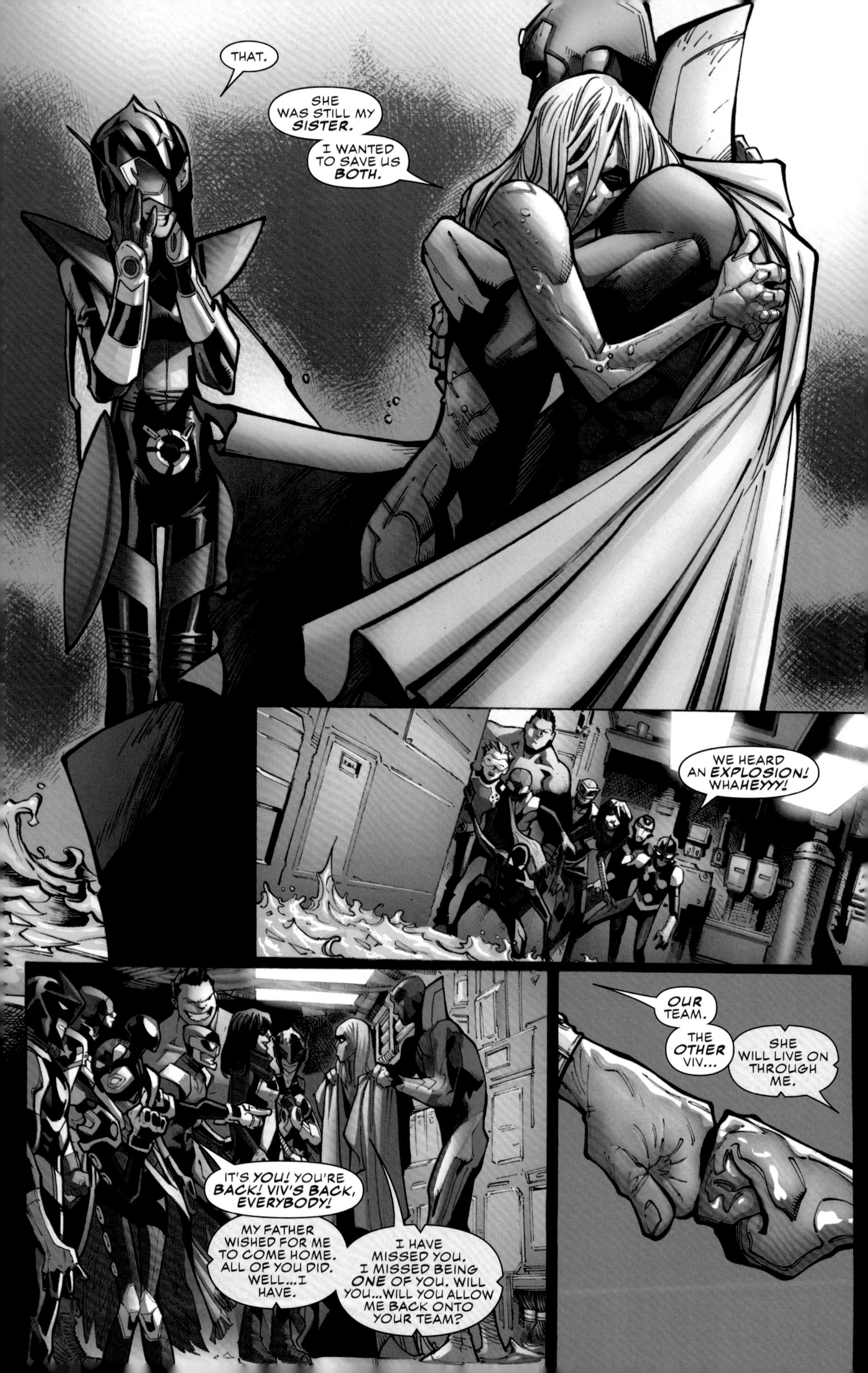
THAT.
SHE WAS STILL MY SISTER.
I WANTED TO SAVE US BOTH.
WE HEARD AN EXPLOSION! WHAHEYYY!
IT'S YOU! YOU'RE BACK! VIV'S BACK, EVERYBODY!
MY FATHER WISHED FOR ME TO COME HOME. ALL OF YOU DID. WELL...I HAVE.
I HAVE MISSED YOU. I MISSED BEING ONE OF YOU. WILL YOU...WILL YOU ALLOW ME BACK ONTO YOUR TEAM?
OUR TEAM.
THE OTHER VIV...
SHE WILL LIVE ON THROUGH ME.

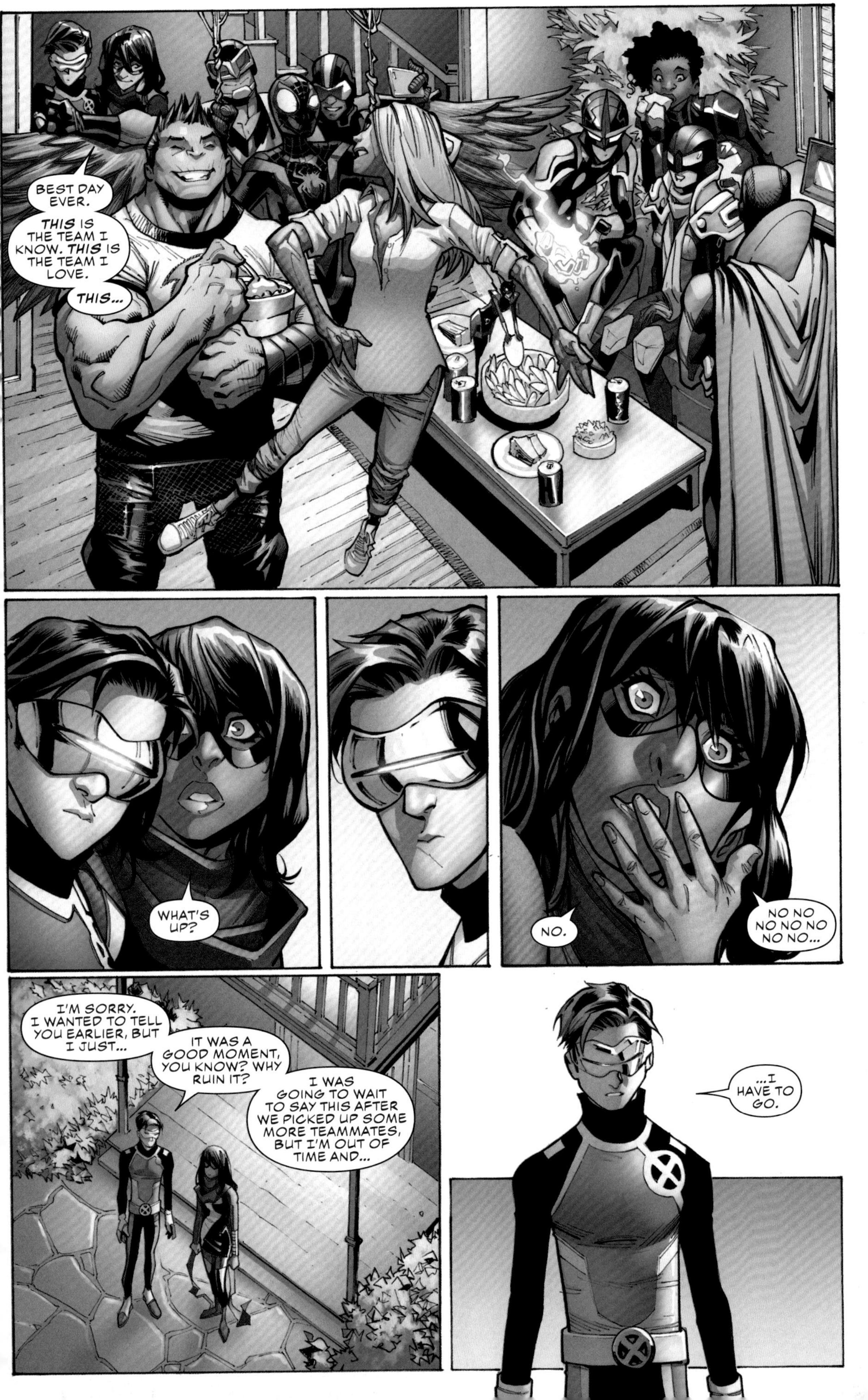
BEST DAY EVER.
THIS IS THE TEAM I KNOW. THIS IS THE TEAM I LOVE.
THIS...
WHAT'S UP?
NO.
NO NO NO NO NO NO NO...
I'M SORRY. I WANTED TO TELL YOU EARLIER, BUT I JUST...
IT WAS A GOOD MOMENT, YOU KNOW? WHY RUIN IT?
I WAS GOING TO WAIT TO SAY THIS AFTER WE PICKED UP SOME MORE TEAMMATES, BUT I'M OUT OF TIME AND...
...I HAVE TO GO.

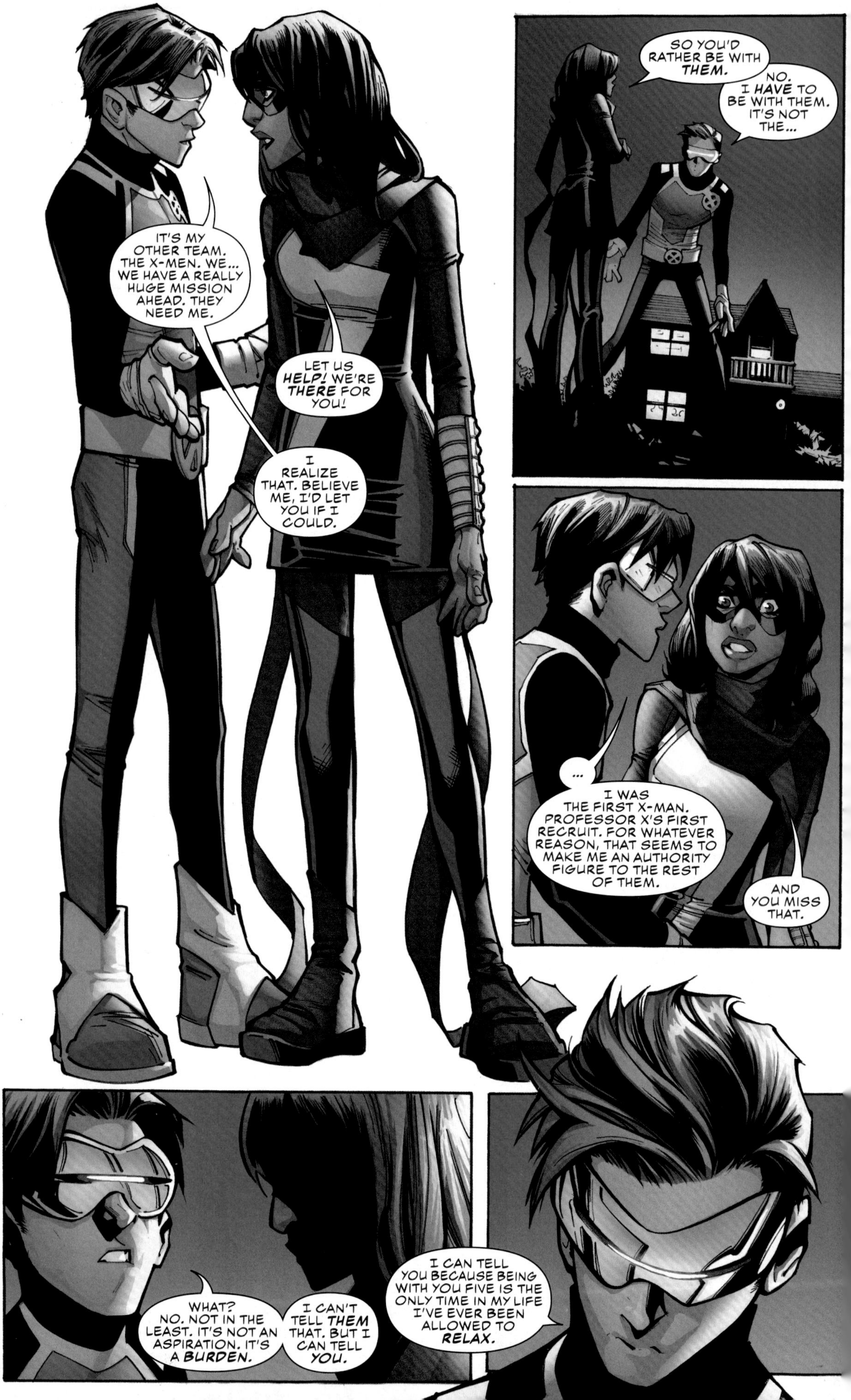
IT'S MY OTHER TEAM. THE X-MEN. WE... WE HAVE A REALLY HUGE MISSION AHEAD. THEY NEED ME.
LET US HELP! WE'RE THERE FOR YOU!
I REALIZE THAT. BELIEVE ME, I'D LET YOU IF I COULD.
SO YOU'D RATHER BE WITH THEM.
NO. I HAVE TO BE WITH THEM. IT'S NOT THE...
...
I WAS THE FIRST X-MAN. PROFESSOR X'S FIRST RECRUIT. FOR WHATEVER REASON, THAT SEEMS TO MAKE ME AN AUTHORITY FIGURE TO THE REST OF THEM.
AND YOU MISS THAT.
WHAT? NO. NOT IN THE LEAST. IT'S NOT AN ASPIRATION. IT'S A BURDEN.
I CAN'T TELL THEM THAT. BUT I CAN TELL YOU.
I CAN TELL YOU BECAUSE BEING WITH YOU FIVE IS THE ONLY TIME IN MY LIFE I'VE EVER BEEN ALLOWED TO RELAX.

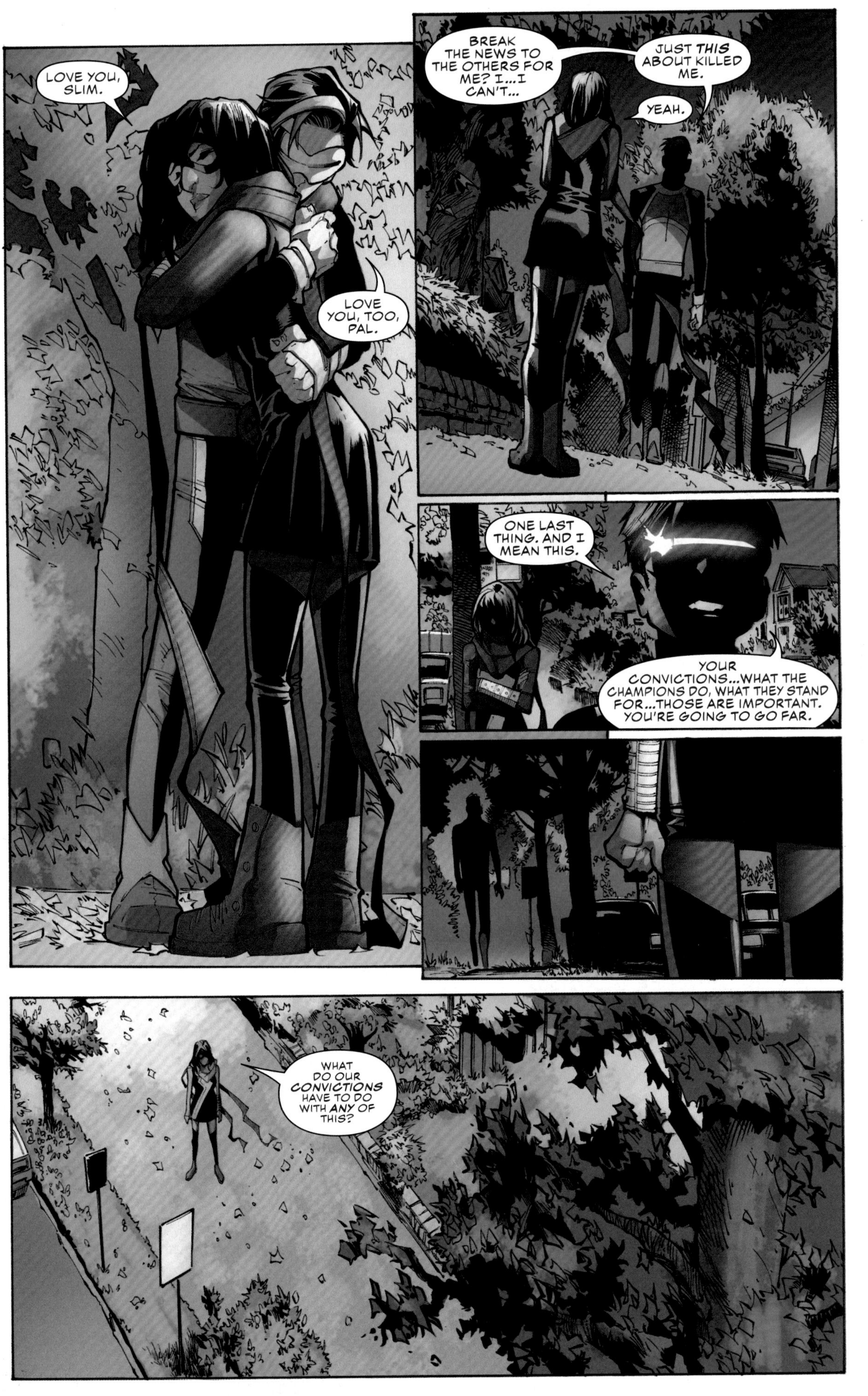
LOVE YOU, SLIM.
LOVE YOU, TOO, PAL.
BREAK THE NEWS TO THE OTHERS FOR ME? I...I CAN'T...
JUST THIS ABOUT KILLED ME.
YEAH.
ONE LAST THING. AND I MEAN THIS.
YOUR CONVICTIONS...WHAT THE CHAMPIONS DO, WHAT THEY STAND FOR...THOSE ARE IMPORTANT. YOU'RE GOING TO GO FAR.
WHAT DO OUR CONVICTIONS HAVE TO DO WITH ANY OF THIS?

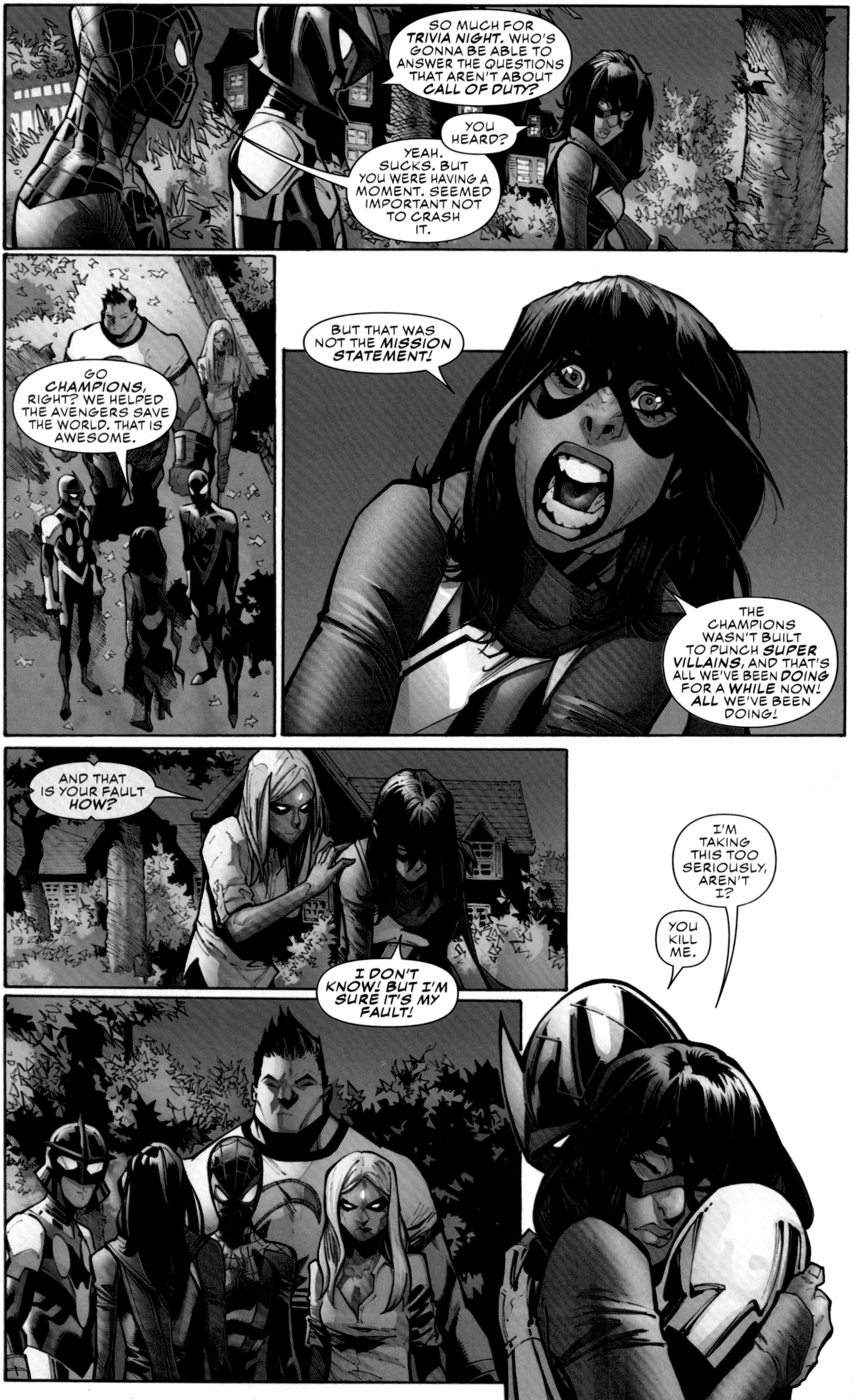
SO MUCH FOR TRIVIA NIGHT. WHO'S GONNA BE ABLE TO ANSWER THE QUESTIONS THAT AREN'T ABOUT CALL OF DUTY?
YOU HEARD?
YEAH. SUCKS. BUT YOU WERE HAVING A MOMENT. SEEMED IMPORTANT NOT TO CRASH IT.
GO CHAMPIONS, RIGHT? WE HELPED THE AVENGERS SAVE THE WORLD. THAT IS AWESOME.
BUT THAT WAS NOT THE MISSION STATEMENT!
THE CHAMPIONS WASN'T BUILT TO PUNCH SUPER VILLAINS, AND THAT'S ALL WE'VE BEEN DOING FOR A WHILE NOW! ALL WE'VE BEEN DOING!
AND THAT IS YOUR FAULT HOW?
I DON'T KNOW! BUT I'M SURE IT'S MY FAULT!
I'M TAKING THIS TOO SERIOUSLY, AREN'T I?
YOU KILL ME.

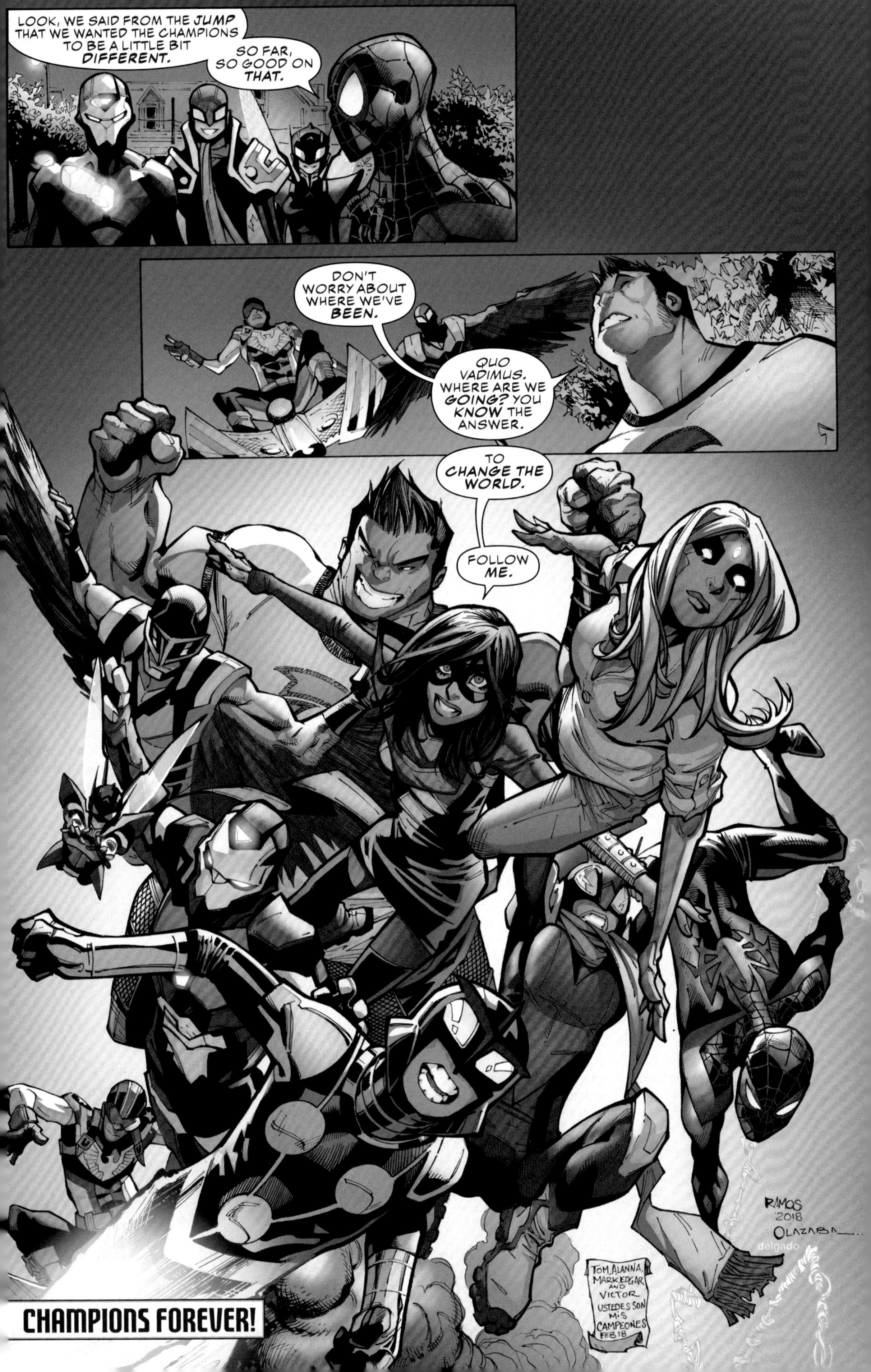
LOOK, WE SAID FROM THE JUMP THAT WE WANTED THE CHAMPIONS TO BE A LITTLE BIT DIFFERENT.
SO FAR, SO GOOD ON THAT.
DON'T WORRY ABOUT WHERE WE'VE BEEN.
QUO VADIMUS. WHERE ARE WE GOING? YOU KNOW THE ANSWER.
TO CHANGE THE WORLD.
FOLLOW ME.
RAMOS 2018
OLAZABA
delgado
TOM, ALANNA, MARK, EDGAR AND VICTOR USTEDES SON MIS CAMPEONES FEB 18
CHAMPIONS FOREVER!

WE ARE THE CHAMPIONS

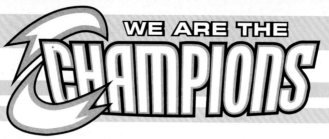

Jobs don't get much more fun than this. Our six Champions, all of them, are a blast to write and ended up being a good mix of personalities and powers. When Editor Tom Brevoort and I talked about spinning this book out of ALL-NEW, ALL-DIFFERENT AVENGERS, we knew the core members would be those departing that team: Ms. Marvel, Spider-Miles and Nova. Building from there, we needed a powerhouse, so Amadeus Cho was an obvious choice. Viv Vision, coming off of Tom King's excellent VISION series, was also an intriguing pick--we thought that if we temporarily gave her a slightly colder personality like her father's, for a good reason that would pay off in the series as it went along, she'd fit right in. Cyclops was our wild card; as everyone at Marvel will tell you, Scott Summers is hands-down one of my favorite characters in all of comics, and I'm grateful to the X-Men office for letting Slim come to the party. Extra added bonus from the mix: by coincidence less than design, we'd backed into a super-team with only one white male on it, which was an exciting reflection of how inclusive American society is becoming.

The real joy, though, has been working with my longtime partner Humberto Ramos and his posse, Victor and Edgar. Month after month, they made me look like I kinda knew what I was doing, as did Assistant Editor Alanna Smith. Editor Tom Brevoort wears his famous hat so he can slide it down over his face during the day to hide the fact that he's sleeping, but even he piped in from time to time with aid and assistance.

I hope you enjoyed our work. Some issues were easier to write than others (though the Cyclops issue, #12, was a breeze and my favorite), but the overall experience was terrific. Now it's up to writer Jim Zub and artist Sean Izaakse to carry on, and I know they'll keep you entertained. Thanks for reading!

Mark Waid

The saying goes that lighting never strikes twice...in the same spot.

That's actually not true--a long, long time ago in a galaxy far, far away called DC comics, I once had the biggest stroke of good luck when they offered my me the job of penciling a little book called *Impulse*. I couldn't fathom that it was the beginning of a series of fortunate events, not only to have for the first time the honor to be the lead artist in an ongoing comic book series, but like in the heroic journey, I got to meet both my Ben Kenobi and Yoda who goes by the name of Mark Waid. After an amazing run of joy and growth, that book came to an end and we followed our paths elsewhere. Mark became a living legend and I got to draw SPIDER-MAN--not bad, huh?

But like in a decent epic tale, the journey is not complete until you go back home with the wisdom learned through the many adventures you've lived. That couldn't happen without the call of the essential elders of the MARVEL reign. Axel and Tom are the names of these beings.

They summoned me to draw this "little" book called CHAMPIONS, and the idea of working again with Obi-Mark Kenobi put a huge smile on my face--but then when Alanna Smith, the fairest assistant editor, explained to me what the book was all about, I suddenly had a *Ratatouille* moment and instantly returned back to those early years in comics. Our mission was to bring togetherness to this band of cool young super heroes and make something fun and encouraging at the same time, a story that brought joy and hope to those who would read it, and that is how CHAMPIONS happened. Edgar and Victor brought their best to make CHAMPIONS what it is...

...A BREATH OF FRESH AIR ON THE FIRST DAY OF SUMMER!

Just what comic books are meant to be.

I was lucky enough to grow and have a great career after *Impulse*, good enough to make that lighting strike again and impact me right in my heart where I'll keep my eternal love for Viv, Kamala, Scott, Miles, Amadeus and Sam.

Thank you, Champions!

You rule my world.

Humberto Ramos

Usually when I look back at a series I worked on, I remember stuff that happened while I was coloring, like déjà vu. Most of the time it is music or a certain movie that I was watching on repeat during those days.

With CHAMPIONS, I will always remember the meaning of the word "change," not only because the world is going through many changes but because this book is all about that: the new generation demanding the older one to make changes to better the world, and if they don't listen, it's time for the kids to take charge. Also, I had a lot of personal and professional changes going on while working on this book, changes I resisted at first, but in the end all of them turned out for the better.

So I think that's what I will remember the most whenever I look back at this excellent run (besides the opportunity to work with the amazing Mark Waid and my brothers Humberto and Victor), that change is always necessary or else you'll go insane.

Thanks, Marvel!

Edgar Delgado

Teamwork--that's what I learned every time we finished an issue, and each has been fun... Something that always will stay in my mind is last year at La Conque show in Queretaro, Mexico. We were at that show to do a panel and a signing, and Mark was announced to be there too. He flew out just for that and stayed 'til the last person in line to sign books. Right after that, they had to take him to the airport so he could make his flight back home and be at another signing--that's what I call real professionalism! So, for me, being part of this team is an honor...

Tom, Alanna, Mark and my brothers Humberto and Edgar! You guys are the Champions in my book. I enjoyed this long summer ride, and for that...

GRACIAS!!!

Victor Olazaba

Send letters to MHEROES@MARVEL.COM marked "OKAY TO PRINT."

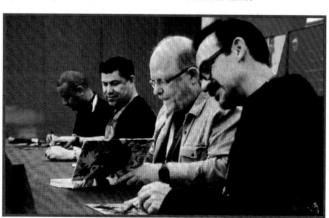

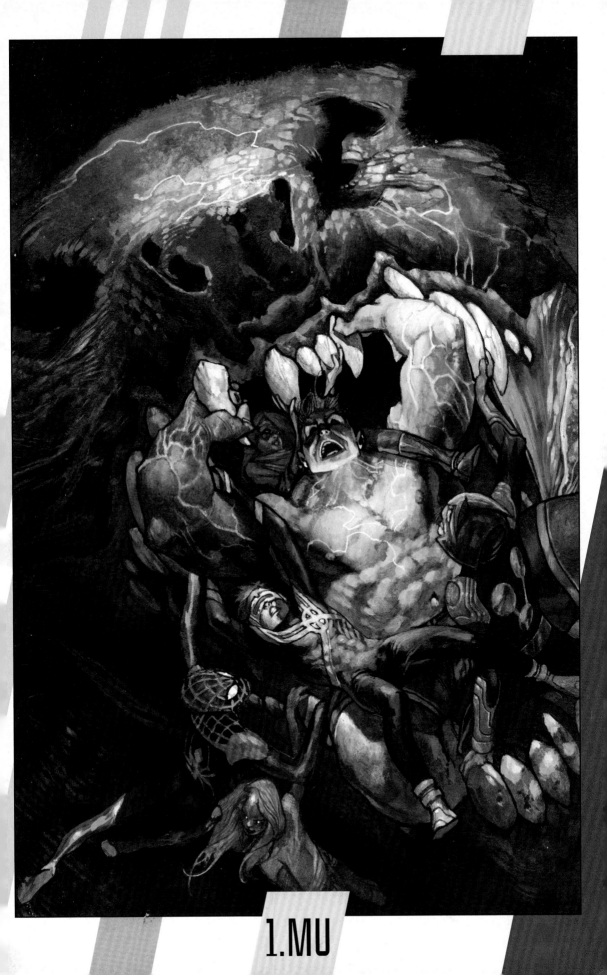

1.MU

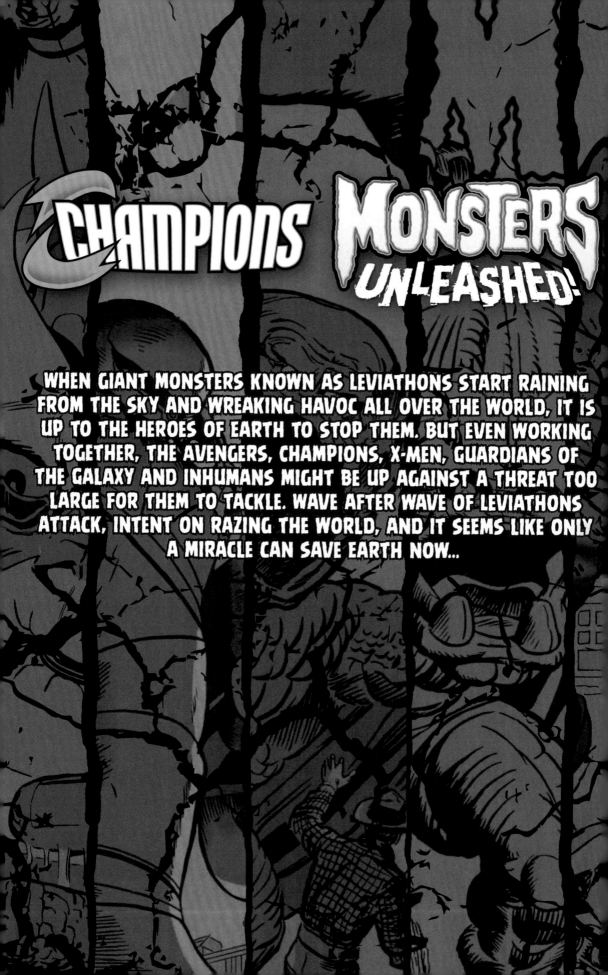

CHAMPIONS

MONSTERS UNLEASHED!

WHEN GIANT MONSTERS KNOWN AS LEVIATHONS START RAINING FROM THE SKY AND WREAKING HAVOC ALL OVER THE WORLD, IT IS UP TO THE HEROES OF EARTH TO STOP THEM. BUT EVEN WORKING TOGETHER, THE AVENGERS, CHAMPIONS, X-MEN, GUARDIANS OF THE GALAXY AND INHUMANS MIGHT BE UP AGAINST A THREAT TOO LARGE FOR THEM TO TACKLE. WAVE AFTER WAVE OF LEVIATHONS ATTACK, INTENT ON RAZING THE WORLD, AND IT SEEMS LIKE ONLY A MIRACLE CAN SAVE EARTH NOW...

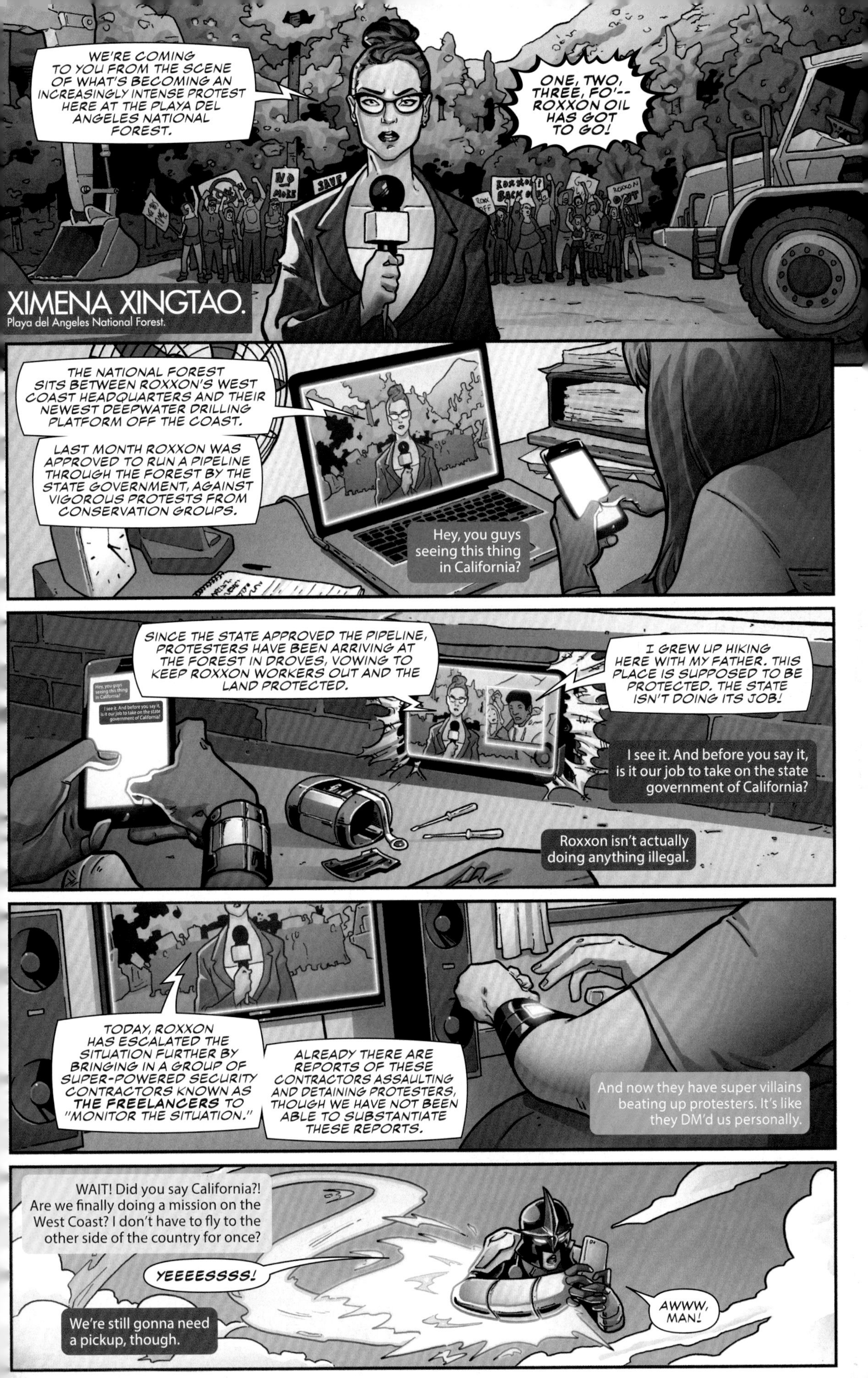
WE'RE COMING TO YOU FROM THE SCENE OF WHAT'S BECOMING AN INCREASINGLY INTENSE PROTEST HERE AT THE PLAYA DEL ANGELES NATIONAL FOREST.
ONE, TWO, THREE, FO'-- ROXXON OIL HAS GOT TO GO!
XIMENA XINGTAO.
Playa del Angeles National Forest.
THE NATIONAL FOREST SITS BETWEEN ROXXON'S WEST COAST HEADQUARTERS AND THEIR NEWEST DEEPWATER DRILLING PLATFORM OFF THE COAST.
LAST MONTH ROXXON WAS APPROVED TO RUN A PIPELINE THROUGH THE FOREST BY THE STATE GOVERNMENT, AGAINST VIGOROUS PROTESTS FROM CONSERVATION GROUPS.
Hey, you guys seeing this thing in California?
SINCE THE STATE APPROVED THE PIPELINE, PROTESTERS HAVE BEEN ARRIVING AT THE FOREST IN DROVES, VOWING TO KEEP ROXXON WORKERS OUT AND THE LAND PROTECTED.
I GREW UP HIKING HERE WITH MY FATHER. THIS PLACE IS SUPPOSED TO BE PROTECTED. THE STATE ISN'T DOING ITS JOB!
I see it. And before you say it, is it our job to take on the state government of California?
Roxxon isn't actually doing anything illegal.
TODAY, ROXXON HAS ESCALATED THE SITUATION FURTHER BY BRINGING IN A GROUP OF SUPER-POWERED SECURITY CONTRACTORS KNOWN AS **THE FREELANCERS** TO "MONITOR THE SITUATION."
ALREADY THERE ARE REPORTS OF THESE CONTRACTORS ASSAULTING AND DETAINING PROTESTERS, THOUGH WE HAVE NOT BEEN ABLE TO SUBSTANTIATE THESE REPORTS.
And now they have super villains beating up protesters. It's like they DM'd us personally.
WAIT! Did you say California?! Are we finally doing a mission on the West Coast? I don't have to fly to the other side of the country for once?
YEEEESSSS!
We're still gonna need a pickup, though.
AWWW, MAN!

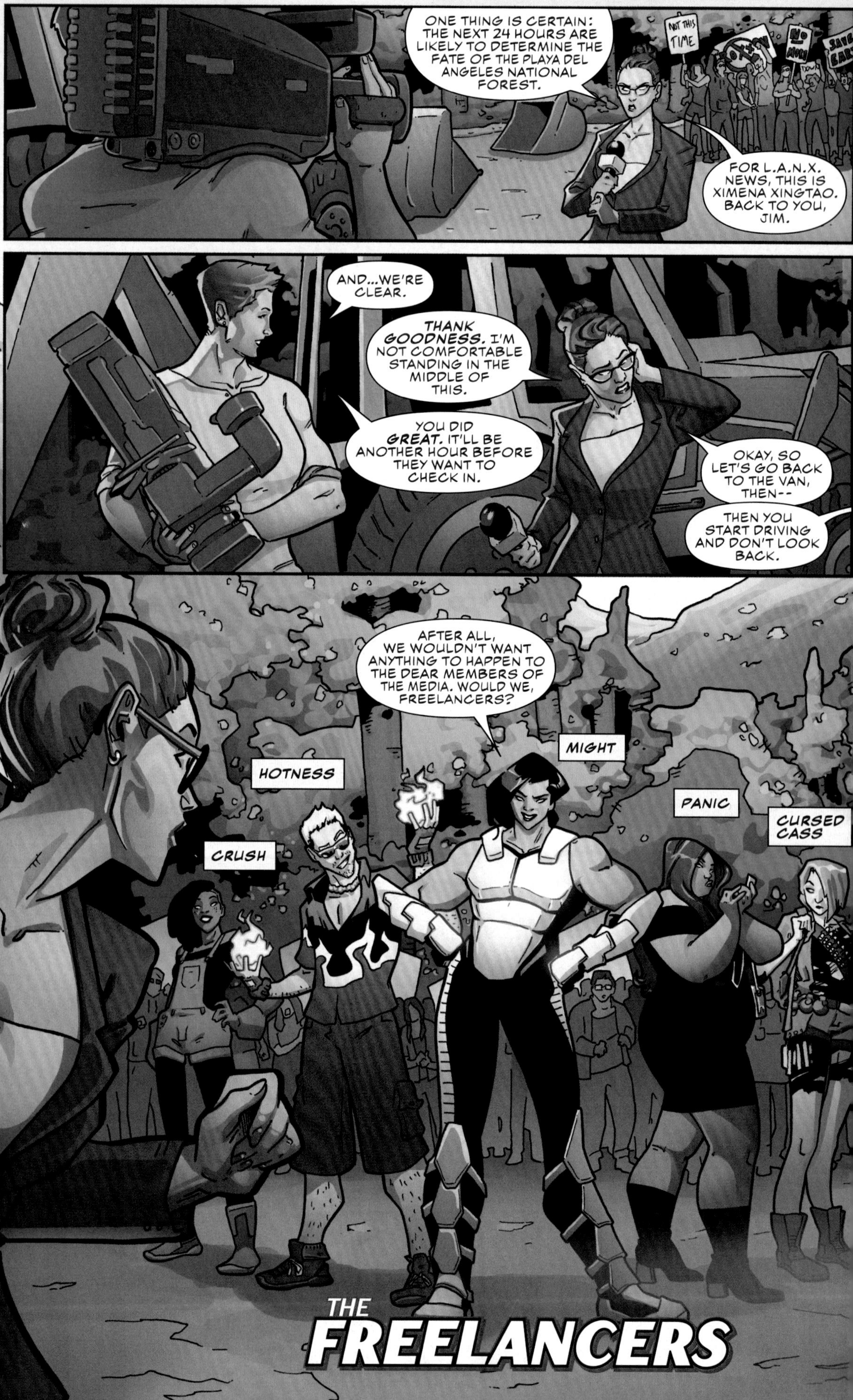
ONE THING IS CERTAIN: THE NEXT 24 HOURS ARE LIKELY TO DETERMINE THE FATE OF THE PLAYA DEL ANGELES NATIONAL FOREST.
NOT THIS TIME
FOR L.A.N.X. NEWS, THIS IS XIMENA XINGTAO. BACK TO YOU, JIM.
AND...WE'RE CLEAR.
THANK GOODNESS. I'M NOT COMFORTABLE STANDING IN THE MIDDLE OF THIS.
YOU DID GREAT. IT'LL BE ANOTHER HOUR BEFORE THEY WANT TO CHECK IN.
OKAY, SO LET'S GO BACK TO THE VAN, THEN--
THEN YOU START DRIVING AND DON'T LOOK BACK.
AFTER ALL, WE WOULDN'T WANT ANYTHING TO HAPPEN TO THE DEAR MEMBERS OF THE MEDIA. WOULD WE, FREELANCERS?
HOTNESS
MIGHT
PANIC
CURSED CASS
CRUSH
THE FREELANCERS

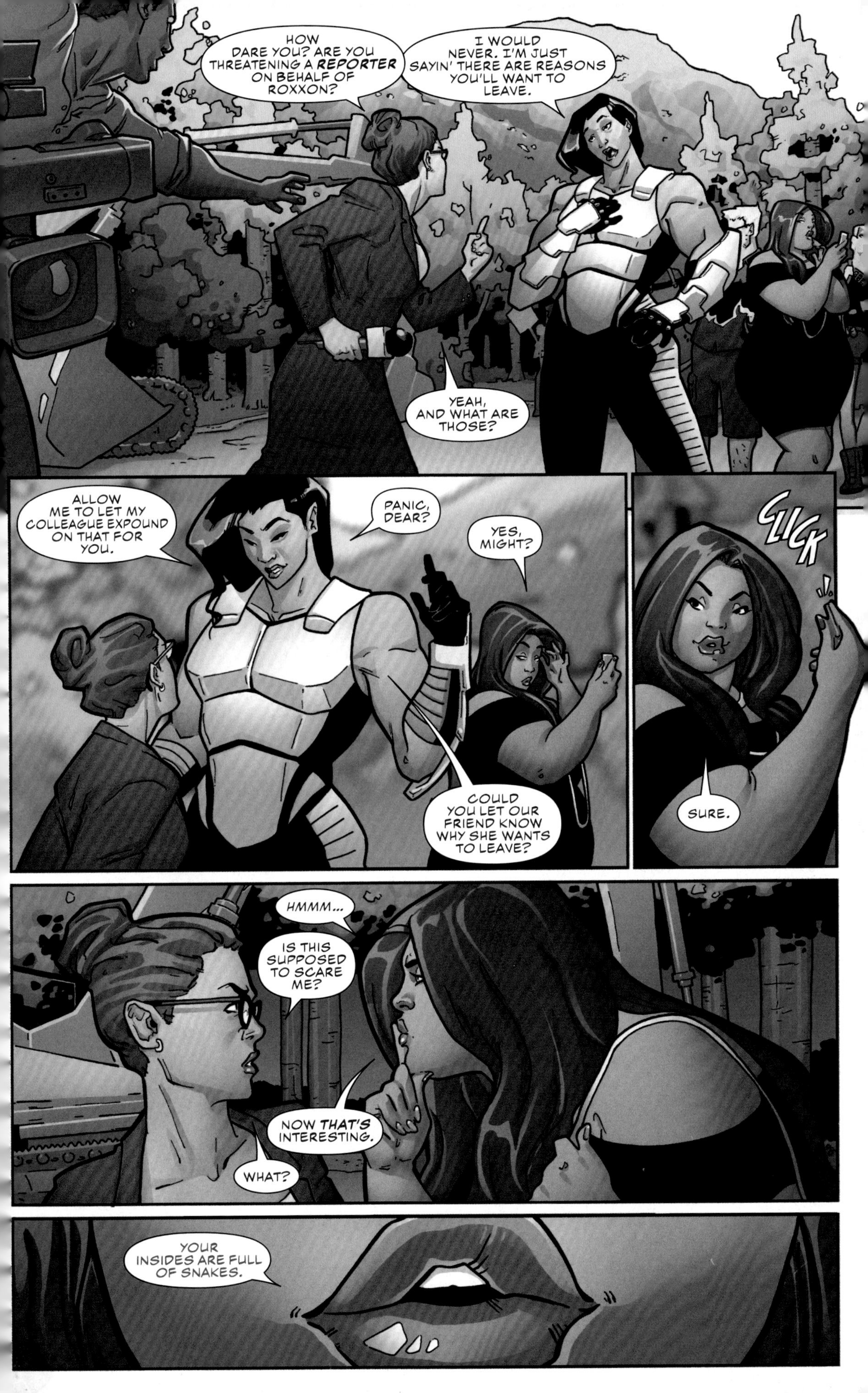
HOW DARE YOU? ARE YOU THREATENING A REPORTER ON BEHALF OF ROXXON?
I WOULD NEVER. I'M JUST SAYIN' THERE ARE REASONS YOU'LL WANT TO LEAVE.
YEAH, AND WHAT ARE THOSE?
ALLOW ME TO LET MY COLLEAGUE EXPOUND ON THAT FOR YOU.
PANIC, DEAR?
YES, MIGHT?
COULD YOU LET OUR FRIEND KNOW WHY SHE WANTS TO LEAVE?
CLICK
SURE.
HMMM...
IS THIS SUPPOSED TO SCARE ME?
NOW THAT'S INTERESTING.
WHAT?
YOUR INSIDES ARE FULL OF SNAKES.

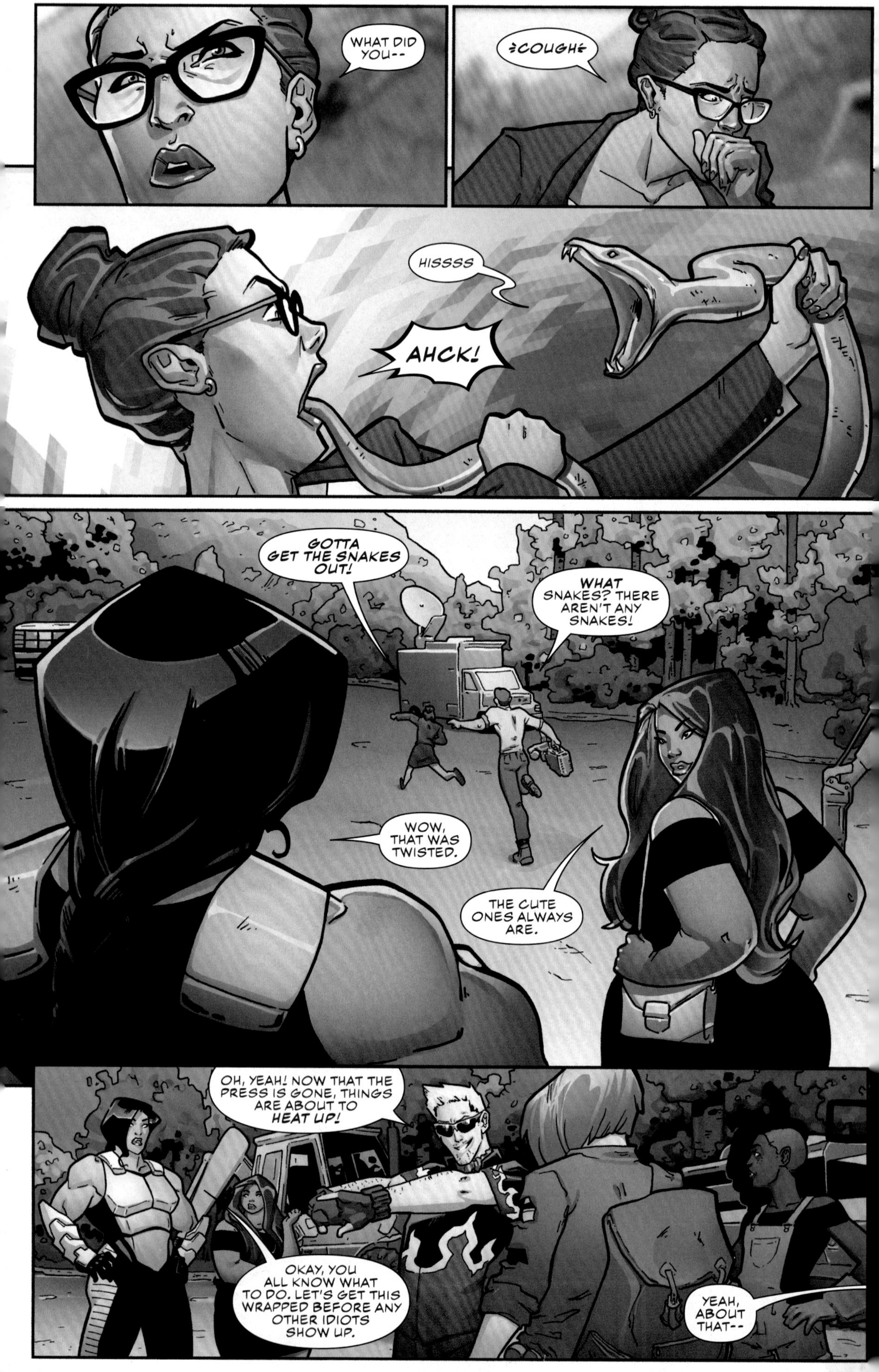
WHAT DID YOU--
COUGH
HISSSS
AHCK!
GOTTA GET THE SNAKES OUT!
WHAT SNAKES? THERE AREN'T ANY SNAKES!
WOW, THAT WAS TWISTED.
THE CUTE ONES ALWAYS ARE.
OH, YEAH! NOW THAT THE PRESS IS GONE, THINGS ARE ABOUT TO HEAT UP!
OKAY, YOU ALL KNOW WHAT TO DO. LET'S GET THIS WRAPPED BEFORE ANY OTHER IDIOTS SHOW UP.
YEAH, ABOUT THAT--

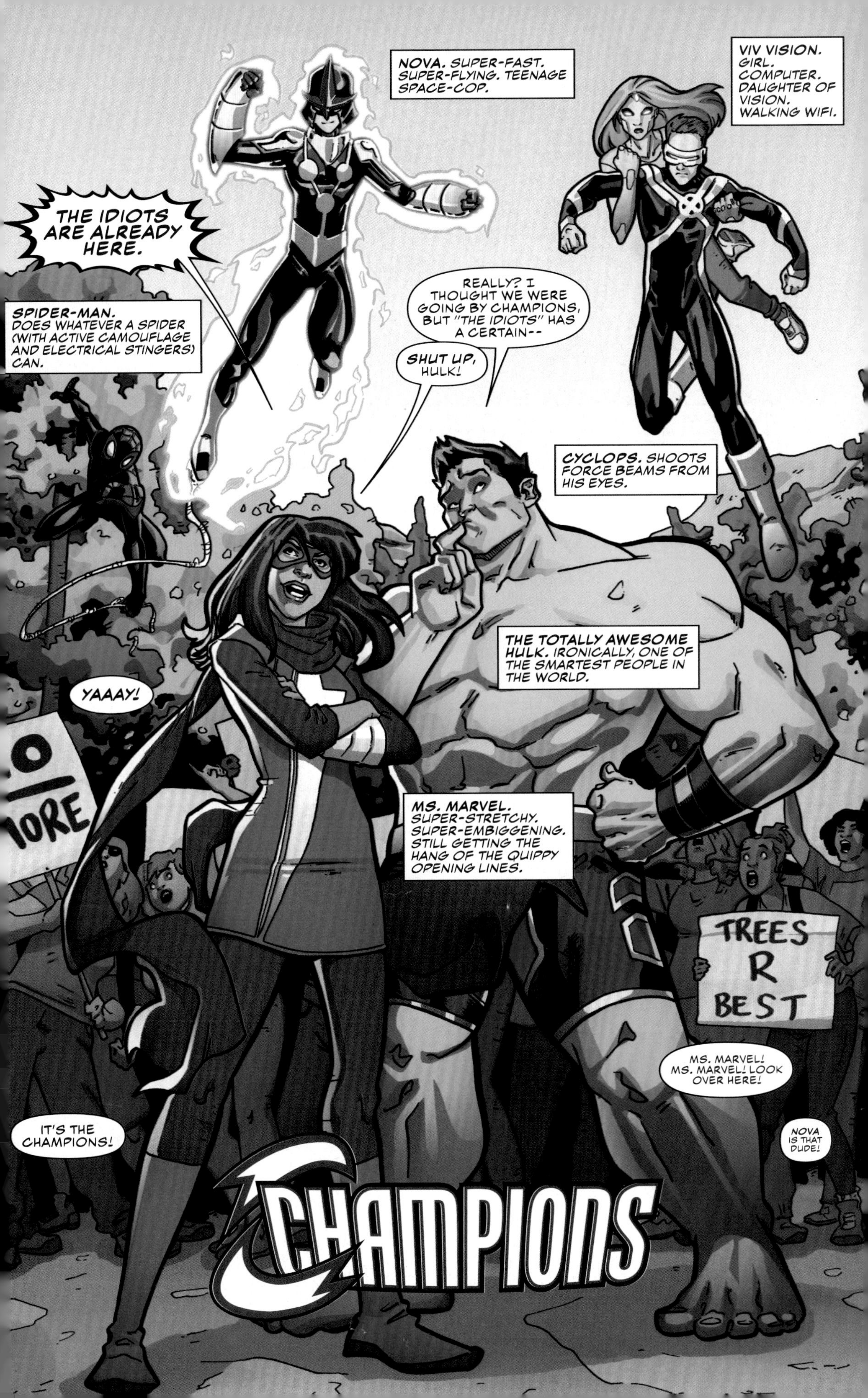
NOVA. SUPER-FAST. SUPER-FLYING. TEENAGE SPACE-COP.
VIV VISION. GIRL. COMPUTER. DAUGHTER OF VISION. WALKING WIFI.
THE IDIOTS ARE ALREADY HERE.
SPIDER-MAN. DOES WHATEVER A SPIDER (WITH ACTIVE CAMOUFLAGE AND ELECTRICAL STINGERS) CAN.
REALLY? I THOUGHT WE WERE GOING BY CHAMPIONS, BUT "THE IDIOTS" HAS A CERTAIN--
SHUT UP, HULK!
CYCLOPS. SHOOTS FORCE BEAMS FROM HIS EYES.
THE TOTALLY AWESOME HULK. IRONICALLY, ONE OF THE SMARTEST PEOPLE IN THE WORLD.
YAAAY!
MS. MARVEL. SUPER-STRETCHY. SUPER-EMBIGGENING. STILL GETTING THE HANG OF THE QUIPPY OPENING LINES.
TREES R BEST
MS. MARVEL! MS. MARVEL! LOOK OVER HERE!
IT'S THE CHAMPIONS!
NOVA IS THAT DUDE!
CHAMPIONS

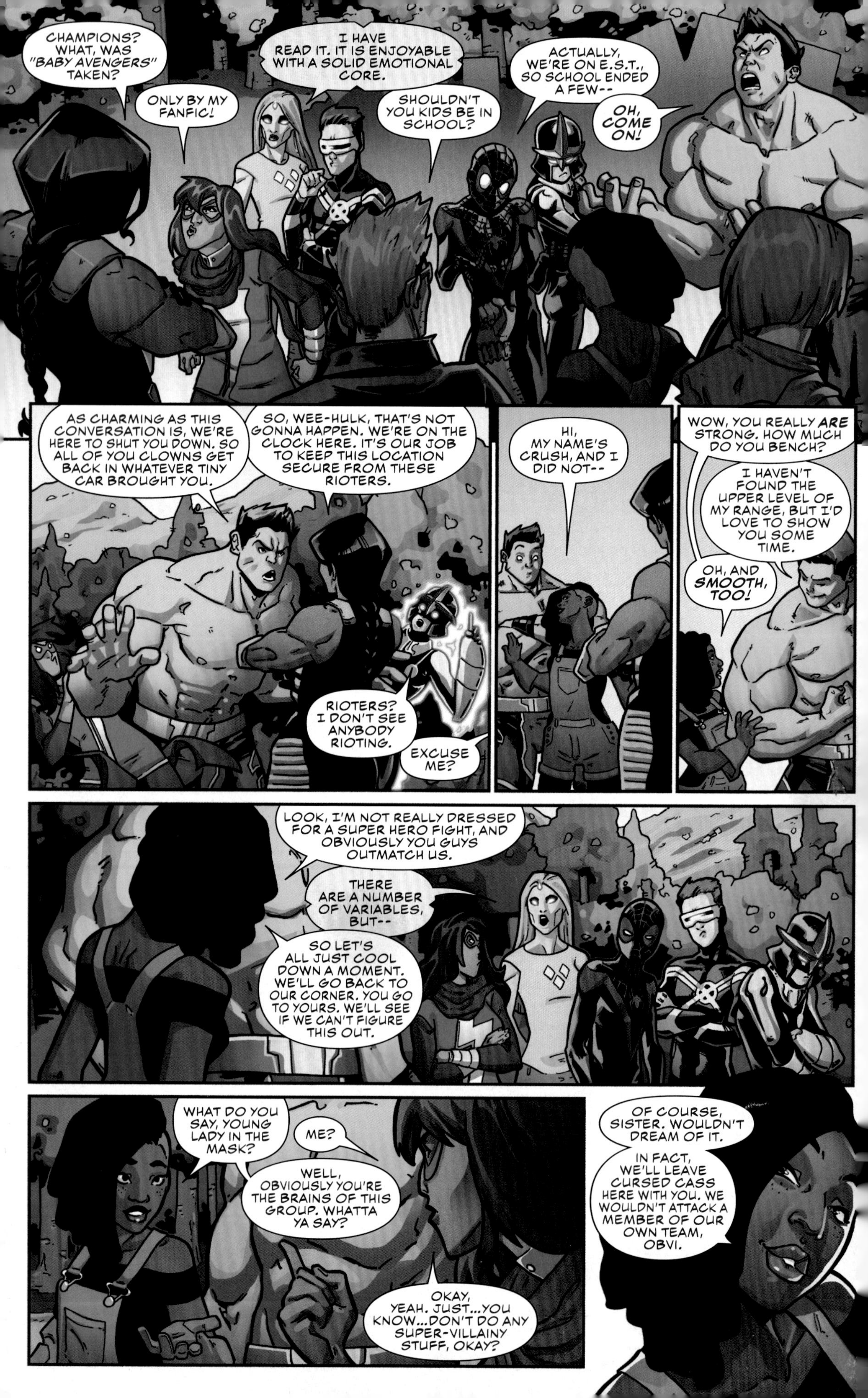
CHAMPIONS? WHAT, WAS "BABY AVENGERS" TAKEN?
ONLY BY MY FANFIC!
I HAVE READ IT. IT IS ENJOYABLE WITH A SOLID EMOTIONAL CORE.
SHOULDN'T YOU KIDS BE IN SCHOOL?
ACTUALLY, WE'RE ON E.S.T., SO SCHOOL ENDED A FEW--
OH, COME ON!
AS CHARMING AS THIS CONVERSATION IS, WE'RE HERE TO SHUT YOU DOWN. SO ALL OF YOU CLOWNS GET BACK IN WHATEVER TINY CAR BROUGHT YOU.
SO, WEE-HULK, THAT'S NOT GONNA HAPPEN. WE'RE ON THE CLOCK HERE. IT'S OUR JOB TO KEEP THIS LOCATION SECURE FROM THESE RIOTERS.
RIOTERS? I DON'T SEE ANYBODY RIOTING.
EXCUSE ME?
HI, MY NAME'S CRUSH, AND I DID NOT--
WOW, YOU REALLY ARE STRONG. HOW MUCH DO YOU BENCH?
I HAVEN'T FOUND THE UPPER LEVEL OF MY RANGE, BUT I'D LOVE TO SHOW YOU SOME TIME.
OH, AND SMOOTH, TOO!
LOOK, I'M NOT REALLY DRESSED FOR A SUPER HERO FIGHT, AND OBVIOUSLY YOU GUYS OUTMATCH US.
THERE ARE A NUMBER OF VARIABLES, BUT--
SO LET'S ALL JUST COOL DOWN A MOMENT. WE'LL GO BACK TO OUR CORNER. YOU GO TO YOURS. WE'LL SEE IF WE CAN'T FIGURE THIS OUT.
WHAT DO YOU SAY, YOUNG LADY IN THE MASK?
ME?
WELL, OBVIOUSLY YOU'RE THE BRAINS OF THIS GROUP. WHATTA YA SAY?
OKAY, YEAH. JUST...YOU KNOW...DON'T DO ANY SUPER-VILLAINY STUFF, OKAY?
OF COURSE, SISTER. WOULDN'T DREAM OF IT.
IN FACT, WE'LL LEAVE CURSED CASS HERE WITH YOU. WE WOULDN'T ATTACK A MEMBER OF OUR OWN TEAM, OBVI.

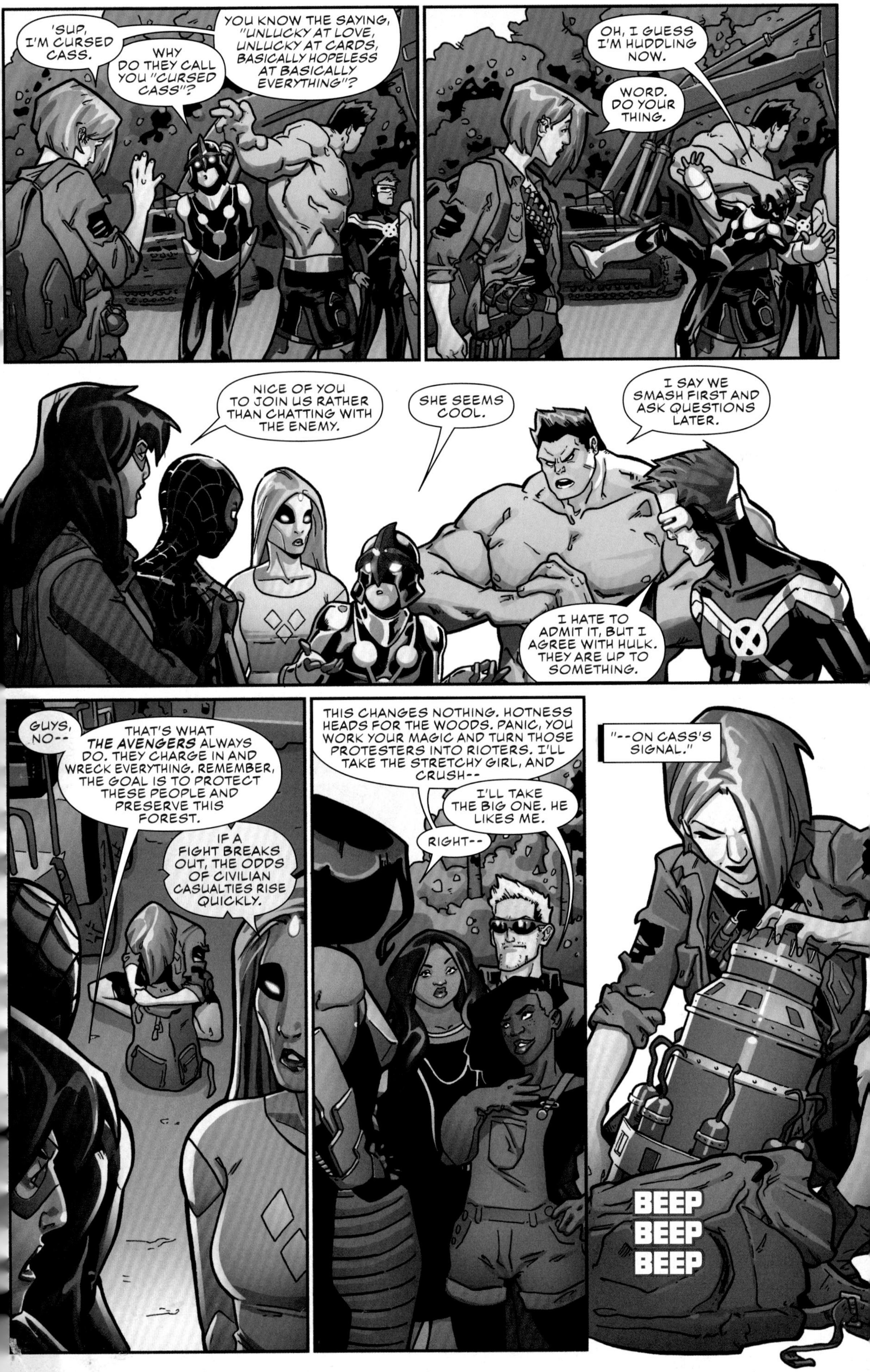
'SUP, I'M CURSED CASS.
WHY DO THEY CALL YOU "CURSED CASS"?
YOU KNOW THE SAYING, "UNLUCKY AT LOVE, UNLUCKY AT CARDS, BASICALLY HOPELESS AT BASICALLY EVERYTHING"?
OH, I GUESS I'M HUDDLING NOW.
WORD. DO YOUR THING.
NICE OF YOU TO JOIN US RATHER THAN CHATTING WITH THE ENEMY.
SHE SEEMS COOL.
I SAY WE SMASH FIRST AND ASK QUESTIONS LATER.
I HATE TO ADMIT IT, BUT I AGREE WITH HULK. THEY ARE UP TO SOMETHING.
GUYS, NO--
THAT'S WHAT THE AVENGERS ALWAYS DO. THEY CHARGE IN AND WRECK EVERYTHING. REMEMBER, THE GOAL IS TO PROTECT THESE PEOPLE AND PRESERVE THIS FOREST.
IF A FIGHT BREAKS OUT, THE ODDS OF CIVILIAN CASUALTIES RISE QUICKLY.
THIS CHANGES NOTHING. HOTNESS HEADS FOR THE WOODS. PANIC, YOU WORK YOUR MAGIC AND TURN THOSE PROTESTERS INTO RIOTERS. I'LL TAKE THE STRETCHY GIRL, AND CRUSH--
I'LL TAKE THE BIG ONE. HE LIKES ME.
RIGHT--
"--ON CASS'S SIGNAL."
BEEP
BEEP
BEEP

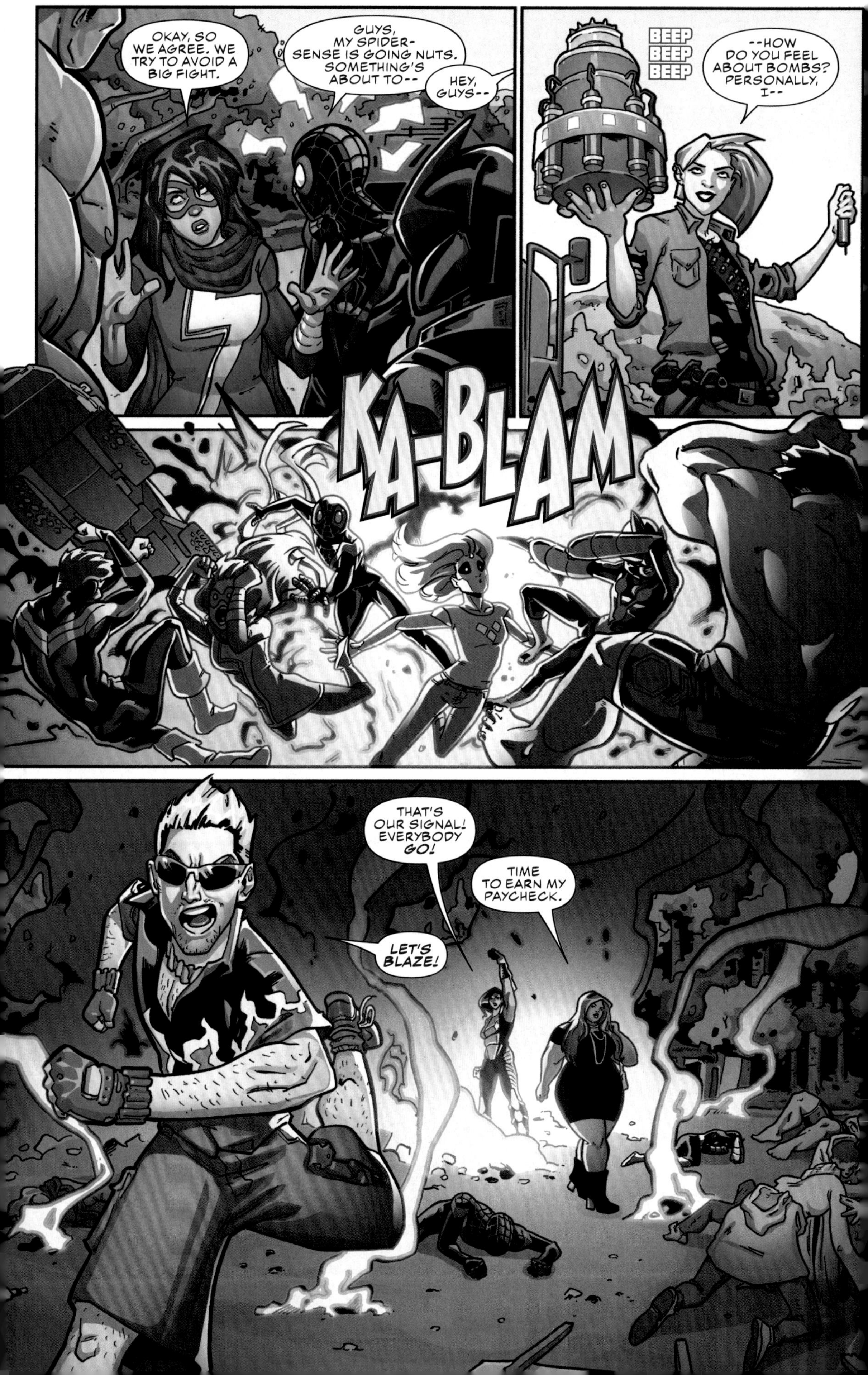
OKAY, SO WE AGREE. WE TRY TO AVOID A BIG FIGHT.
GUYS, MY SPIDER-SENSE IS GOING NUTS. SOMETHING'S ABOUT TO--
HEY, GUYS--
BEEP BEEP BEEP
--HOW DO YOU FEEL ABOUT BOMBS? PERSONALLY, I--
KA-BLAM
THAT'S OUR SIGNAL! EVERYBODY GO!
TIME TO EARN MY PAYCHECK.
LET'S BLAZE!

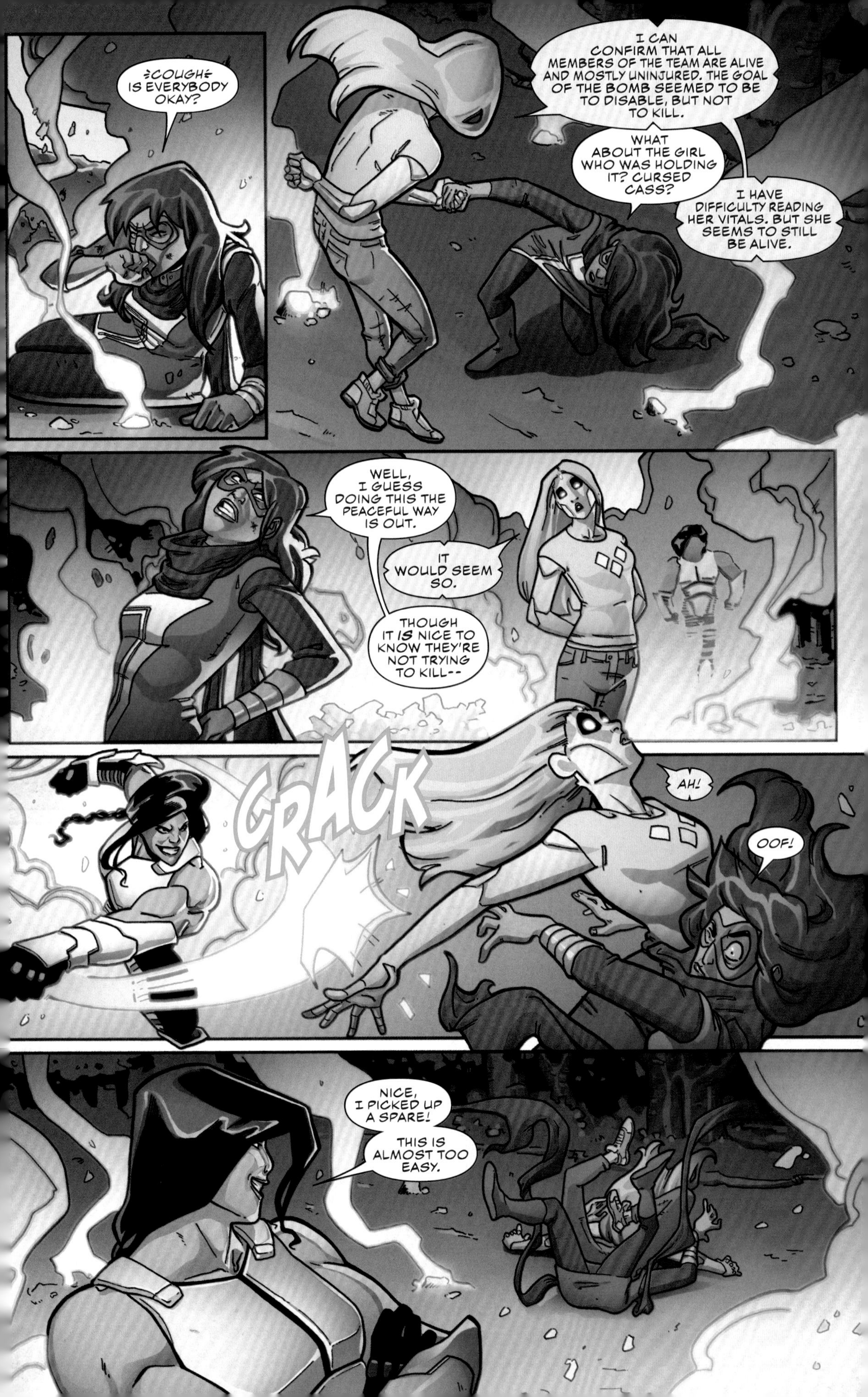

≋COUGH≋ IS EVERYBODY OKAY?
I CAN CONFIRM THAT ALL MEMBERS OF THE TEAM ARE ALIVE AND MOSTLY UNINJURED. THE GOAL OF THE BOMB SEEMED TO BE TO DISABLE, BUT NOT TO KILL.
WHAT ABOUT THE GIRL WHO WAS HOLDING IT? CURSED CASS?
I HAVE DIFFICULTY READING HER VITALS. BUT SHE SEEMS TO STILL BE ALIVE.
WELL, I GUESS DOING THIS THE PEACEFUL WAY IS OUT.
IT WOULD SEEM SO.
THOUGH IT *IS* NICE TO KNOW THEY'RE NOT TRYING TO KILL--
CRACK
AH!
OOF!
NICE, I PICKED UP A SPARE!
THIS IS ALMOST TOO EASY.

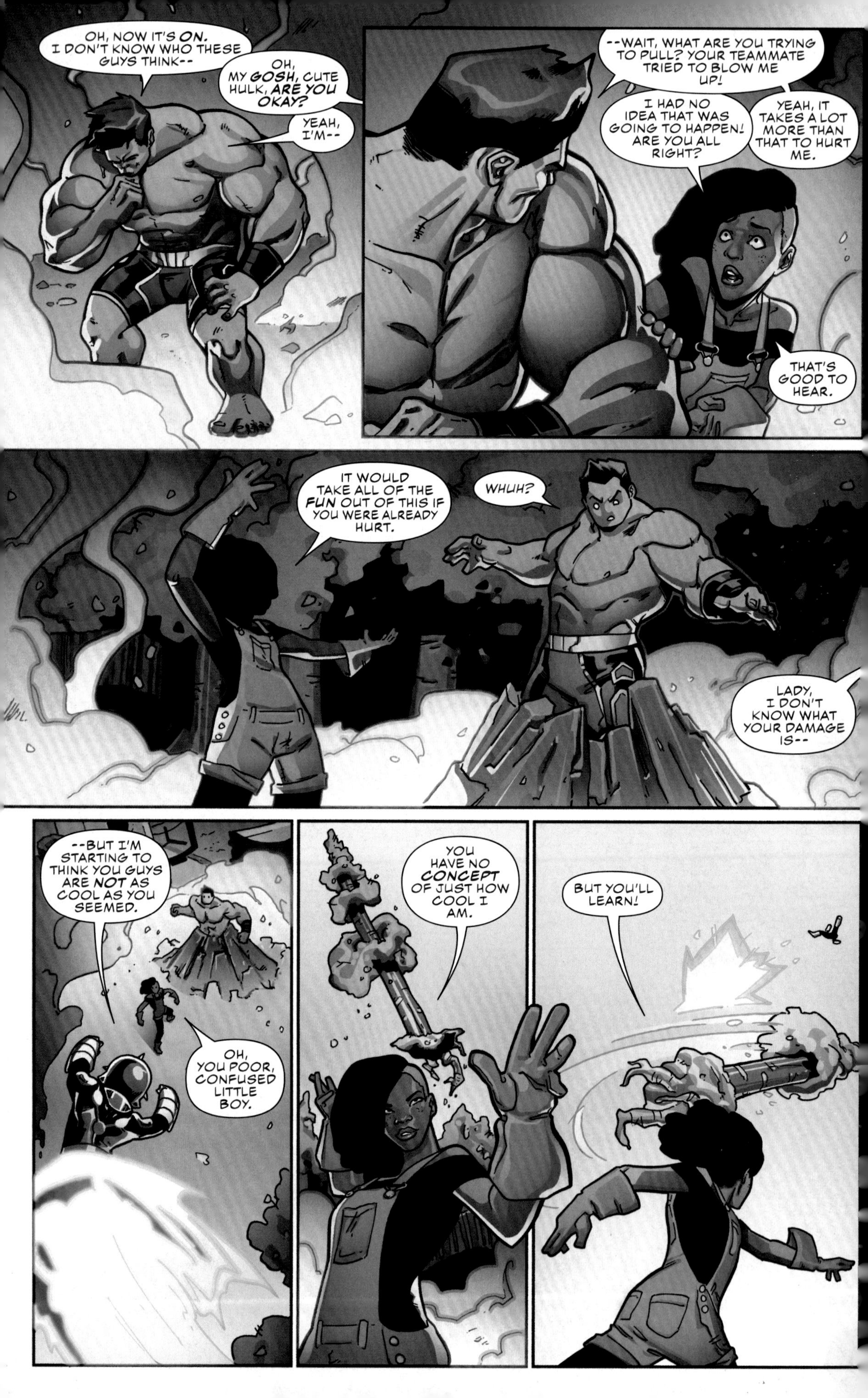
OH, NOW IT'S ON. I DON'T KNOW WHO THESE GUYS THINK--
OH, MY GOSH, CUTE HULK, ARE YOU OKAY?
YEAH, I'M--
--WAIT, WHAT ARE YOU TRYING TO PULL? YOUR TEAMMATE TRIED TO BLOW ME UP!
I HAD NO IDEA THAT WAS GOING TO HAPPEN! ARE YOU ALL RIGHT?
YEAH, IT TAKES A LOT MORE THAN THAT TO HURT ME.
THAT'S GOOD TO HEAR.
IT WOULD TAKE ALL OF THE FUN OUT OF THIS IF YOU WERE ALREADY HURT.
WHUH?
LADY, I DON'T KNOW WHAT YOUR DAMAGE IS--
--BUT I'M STARTING TO THINK YOU GUYS ARE NOT AS COOL AS YOU SEEMED.
OH, YOU POOR, CONFUSED LITTLE BOY.
YOU HAVE NO CONCEPT OF JUST HOW COOL I AM.
BUT YOU'LL LEARN!

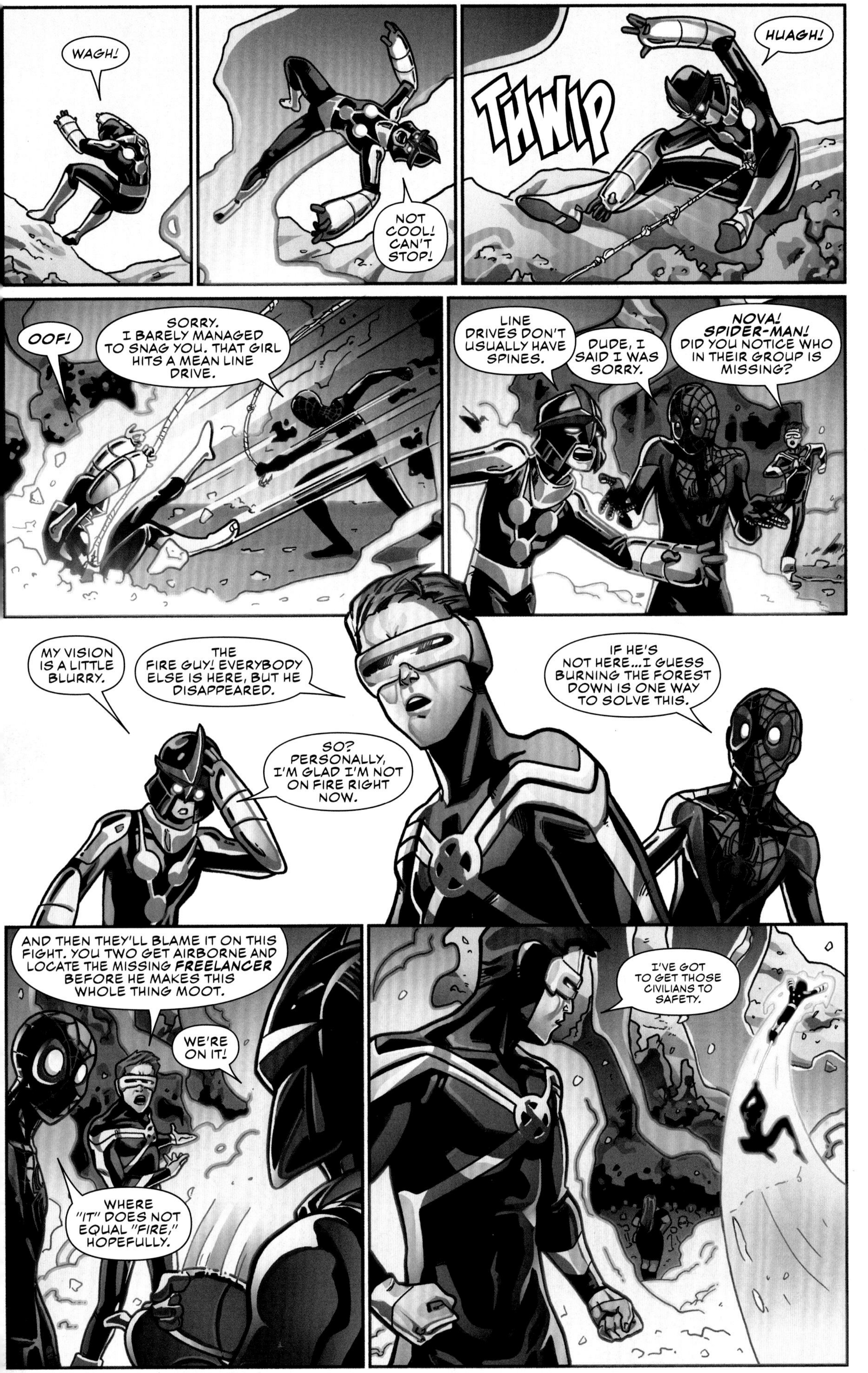
WAGH!
NOT COOL! CAN'T STOP!
THWIP
HUAGH!
OOF!
SORRY. I BARELY MANAGED TO SNAG YOU. THAT GIRL HITS A MEAN LINE DRIVE.
LINE DRIVES DON'T USUALLY HAVE SPINES.
DUDE, I SAID I WAS SORRY.
NOVA! SPIDER-MAN! DID YOU NOTICE WHO IN THEIR GROUP IS MISSING?
MY VISION IS A LITTLE BLURRY.
THE FIRE GUY! EVERYBODY ELSE IS HERE, BUT HE DISAPPEARED.
SO? PERSONALLY, I'M GLAD I'M NOT ON FIRE RIGHT NOW.
IF HE'S NOT HERE...I GUESS BURNING THE FOREST DOWN IS ONE WAY TO SOLVE THIS.
AND THEN THEY'LL BLAME IT ON THIS FIGHT. YOU TWO GET AIRBORNE AND LOCATE THE MISSING FREELANCER BEFORE HE MAKES THIS WHOLE THING MOOT.
WE'RE ON IT!
WHERE "IT" DOES NOT EQUAL "FIRE," HOPEFULLY.
I'VE GOT TO GET THOSE CIVILIANS TO SAFETY.

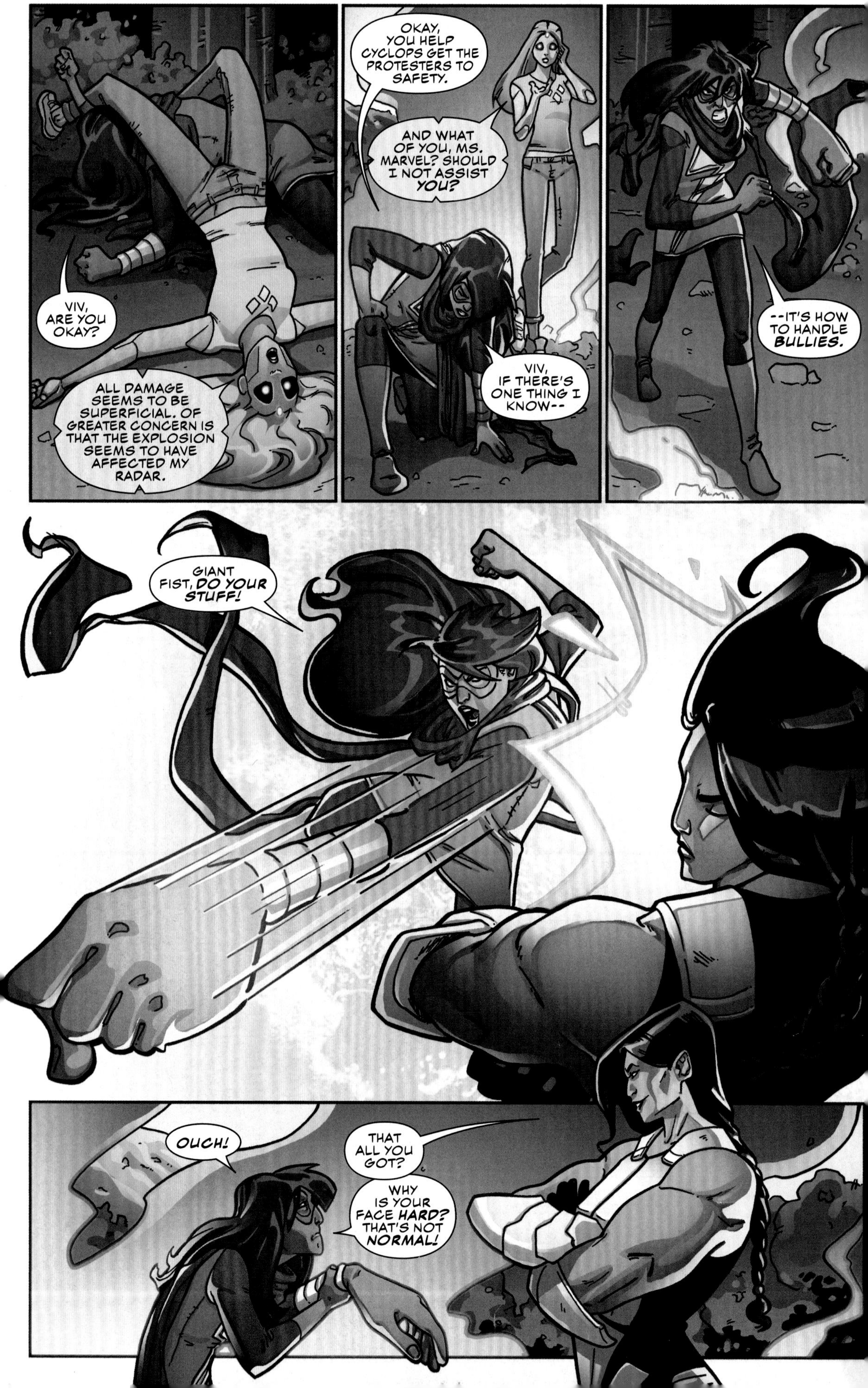
VIV, ARE YOU OKAY?
ALL DAMAGE SEEMS TO BE SUPERFICIAL. OF GREATER CONCERN IS THAT THE EXPLOSION SEEMS TO HAVE AFFECTED MY RADAR.
OKAY, YOU HELP CYCLOPS GET THE PROTESTERS TO SAFETY.
AND WHAT OF YOU, MS. MARVEL? SHOULD I NOT ASSIST YOU?
VIV, IF THERE'S ONE THING I KNOW--
--IT'S HOW TO HANDLE BULLIES.
GIANT FIST, DO YOUR STUFF!
OUCH!
THAT ALL YOU GOT?
WHY IS YOUR FACE HARD? THAT'S NOT NORMAL!

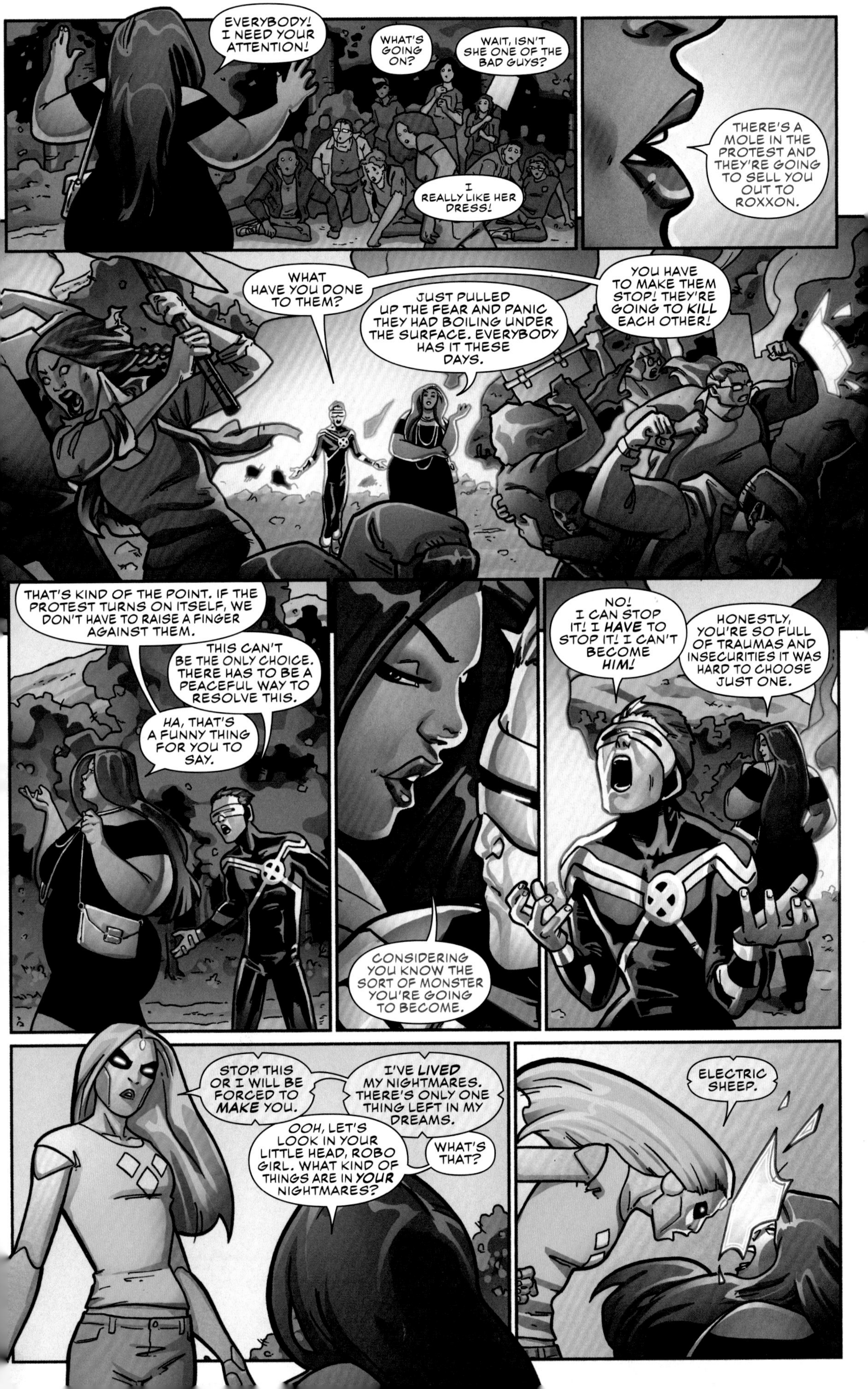
EVERYBODY! I NEED YOUR ATTENTION!
WHAT'S GOING ON?
WAIT, ISN'T SHE ONE OF THE BAD GUYS?
I REALLY LIKE HER DRESS!
THERE'S A MOLE IN THE PROTEST AND THEY'RE GOING TO SELL YOU OUT TO ROXXON.
WHAT HAVE YOU DONE TO THEM?
JUST PULLED UP THE FEAR AND PANIC THEY HAD BOILING UNDER THE SURFACE. EVERYBODY HAS IT THESE DAYS.
YOU HAVE TO MAKE THEM STOP! THEY'RE GOING TO KILL EACH OTHER!
THAT'S KIND OF THE POINT. IF THE PROTEST TURNS ON ITSELF, WE DON'T HAVE TO RAISE A FINGER AGAINST THEM.
THIS CAN'T BE THE ONLY CHOICE. THERE HAS TO BE A PEACEFUL WAY TO RESOLVE THIS.
HA, THAT'S A FUNNY THING FOR YOU TO SAY.
CONSIDERING YOU KNOW THE SORT OF MONSTER YOU'RE GOING TO BECOME.
NO! I CAN STOP IT! I HAVE TO STOP IT! I CAN'T BECOME HIM!
HONESTLY, YOU'RE SO FULL OF TRAUMAS AND INSECURITIES IT WAS HARD TO CHOOSE JUST ONE.
STOP THIS OR I WILL BE FORCED TO MAKE YOU.
OOH, LET'S LOOK IN YOUR LITTLE HEAD, ROBO GIRL. WHAT KIND OF THINGS ARE IN YOUR NIGHTMARES?
I'VE LIVED MY NIGHTMARES. THERE'S ONLY ONE THING LEFT IN MY DREAMS.
WHAT'S THAT?
ELECTRIC SHEEP.

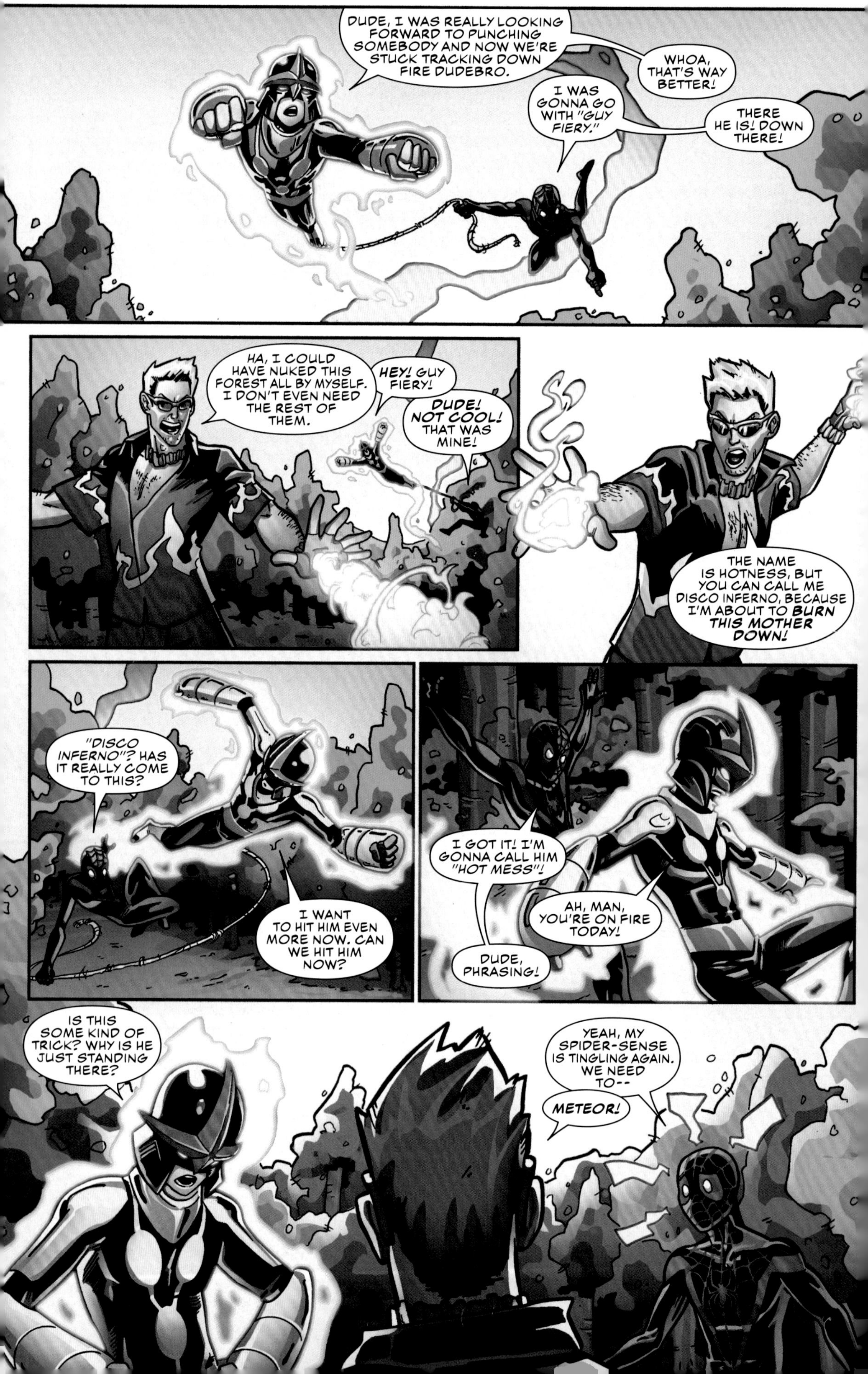
DUDE, I WAS REALLY LOOKING FORWARD TO PUNCHING SOMEBODY AND NOW WE'RE STUCK TRACKING DOWN FIRE DUDEBRO.
WHOA, THAT'S WAY BETTER!
I WAS GONNA GO WITH "GUY FIERY."
THERE HE IS! DOWN THERE!
HA, I COULD HAVE NUKED THIS FOREST ALL BY MYSELF. I DON'T EVEN NEED THE REST OF THEM.
HEY! GUY FIERY!
DUDE! NOT COOL! THAT WAS MINE!
THE NAME IS HOTNESS, BUT YOU CAN CALL ME DISCO INFERNO, BECAUSE I'M ABOUT TO BURN THIS MOTHER DOWN!
"DISCO INFERNO"? HAS IT REALLY COME TO THIS?
I WANT TO HIT HIM EVEN MORE NOW. CAN WE HIT HIM NOW?
I GOT IT! I'M GONNA CALL HIM "HOT MESS"!
AH, MAN, YOU'RE ON FIRE TODAY!
DUDE, PHRASING!
IS THIS SOME KIND OF TRICK? WHY IS HE JUST STANDING THERE?
YEAH, MY SPIDER-SENSE IS TINGLING AGAIN. WE NEED TO--
METEOR!

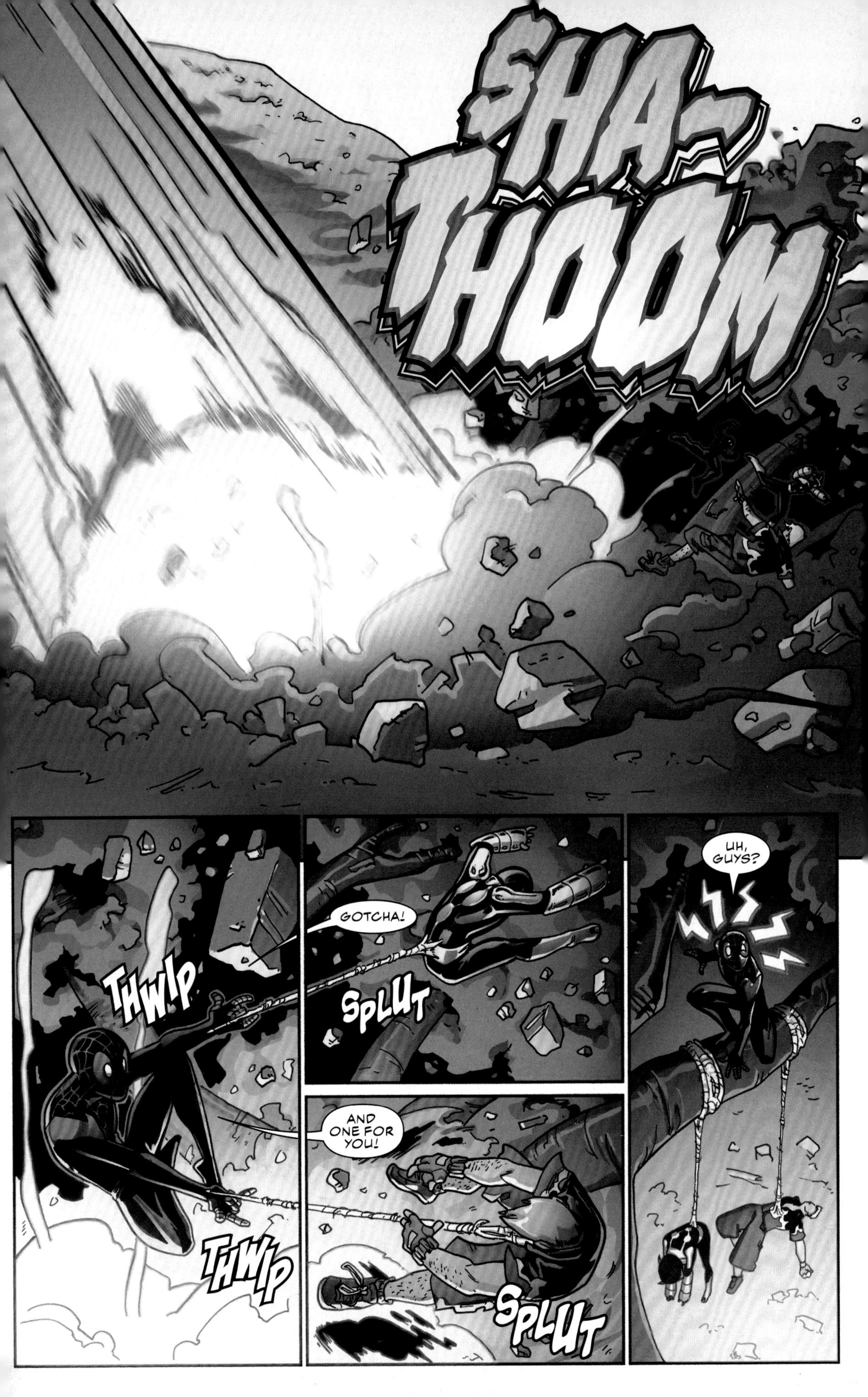
SHA-THOOM
THWIP
GOTCHA!
SPLUT
THWIP
AND ONE FOR YOU!
SPLUT
UH, GUYS?

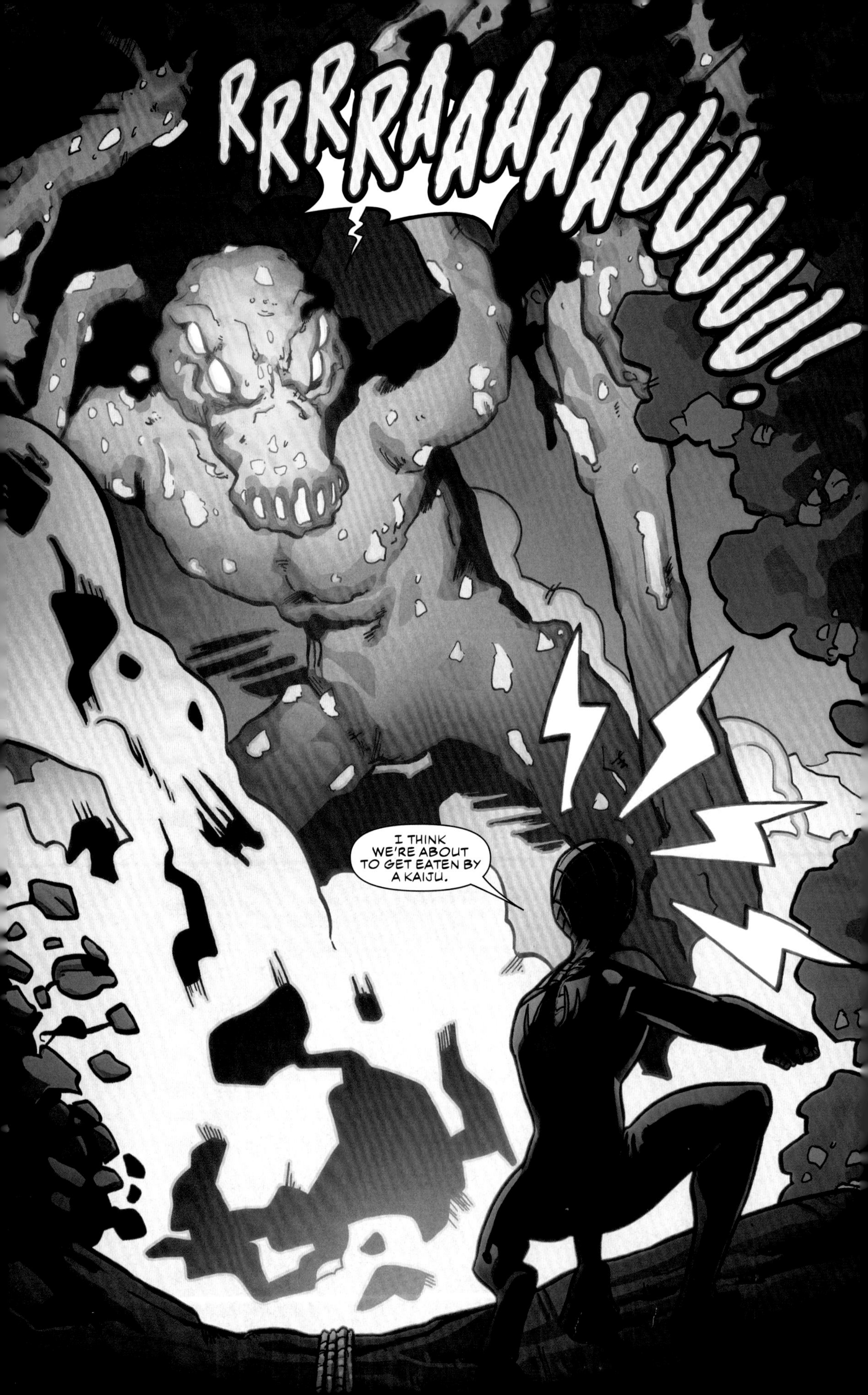
RRRRAAAAAUUUUU!!
I THINK WE'RE ABOUT TO GET EATEN BY A KAIJU.

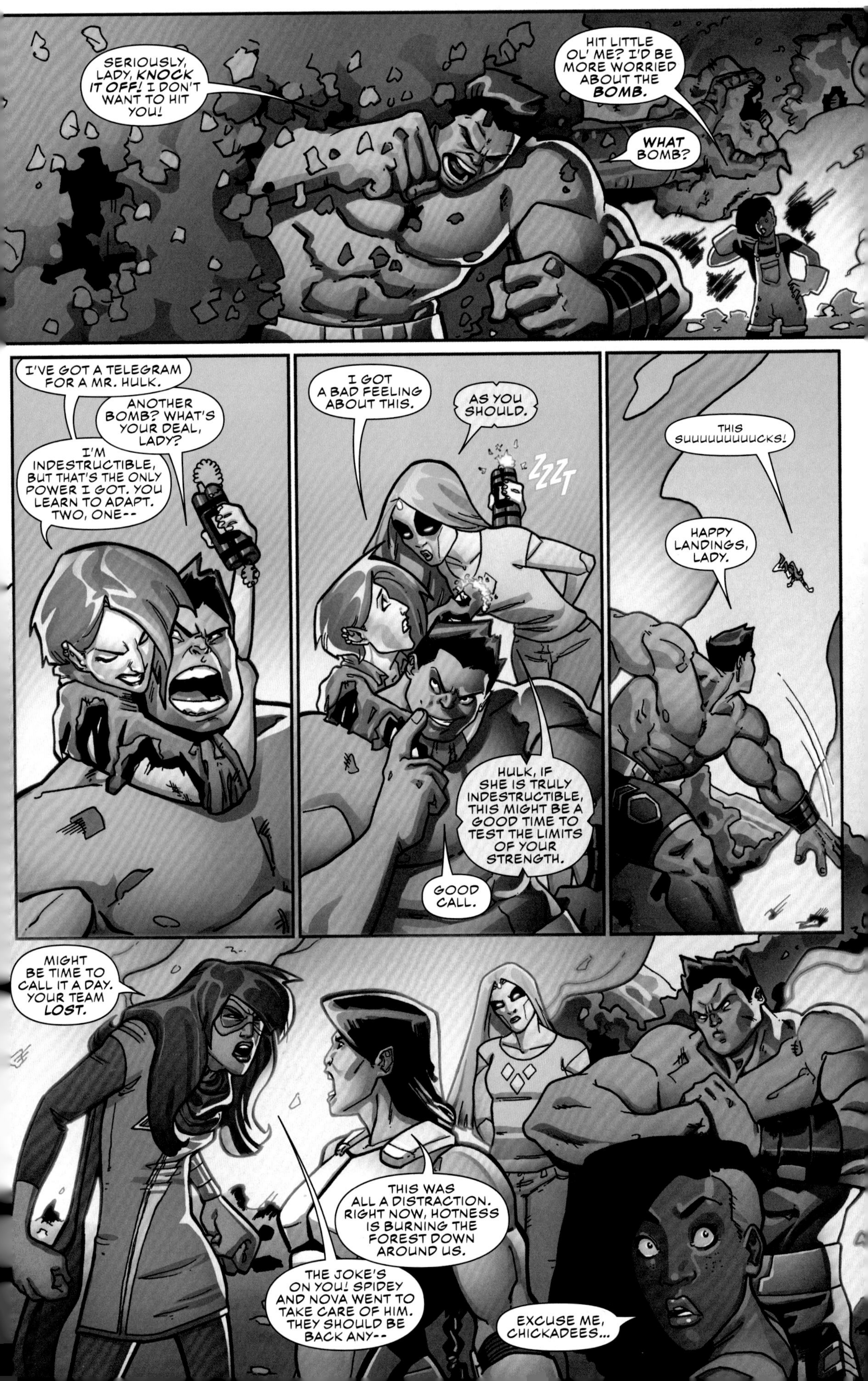
SERIOUSLY, LADY, KNOCK IT OFF! I DON'T WANT TO HIT YOU!
HIT LITTLE OL' ME? I'D BE MORE WORRIED ABOUT THE BOMB.
WHAT BOMB?
I'VE GOT A TELEGRAM FOR A MR. HULK.
ANOTHER BOMB? WHAT'S YOUR DEAL, LADY?
I'M INDESTRUCTIBLE, BUT THAT'S THE ONLY POWER I GOT. YOU LEARN TO ADAPT. TWO, ONE--
I GOT A BAD FEELING ABOUT THIS.
AS YOU SHOULD.
ZZZT
HULK, IF SHE IS TRULY INDESTRUCTIBLE, THIS MIGHT BE A GOOD TIME TO TEST THE LIMITS OF YOUR STRENGTH.
GOOD CALL.
THIS SUUUUUUUUUCKS!
HAPPY LANDINGS, LADY.
MIGHT BE TIME TO CALL IT A DAY. YOUR TEAM LOST.
THIS WAS ALL A DISTRACTION. RIGHT NOW, HOTNESS IS BURNING THE FOREST DOWN AROUND US.
THE JOKE'S ON YOU! SPIDEY AND NOVA WENT TO TAKE CARE OF HIM. THEY SHOULD BE BACK ANY--
EXCUSE ME, CHICKADEES...

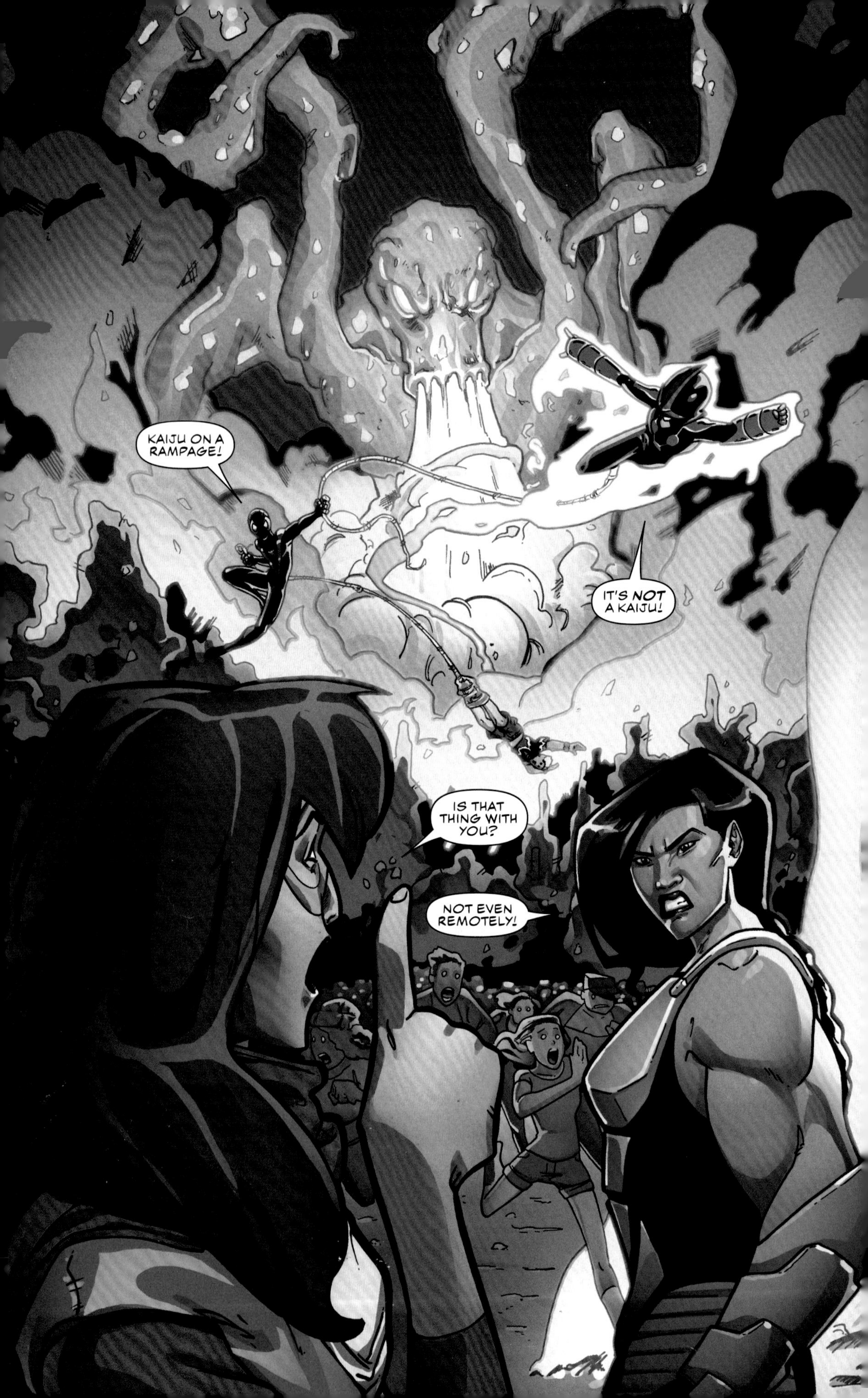
KAIJU ON A RAMPAGE!
IT'S NOT A KAIJU!
IS THAT THING WITH YOU?
NOT EVEN REMOTELY!

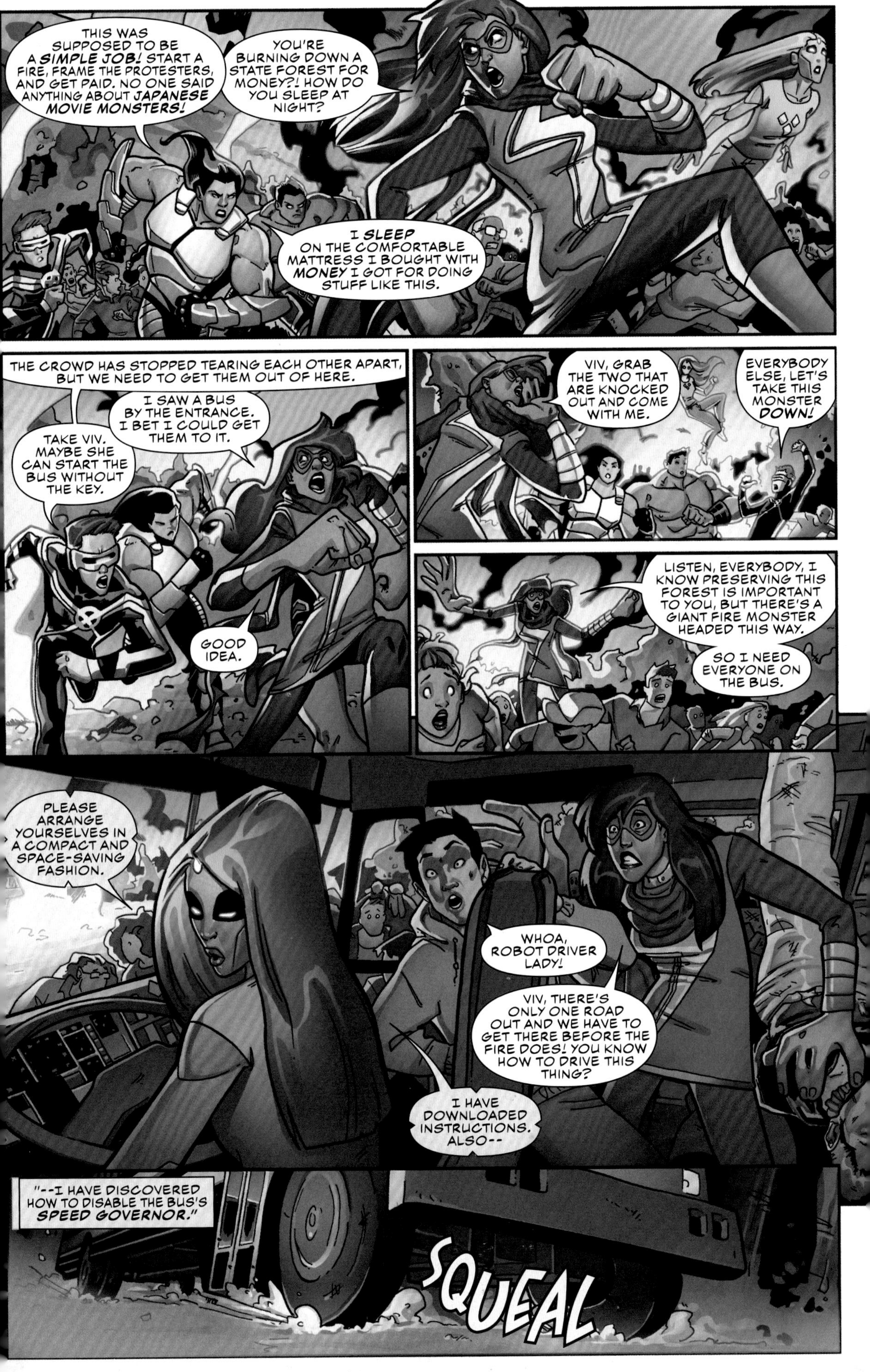
THIS WAS SUPPOSED TO BE A SIMPLE JOB! START A FIRE, FRAME THE PROTESTERS, AND GET PAID. NO ONE SAID ANYTHING ABOUT JAPANESE MOVIE MONSTERS!
YOU'RE BURNING DOWN A STATE FOREST FOR MONEY?! HOW DO YOU SLEEP AT NIGHT?
I SLEEP ON THE COMFORTABLE MATTRESS I BOUGHT WITH MONEY I GOT FOR DOING STUFF LIKE THIS.
THE CROWD HAS STOPPED TEARING EACH OTHER APART, BUT WE NEED TO GET THEM OUT OF HERE.
I SAW A BUS BY THE ENTRANCE. I BET I COULD GET THEM TO IT.
TAKE VIV. MAYBE SHE CAN START THE BUS WITHOUT THE KEY.
GOOD IDEA.
VIV, GRAB THE TWO THAT ARE KNOCKED OUT AND COME WITH ME.
EVERYBODY ELSE, LET'S TAKE THIS MONSTER DOWN!
LISTEN, EVERYBODY, I KNOW PRESERVING THIS FOREST IS IMPORTANT TO YOU, BUT THERE'S A GIANT FIRE MONSTER HEADED THIS WAY.
SO I NEED EVERYONE ON THE BUS.
PLEASE ARRANGE YOURSELVES IN A COMPACT AND SPACE-SAVING FASHION.
WHOA, ROBOT DRIVER LADY!
VIV, THERE'S ONLY ONE ROAD OUT AND WE HAVE TO GET THERE BEFORE THE FIRE DOES! YOU KNOW HOW TO DRIVE THIS THING?
I HAVE DOWNLOADED INSTRUCTIONS. ALSO--
"--I HAVE DISCOVERED HOW TO DISABLE THE BUS'S SPEED GOVERNOR."
SQUEAL

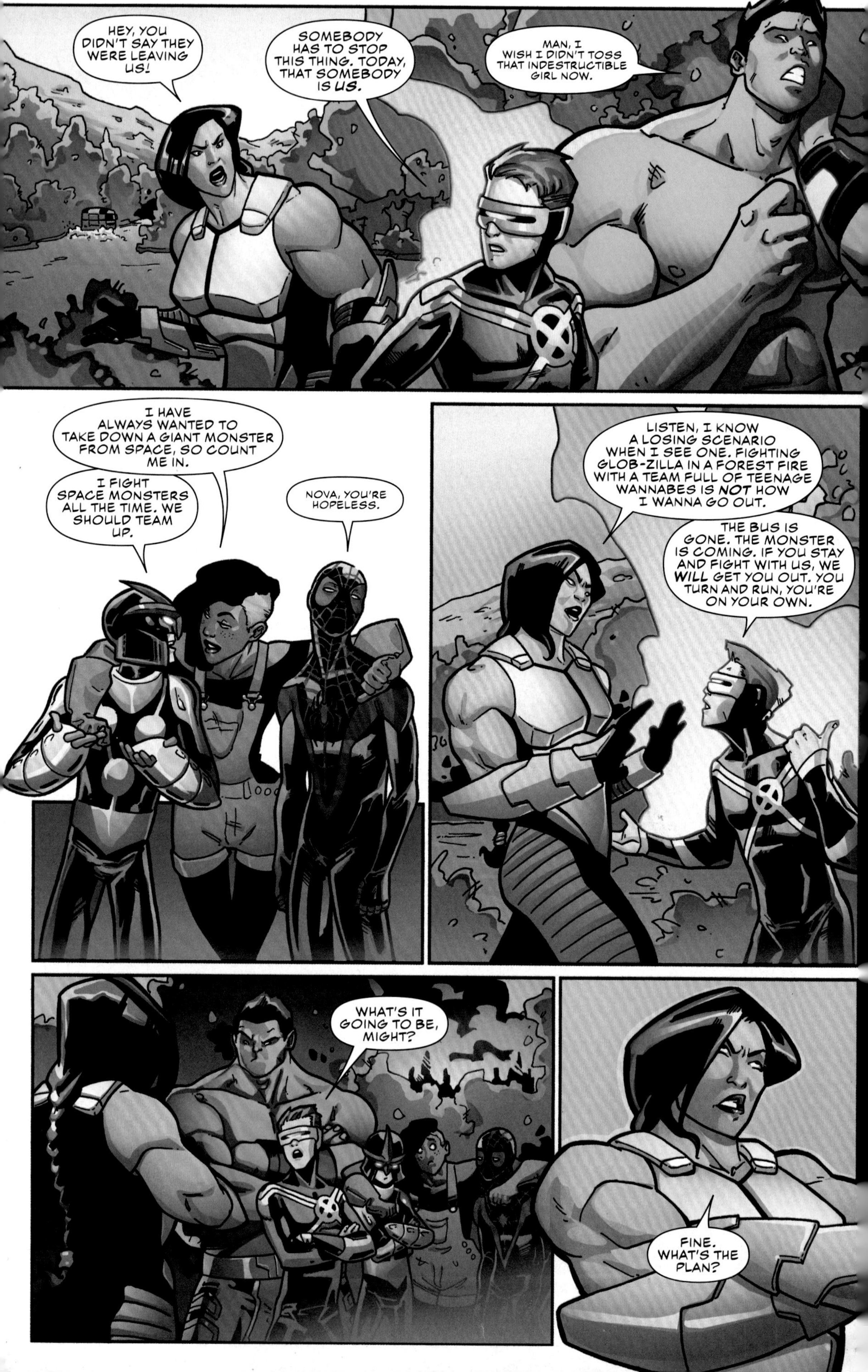
HEY, YOU DIDN'T SAY THEY WERE LEAVING US!
SOMEBODY HAS TO STOP THIS THING. TODAY, THAT SOMEBODY IS US.
MAN, I WISH I DIDN'T TOSS THAT INDESTRUCTIBLE GIRL NOW.
I HAVE ALWAYS WANTED TO TAKE DOWN A GIANT MONSTER FROM SPACE, SO COUNT ME IN.
I FIGHT SPACE MONSTERS ALL THE TIME. WE SHOULD TEAM UP.
NOVA, YOU'RE HOPELESS.
LISTEN, I KNOW A LOSING SCENARIO WHEN I SEE ONE. FIGHTING GLOB-ZILLA IN A FOREST FIRE WITH A TEAM FULL OF TEENAGE WANNABES IS NOT HOW I WANNA GO OUT.
THE BUS IS GONE. THE MONSTER IS COMING. IF YOU STAY AND FIGHT WITH US, WE WILL GET YOU OUT. YOU TURN AND RUN, YOU'RE ON YOUR OWN.
WHAT'S IT GOING TO BE, MIGHT?
FINE. WHAT'S THE PLAN?

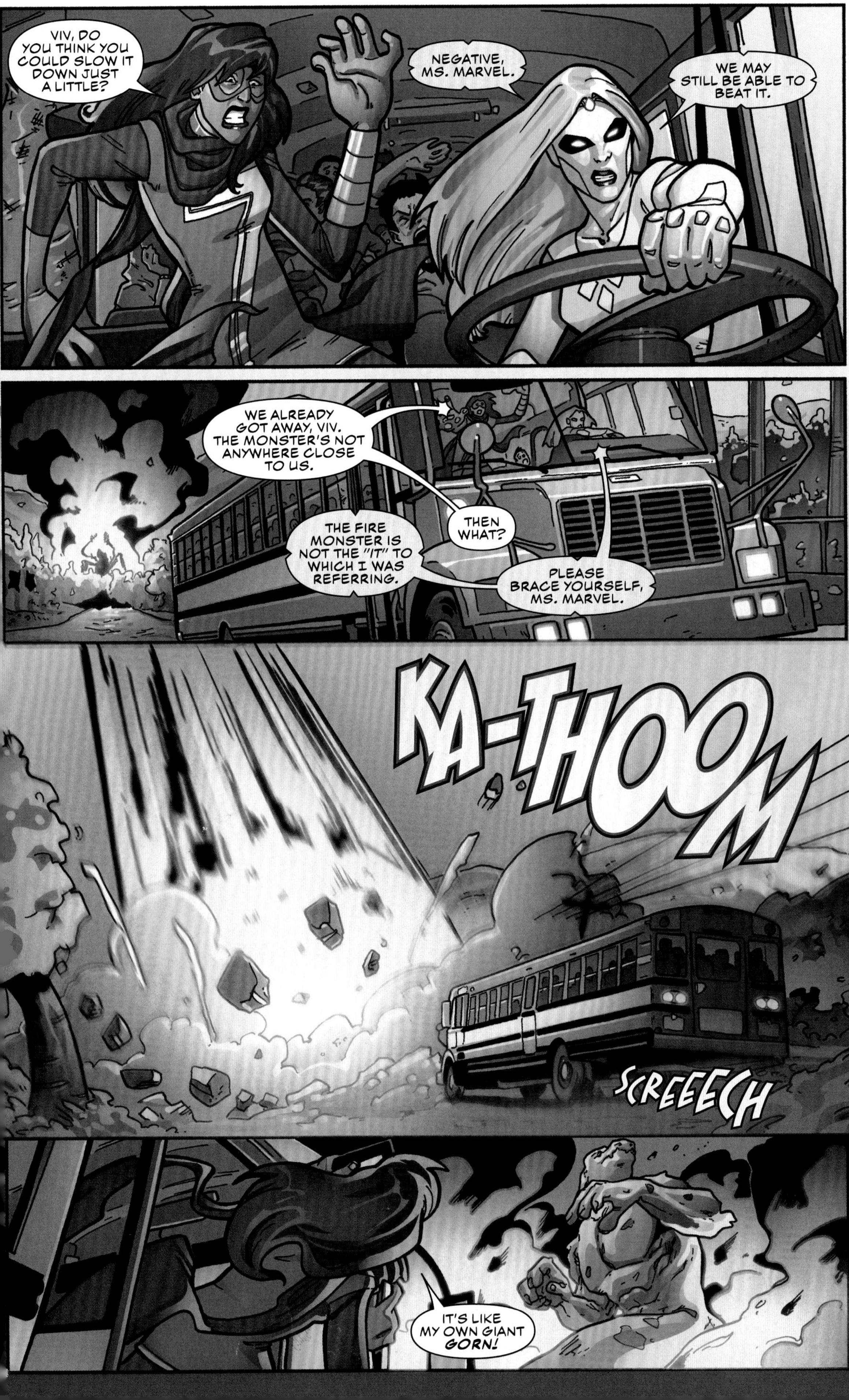
VIV, DO YOU THINK YOU COULD SLOW IT DOWN JUST A LITTLE?
NEGATIVE, MS. MARVEL.
WE MAY STILL BE ABLE TO BEAT IT.
WE ALREADY GOT AWAY, VIV. THE MONSTER'S NOT ANYWHERE CLOSE TO US.
THEN WHAT?
THE FIRE MONSTER IS NOT THE "IT" TO WHICH I WAS REFERRING.
PLEASE BRACE YOURSELF, MS. MARVEL.
KA-THOOM
SCREEECH
IT'S LIKE MY OWN GIANT GORN!

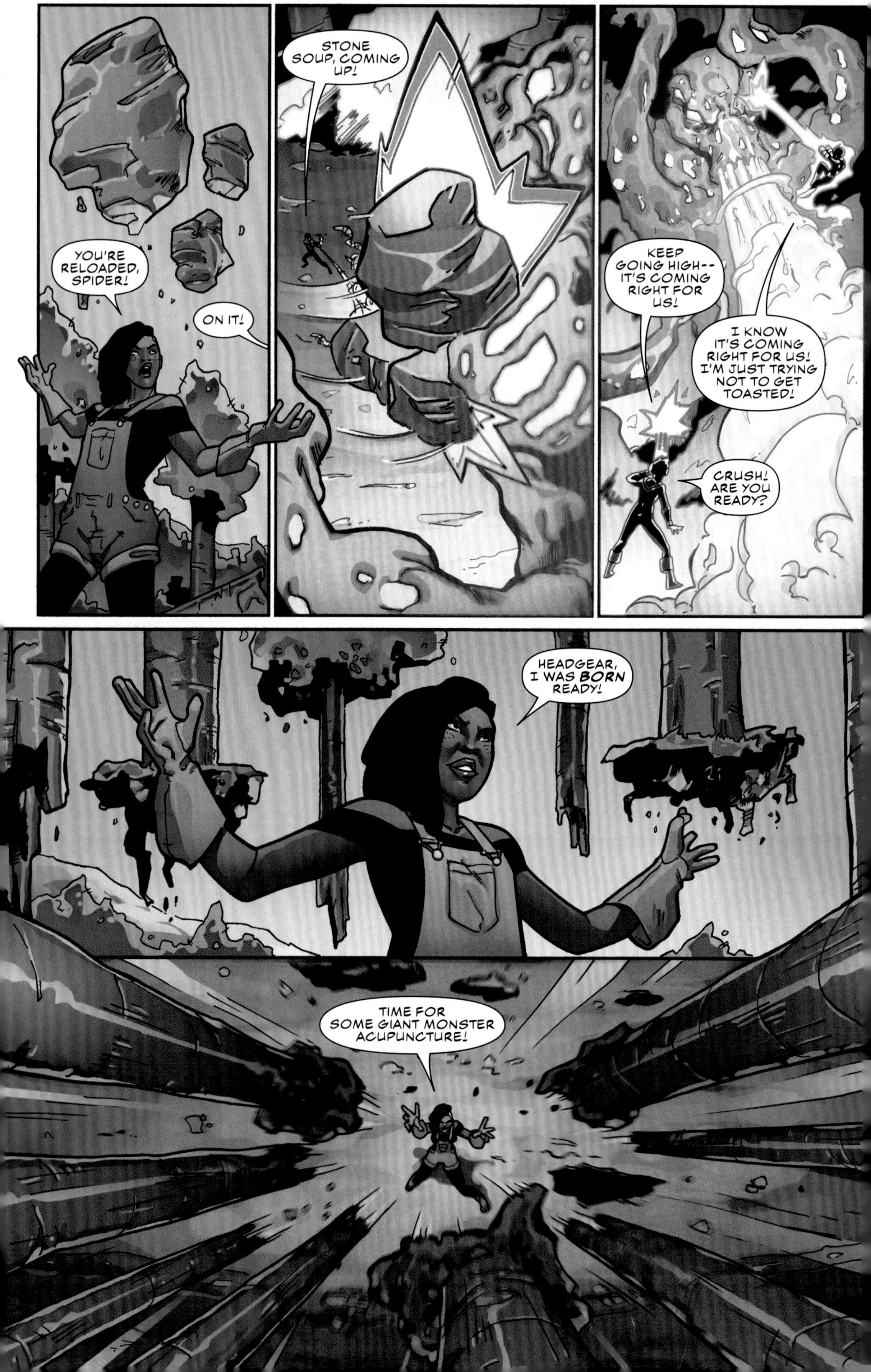
YOU'RE RELOADED, SPIDER!
ON IT!
STONE SOUP, COMING UP!
KEEP GOING HIGH-- IT'S COMING RIGHT FOR US!
I KNOW IT'S COMING RIGHT FOR US! I'M JUST TRYING NOT TO GET TOASTED!
CRUSH! ARE YOU READY?
HEADGEAR, I WAS **BORN** READY!
TIME FOR SOME GIANT MONSTER ACUPUNCTURE!

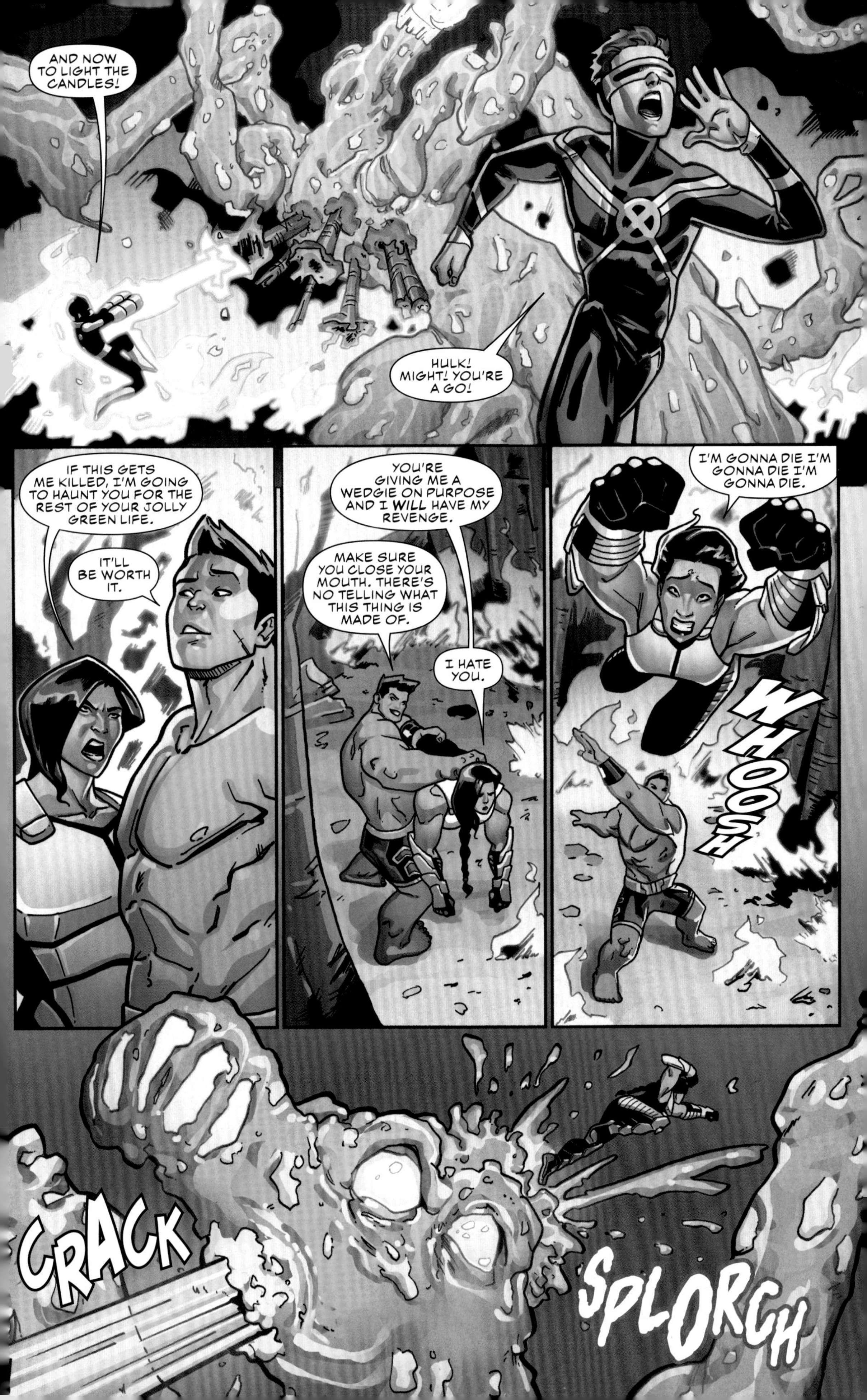
AND NOW TO LIGHT THE CANDLES!
HULK! MIGHT! YOU'RE A GO!
IF THIS GETS ME KILLED, I'M GOING TO HAUNT YOU FOR THE REST OF YOUR JOLLY GREEN LIFE.
IT'LL BE WORTH IT.
YOU'RE GIVING ME A WEDGIE ON PURPOSE AND I **WILL** HAVE MY REVENGE.
MAKE SURE YOU CLOSE YOUR MOUTH. THERE'S NO TELLING WHAT THIS THING IS MADE OF.
I HATE YOU.
I'M GONNA DIE I'M GONNA DIE I'M GONNA DIE.
WHOOSH
CRACK
SPLORCH

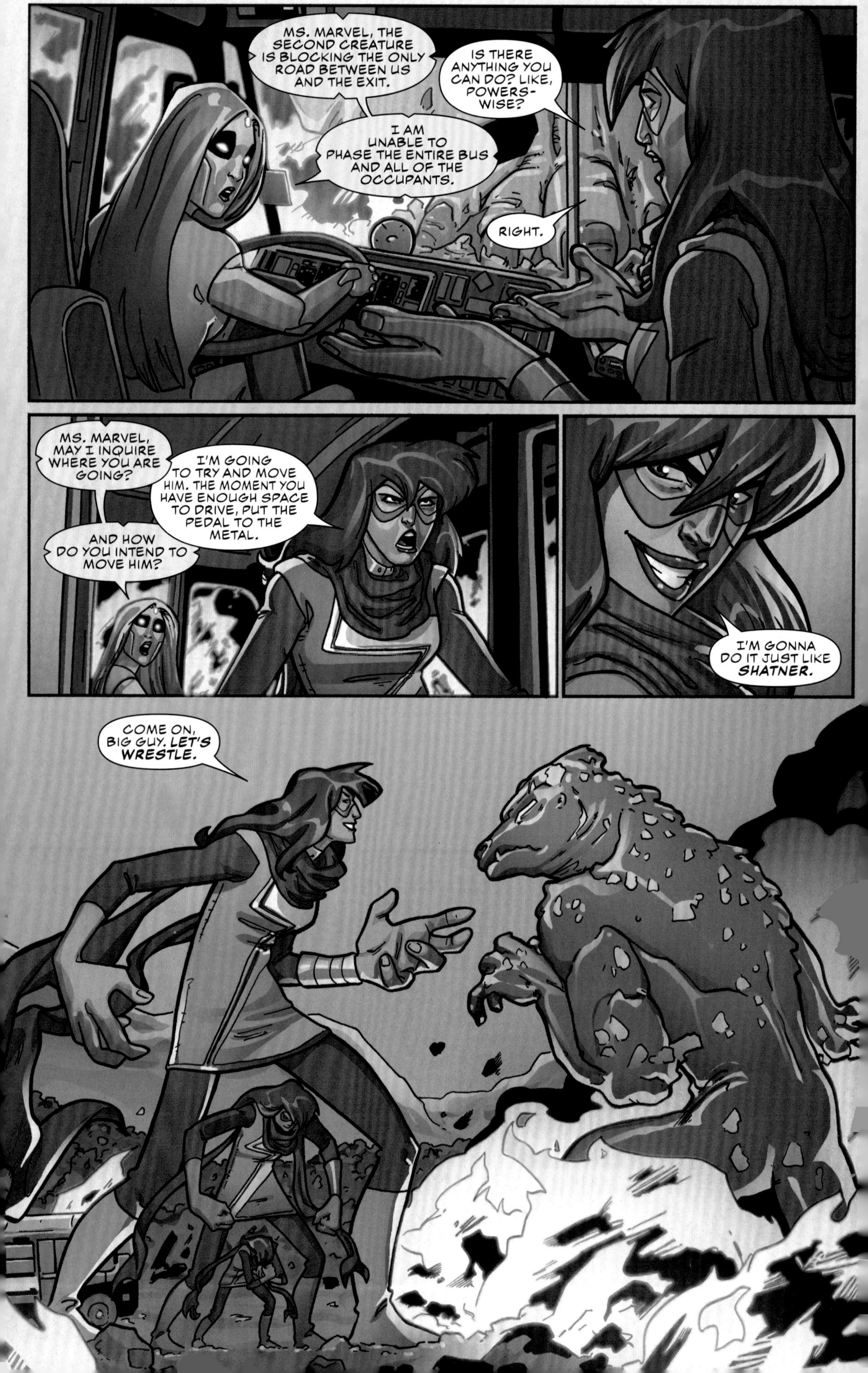
MS. MARVEL, THE SECOND CREATURE IS BLOCKING THE ONLY ROAD BETWEEN US AND THE EXIT.
IS THERE ANYTHING YOU CAN DO? LIKE, POWERS-WISE?
I AM UNABLE TO PHASE THE ENTIRE BUS AND ALL OF THE OCCUPANTS.
RIGHT.
MS. MARVEL, MAY I INQUIRE WHERE YOU ARE GOING?
I'M GOING TO TRY AND MOVE HIM. THE MOMENT YOU HAVE ENOUGH SPACE TO DRIVE, PUT THE PEDAL TO THE METAL.
AND HOW DO YOU INTEND TO MOVE HIM?
I'M GONNA DO IT JUST LIKE SHATNER.
COME ON, BIG GUY. LET'S WRESTLE.

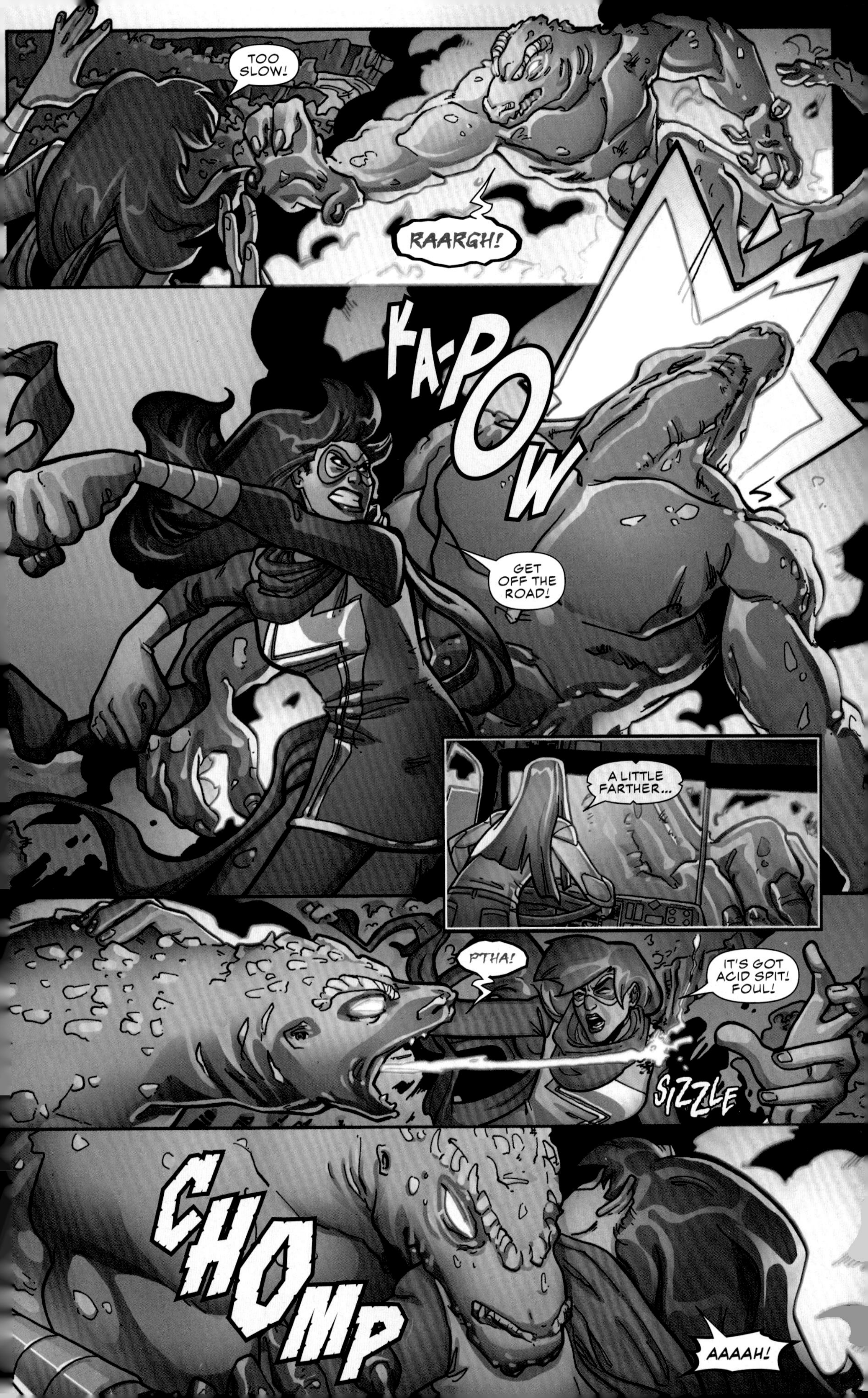
TOO SLOW!
RAARGH!
KA-POW
GET OFF THE ROAD!
A LITTLE FARTHER...
PTHA!
IT'S GOT ACID SPIT! FOUL!
SIZZLE
CHOMP
AAAAH!

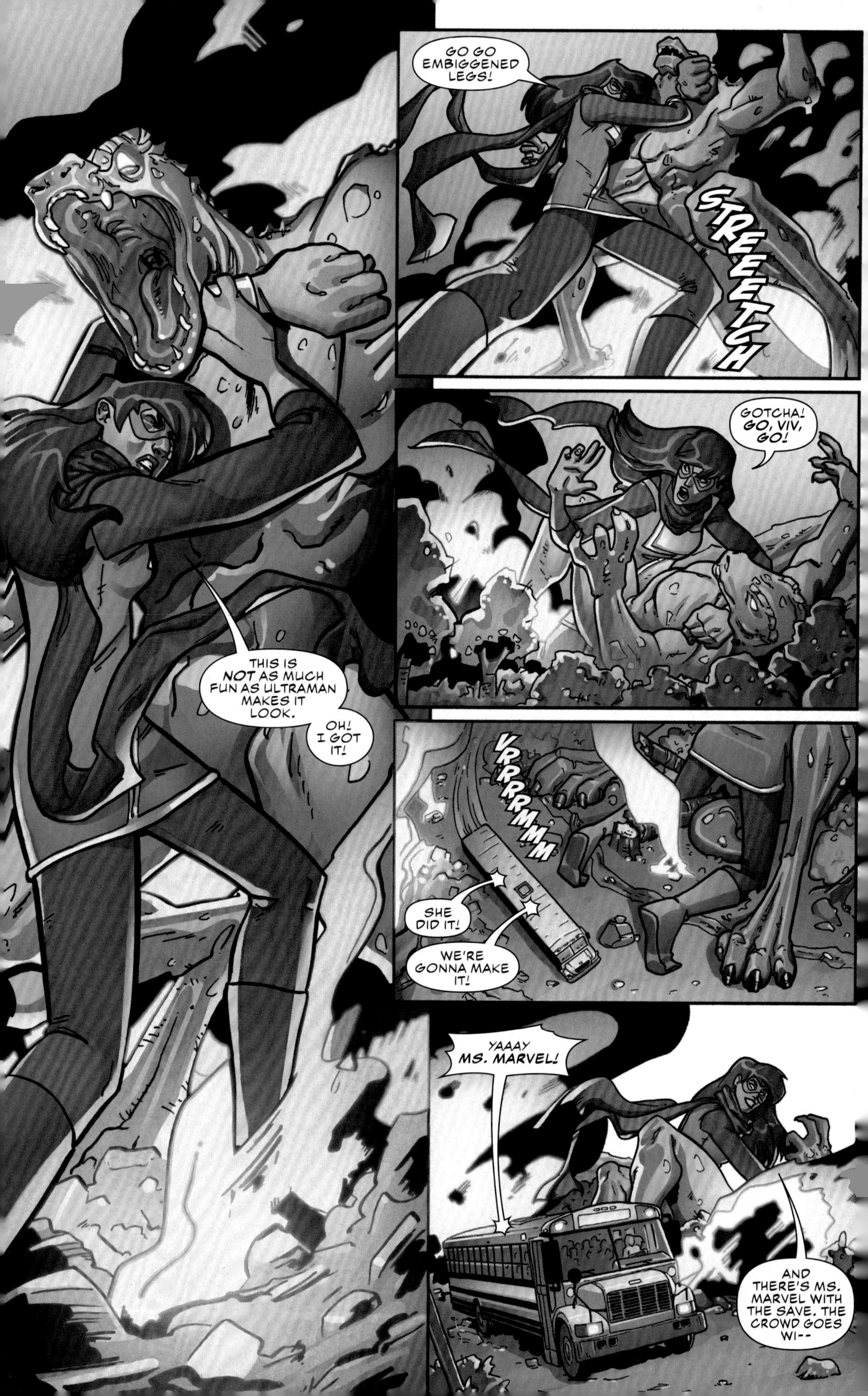
GO GO EMBIGGENED LEGS!
STREEETCH
THIS IS NOT AS MUCH FUN AS ULTRAMAN MAKES IT LOOK.
OH! I GOT IT!
GOTCHA! GO, VIV, GO!
VRRRMMM
SHE DID IT!
WE'RE GONNA MAKE IT!
YAAAY MS. MARVEL!
AND THERE'S MS. MARVEL WITH THE SAVE. THE CROWD GOES WI--

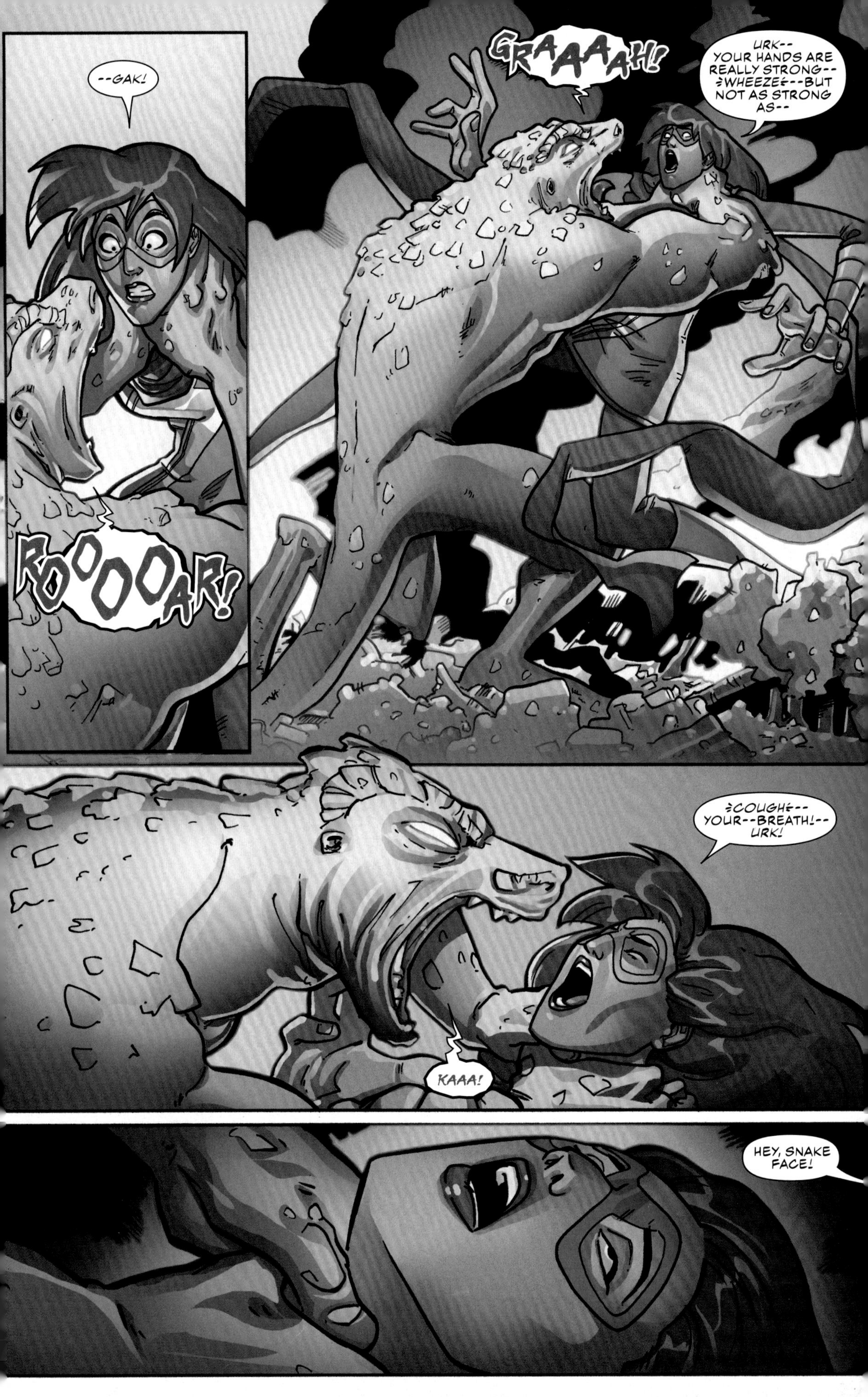
--GAK!
ROOOOAR!
GRAAAAH!
URK-- YOUR HANDS ARE REALLY STRONG-- ⋛WHEEZE⋚--BUT NOT AS STRONG AS--
⋛COUGH⋚-- YOUR--BREATH!-- URK!
KAAA!
HEY, SNAKE FACE!

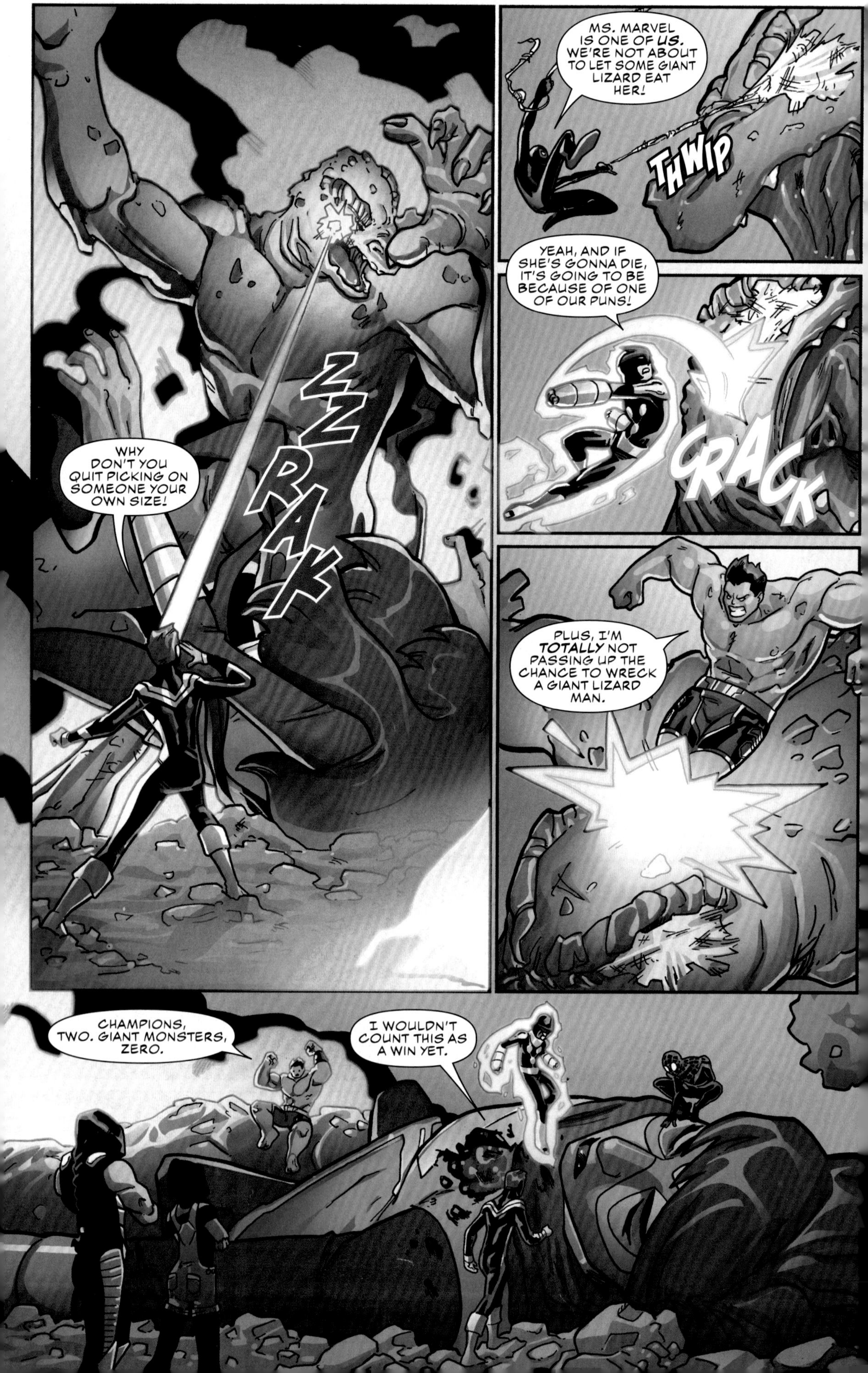
WHY DON'T YOU QUIT PICKING ON SOMEONE YOUR OWN SIZE!
ZZRAK
MS. MARVEL IS ONE OF US. WE'RE NOT ABOUT TO LET SOME GIANT LIZARD EAT HER!
THWIP
YEAH, AND IF SHE'S GONNA DIE, IT'S GOING TO BE BECAUSE OF ONE OF OUR PUNS!
CRACK
PLUS, I'M TOTALLY NOT PASSING UP THE CHANCE TO WRECK A GIANT LIZARD MAN.
CHAMPIONS, TWO. GIANT MONSTERS, ZERO.
I WOULDN'T COUNT THIS AS A WIN YET.

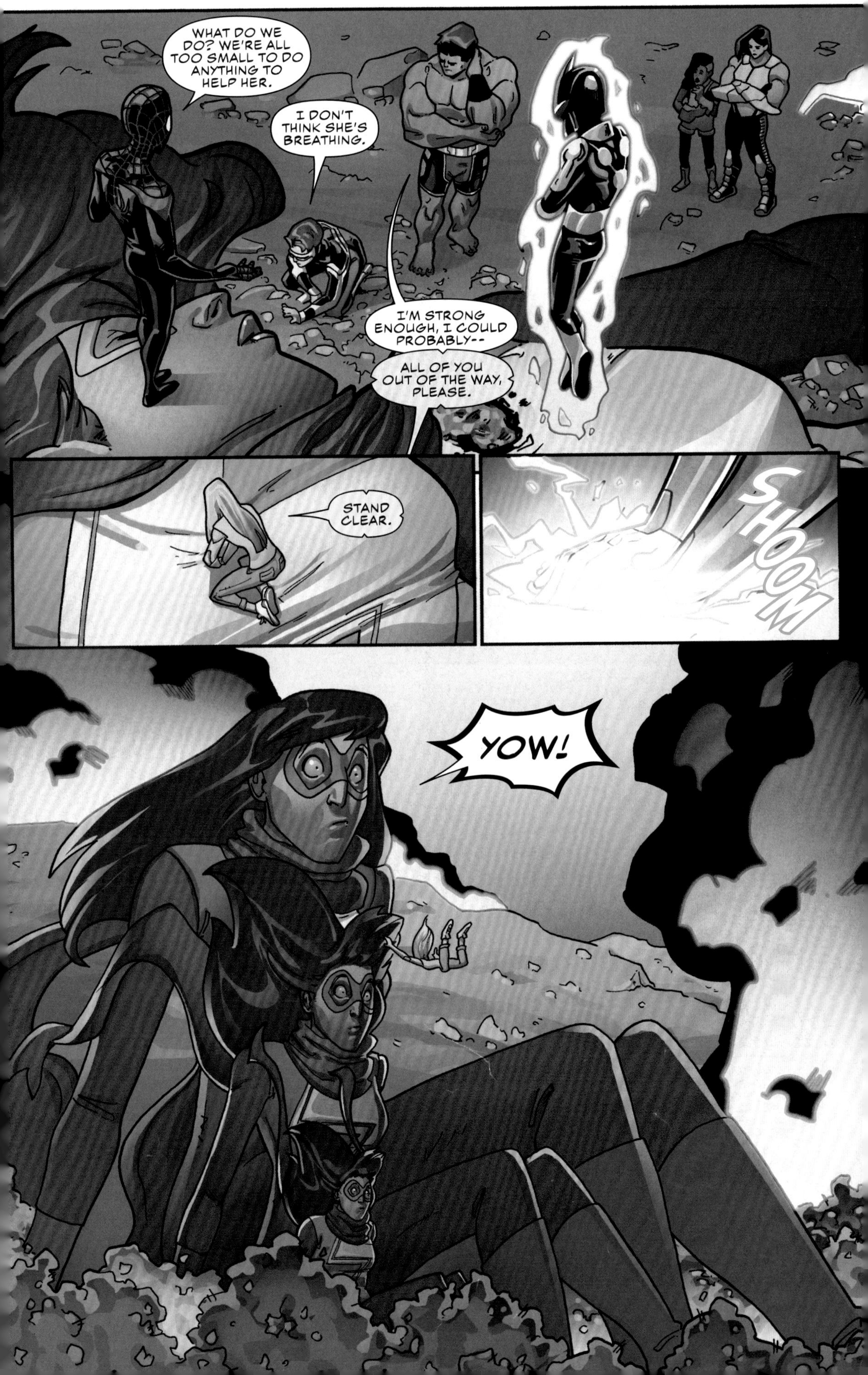

WHAT DO WE DO? WE'RE ALL TOO SMALL TO DO ANYTHING TO HELP HER.
I DON'T THINK SHE'S BREATHING.
I'M STRONG ENOUGH, I COULD PROBABLY--
ALL OF YOU OUT OF THE WAY, PLEASE.
STAND CLEAR.
SHOOM
YOW!

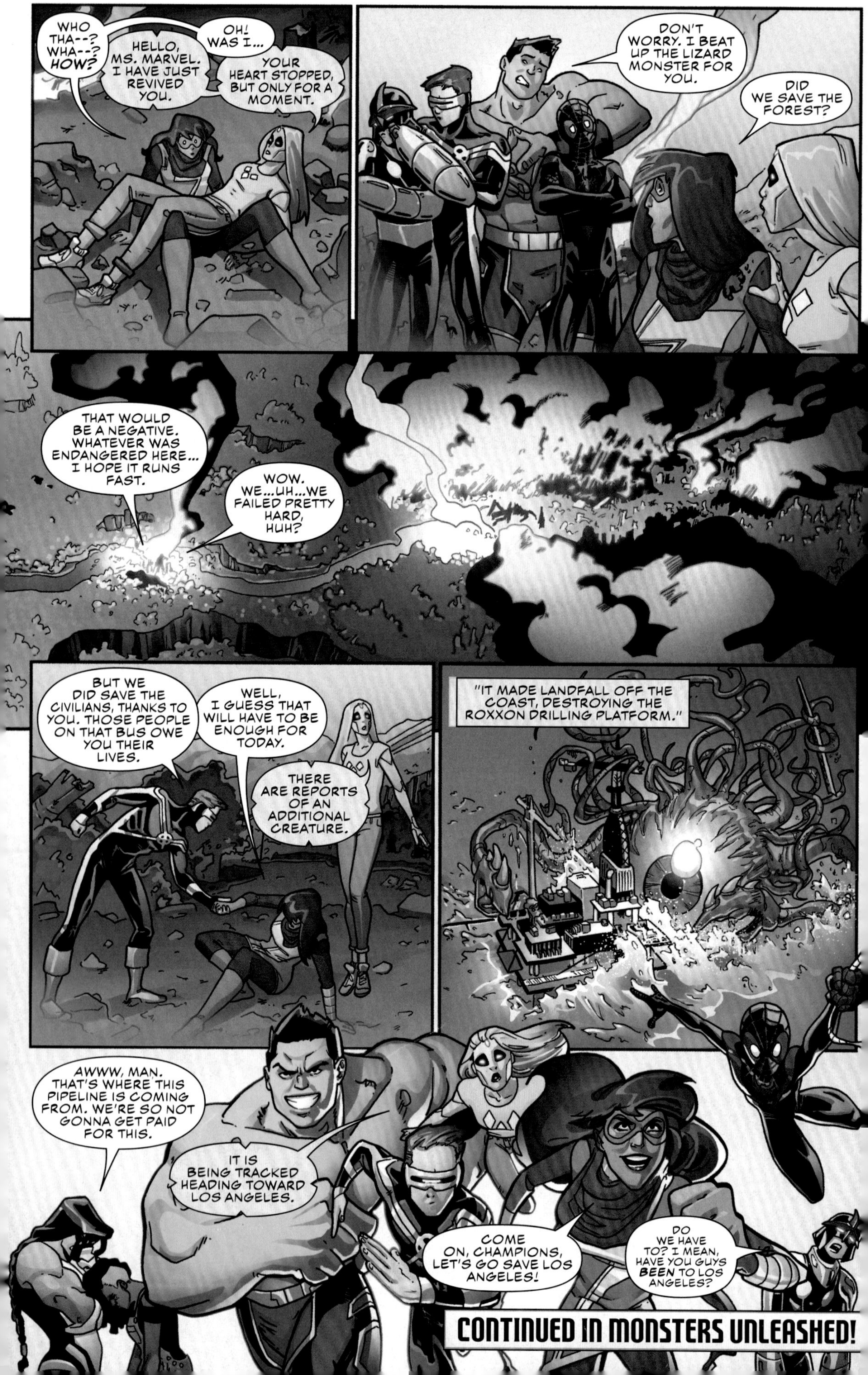
WHO THA--? WHA--? HOW?
HELLO, MS. MARVEL. I HAVE JUST REVIVED YOU.
OH! WAS I...
YOUR HEART STOPPED, BUT ONLY FOR A MOMENT.
DON'T WORRY. I BEAT UP THE LIZARD MONSTER FOR YOU.
DID WE SAVE THE FOREST?
THAT WOULD BE A NEGATIVE. WHATEVER WAS ENDANGERED HERE... I HOPE IT RUNS FAST.
WOW. WE...UH...WE FAILED PRETTY HARD, HUH?
BUT WE DID SAVE THE CIVILIANS, THANKS TO YOU. THOSE PEOPLE ON THAT BUS OWE YOU THEIR LIVES.
WELL, I GUESS THAT WILL HAVE TO BE ENOUGH FOR TODAY.
THERE ARE REPORTS OF AN ADDITIONAL CREATURE.
"IT MADE LANDFALL OFF THE COAST, DESTROYING THE ROXXON DRILLING PLATFORM."
AWWW, MAN. THAT'S WHERE THIS PIPELINE IS COMING FROM. WE'RE SO NOT GONNA GET PAID FOR THIS.
IT IS BEING TRACKED HEADING TOWARD LOS ANGELES.
COME ON, CHAMPIONS, LET'S GO SAVE LOS ANGELES!
DO WE HAVE TO? I MEAN, HAVE YOU GUYS BEEN TO LOS ANGELES?
CONTINUED IN MONSTERS UNLEASHED!

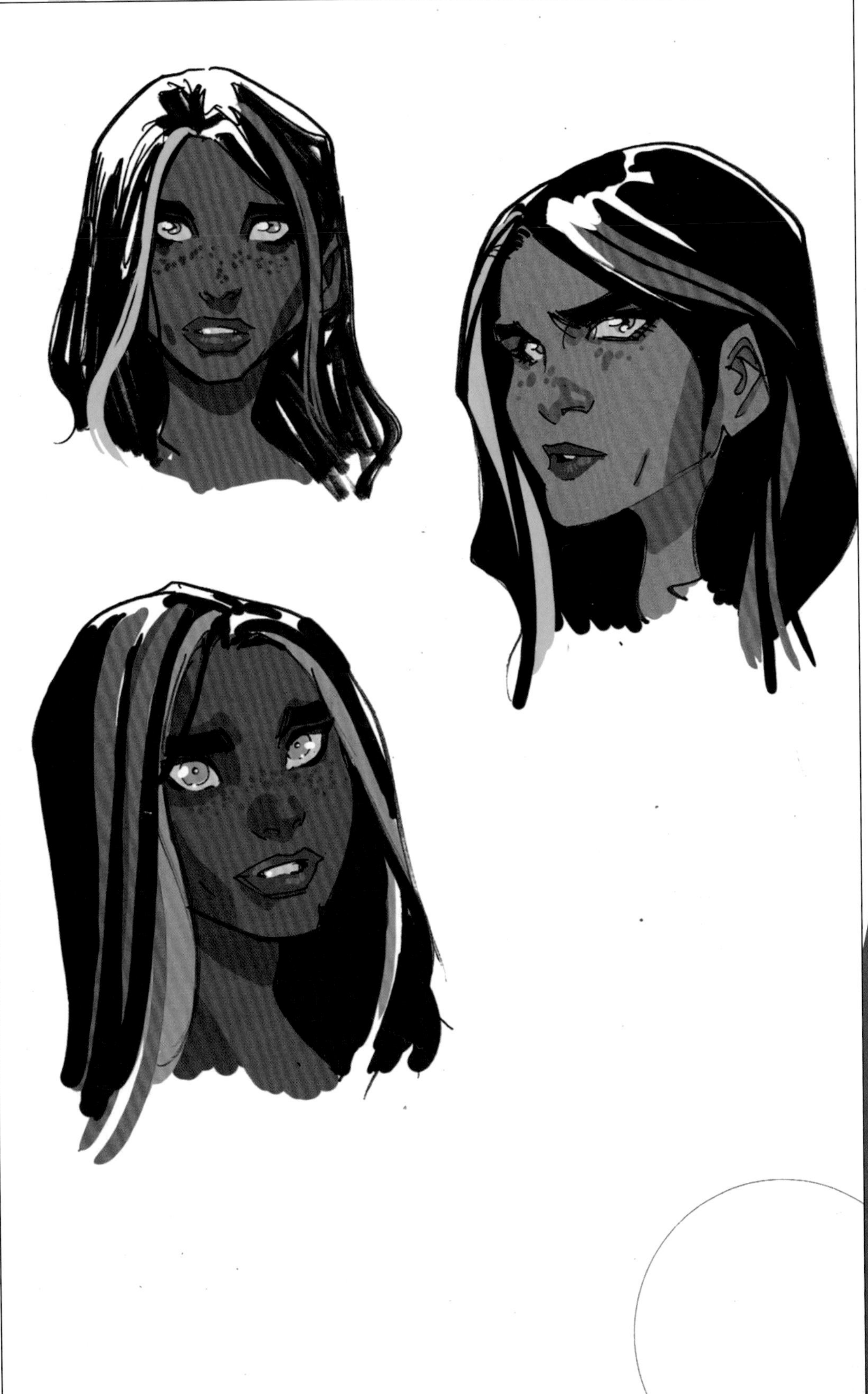

VIV DESIGNS BY **HUMBERTO RAMOS**

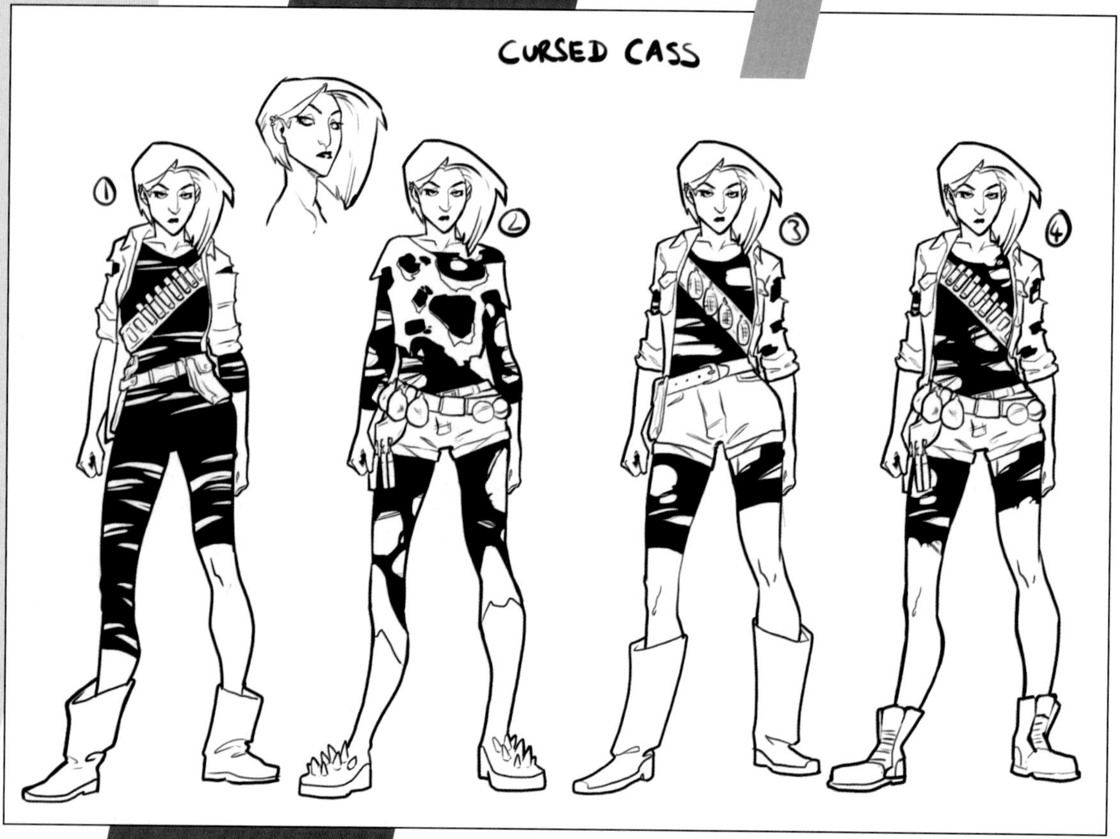
CURSED CASS
1
2
3
4

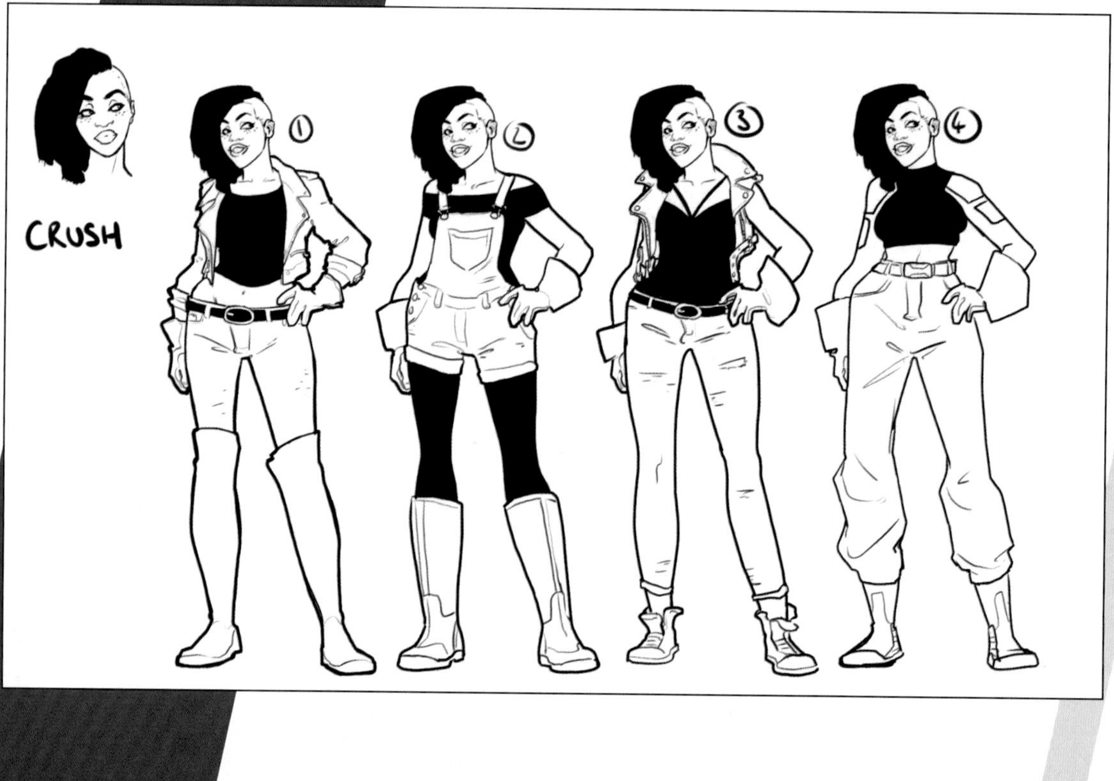
CRUSH
1
2
3
4

MONSTERS UNLEASHED CHARACTER DESIGNS BY RO STEIN & TED BRANDT

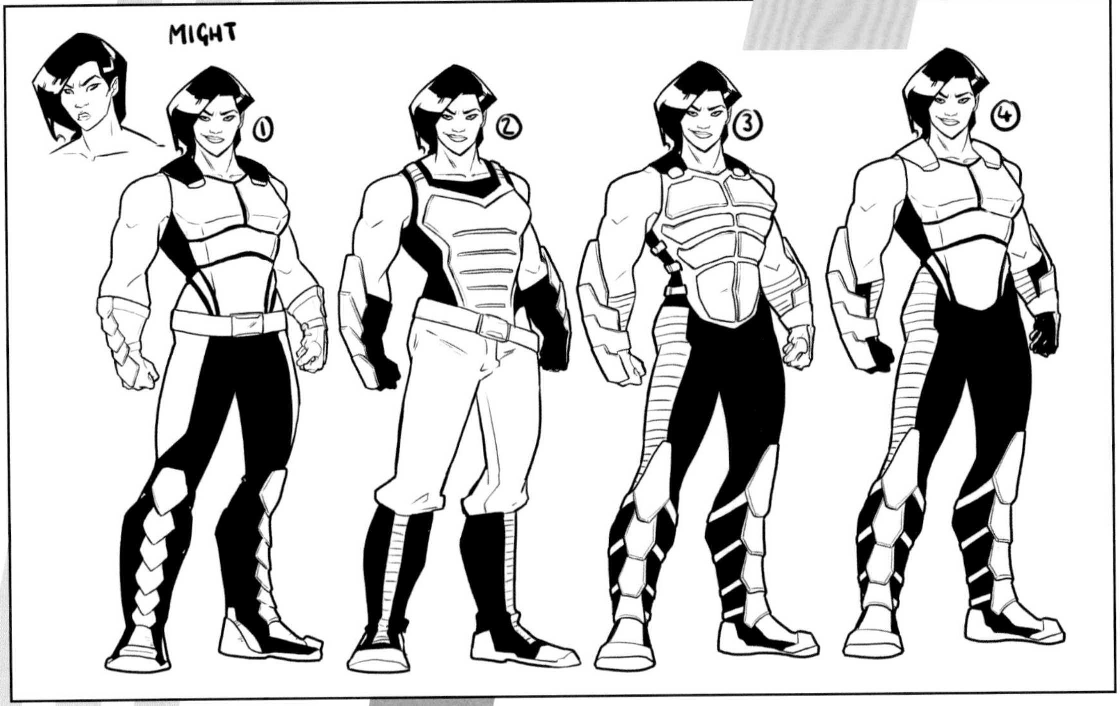
MIGHT
1
2
3
4

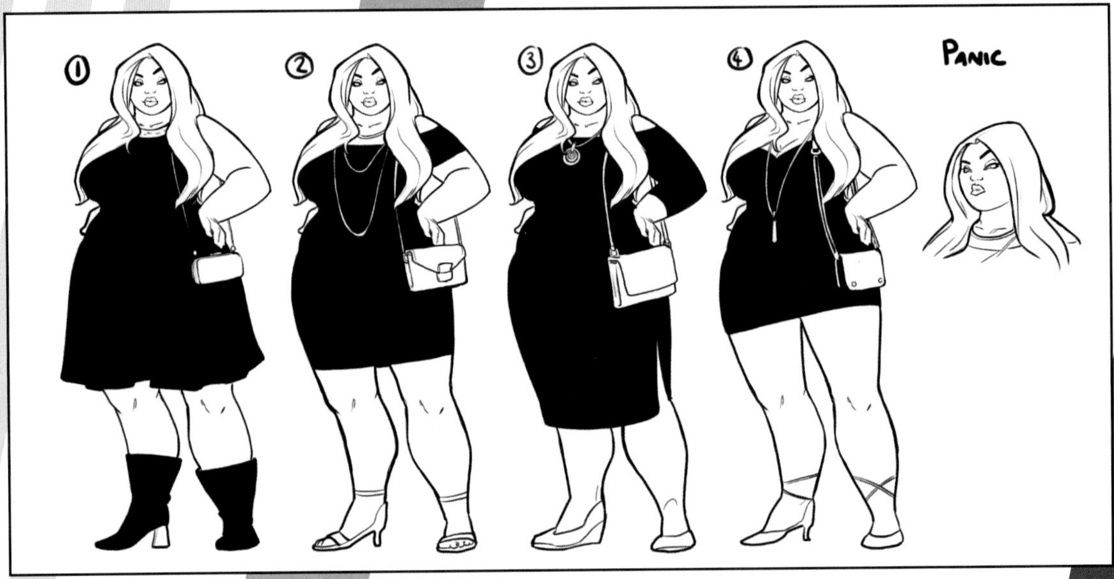
1
2
3
4
PANIC

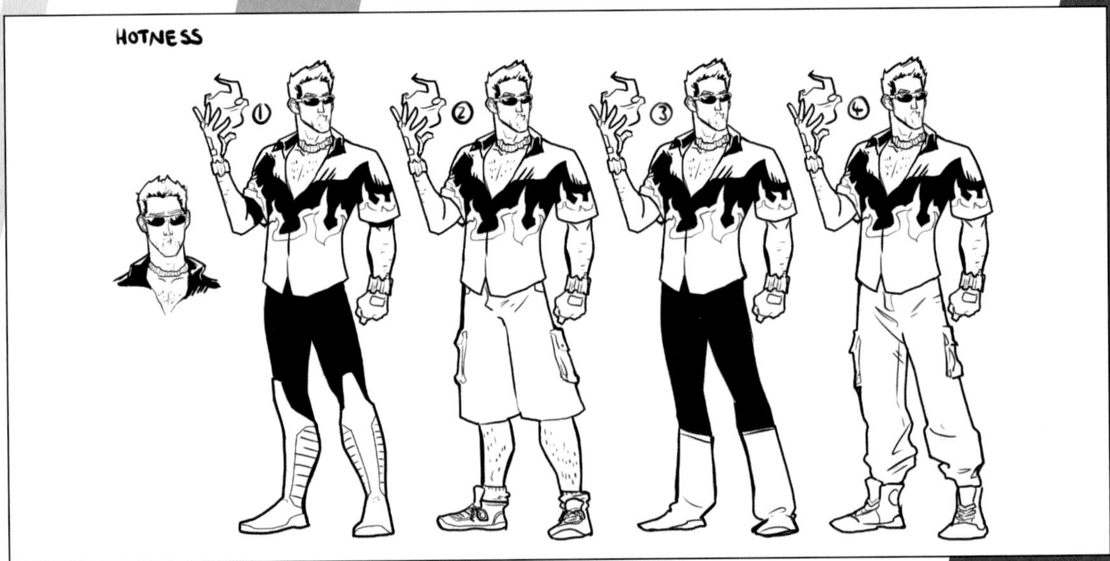
HOTNESS
1
2
3
4

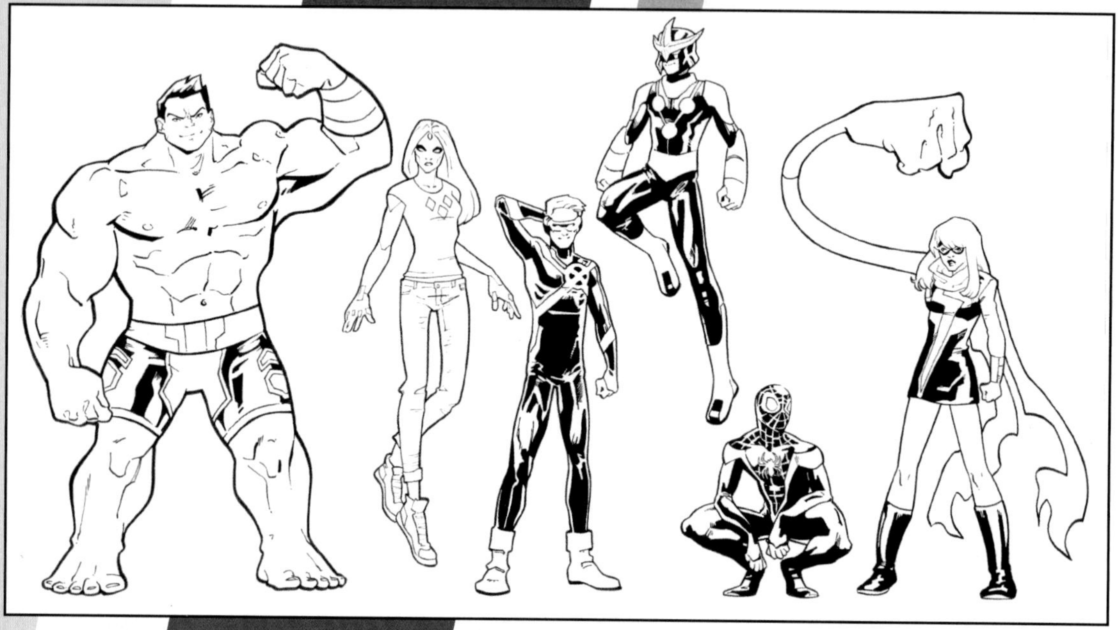

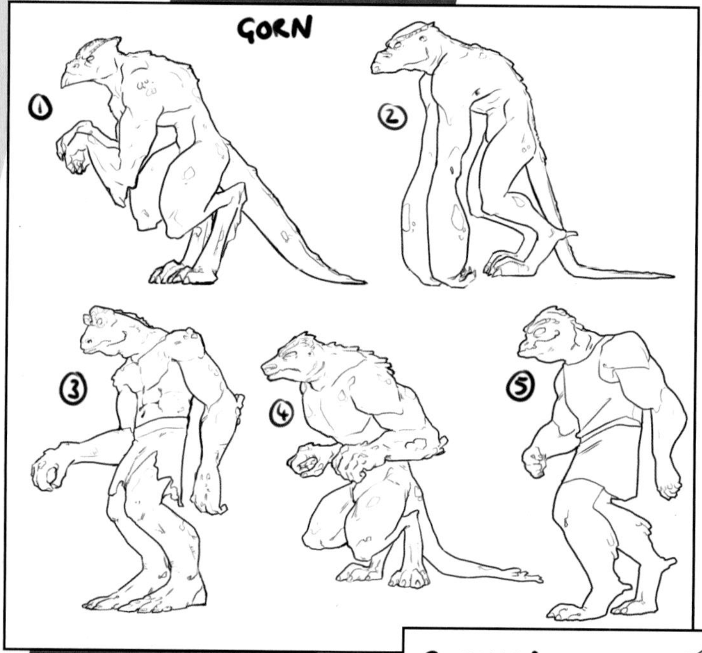
GORN
1
2
3
4
5

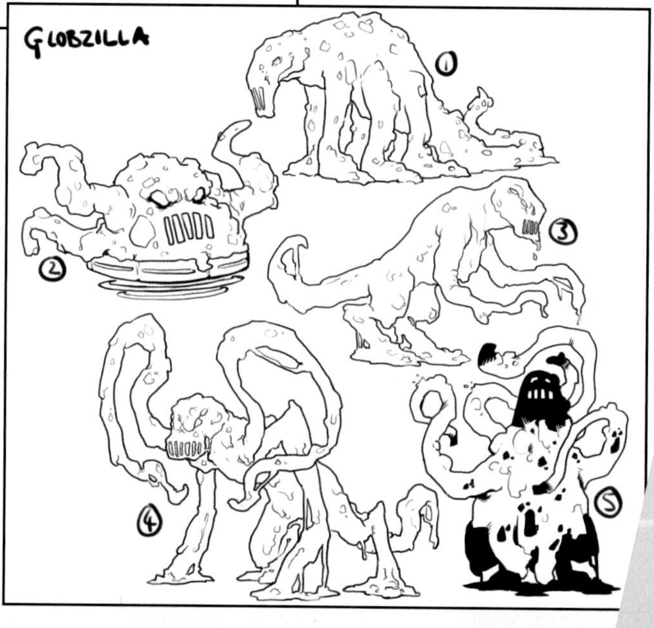
GLOBZILLA
1
2
3
4
5

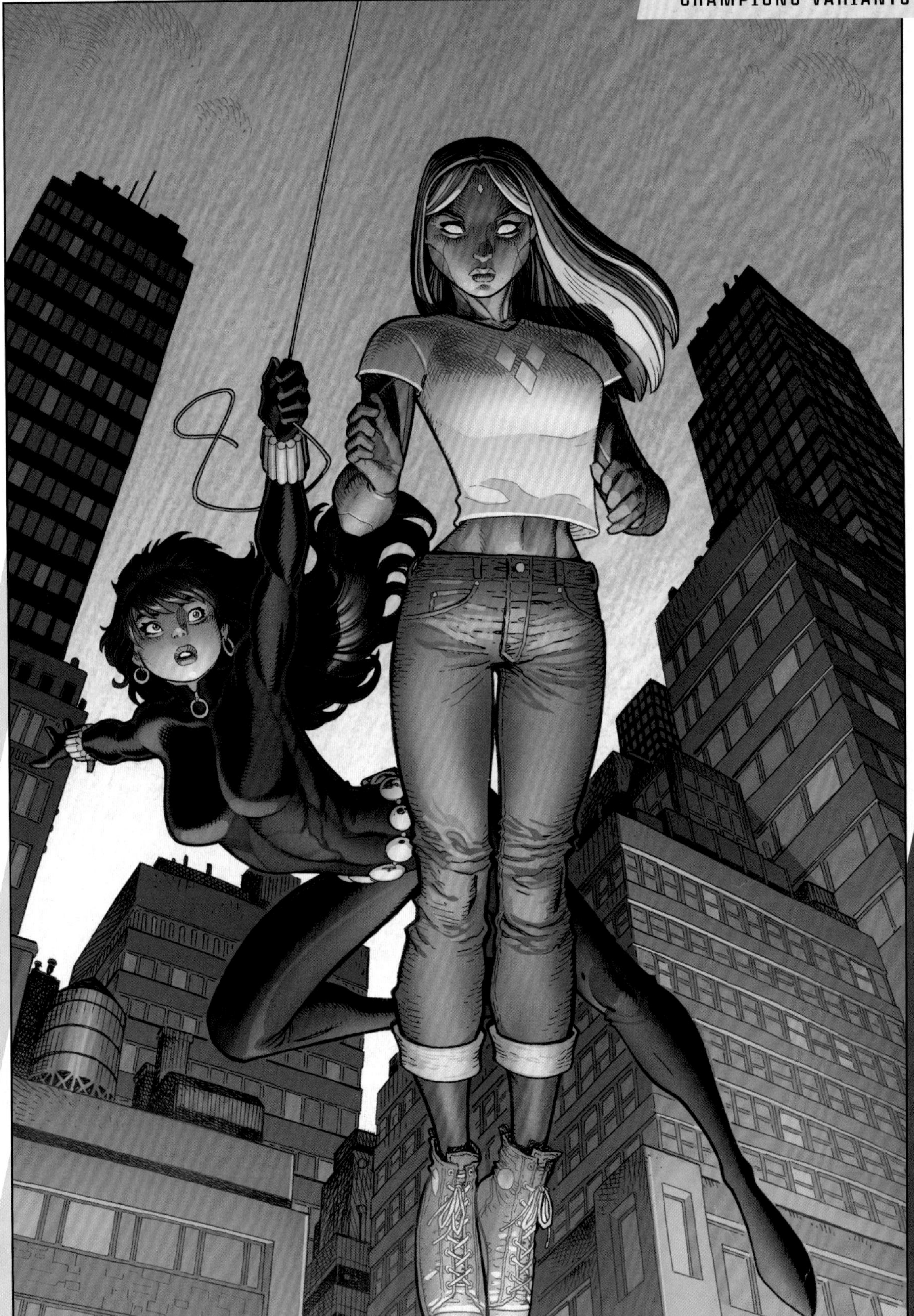

ALL-NEW WOLVERINE #13 BY **ARTHUR ADAMS & MARTE GRACIA**

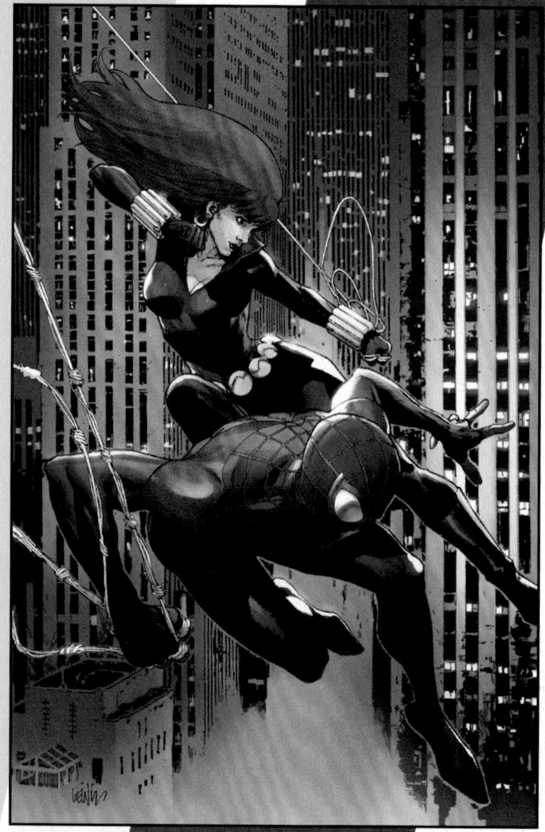

BLACK PANTHER #7 BY
LEINIL FRANCIS YU & JASON KEITH

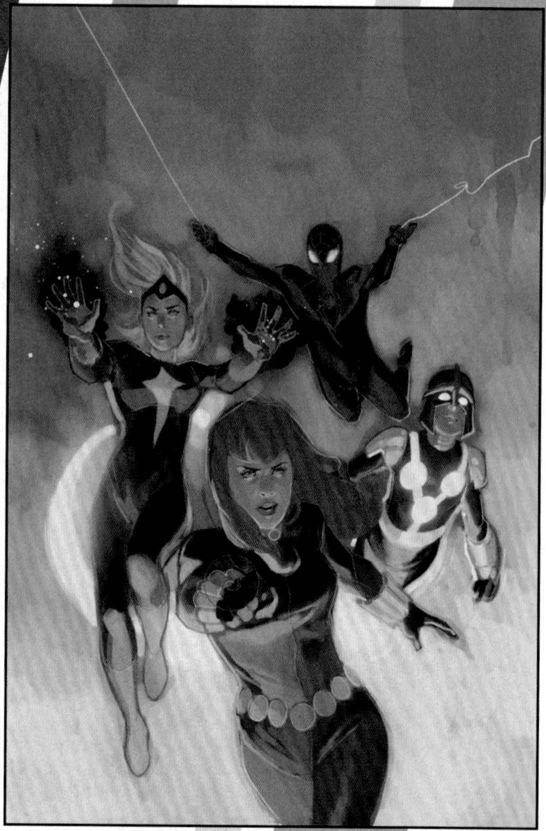

BLACK WIDOW #7 BY
PHIL NOTO

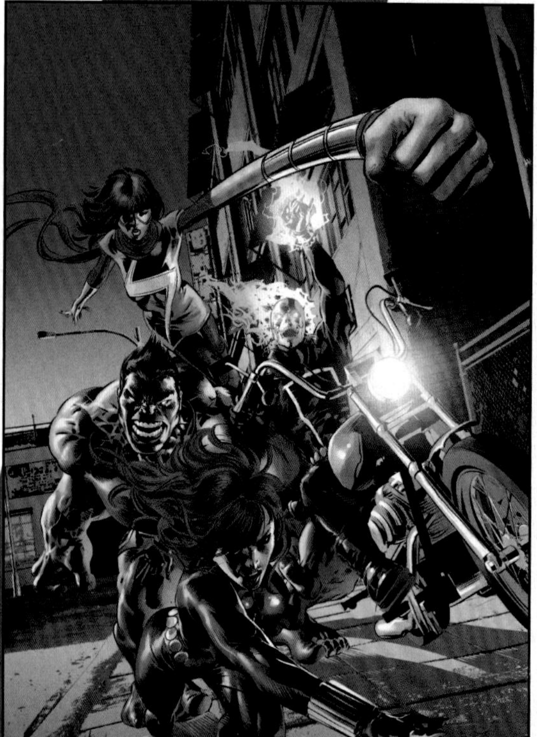

CAPTAI[illegible]A: SAM WILSON#7 BY
MIKE D[illegible] JR. & RAIN BEREDO

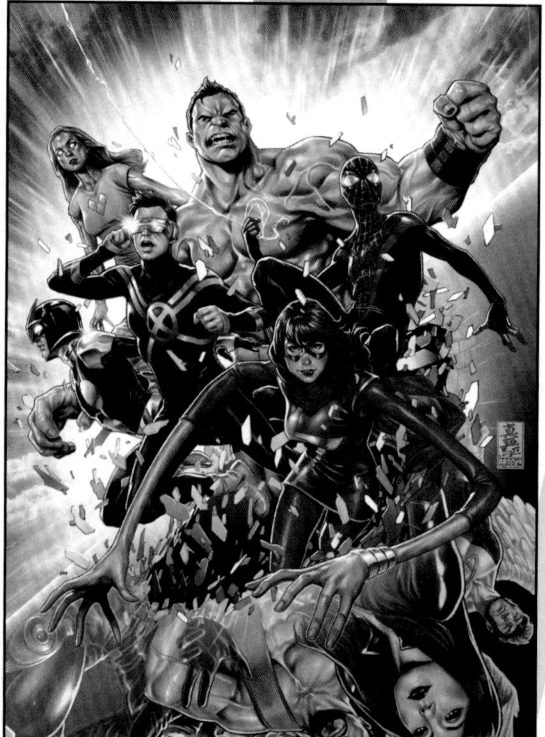

CHAMPIONS #1 BY
MARK BROOKS

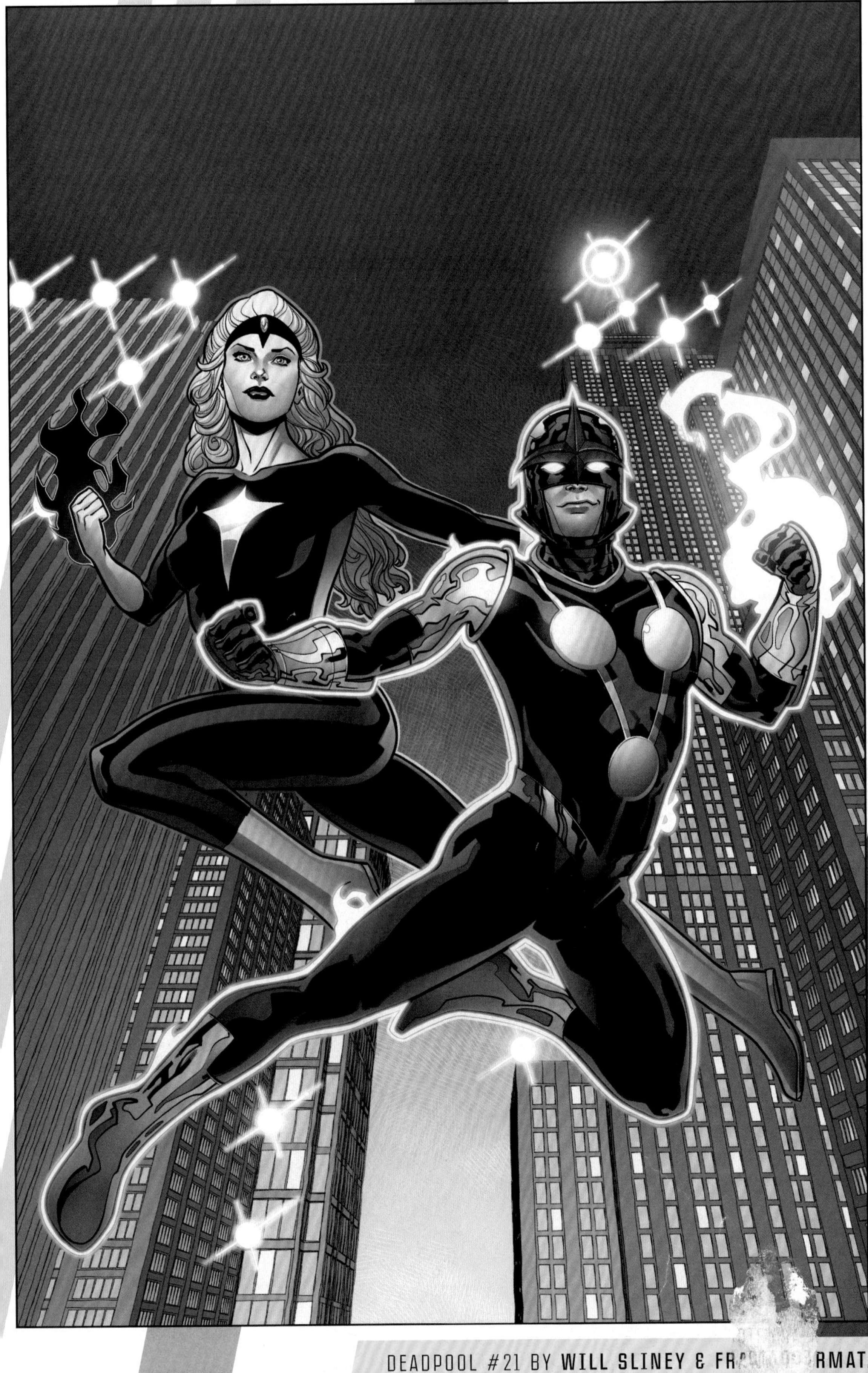

DEADPOOL #21 BY **WILL SLINEY & FRA[illegible]RMATA**

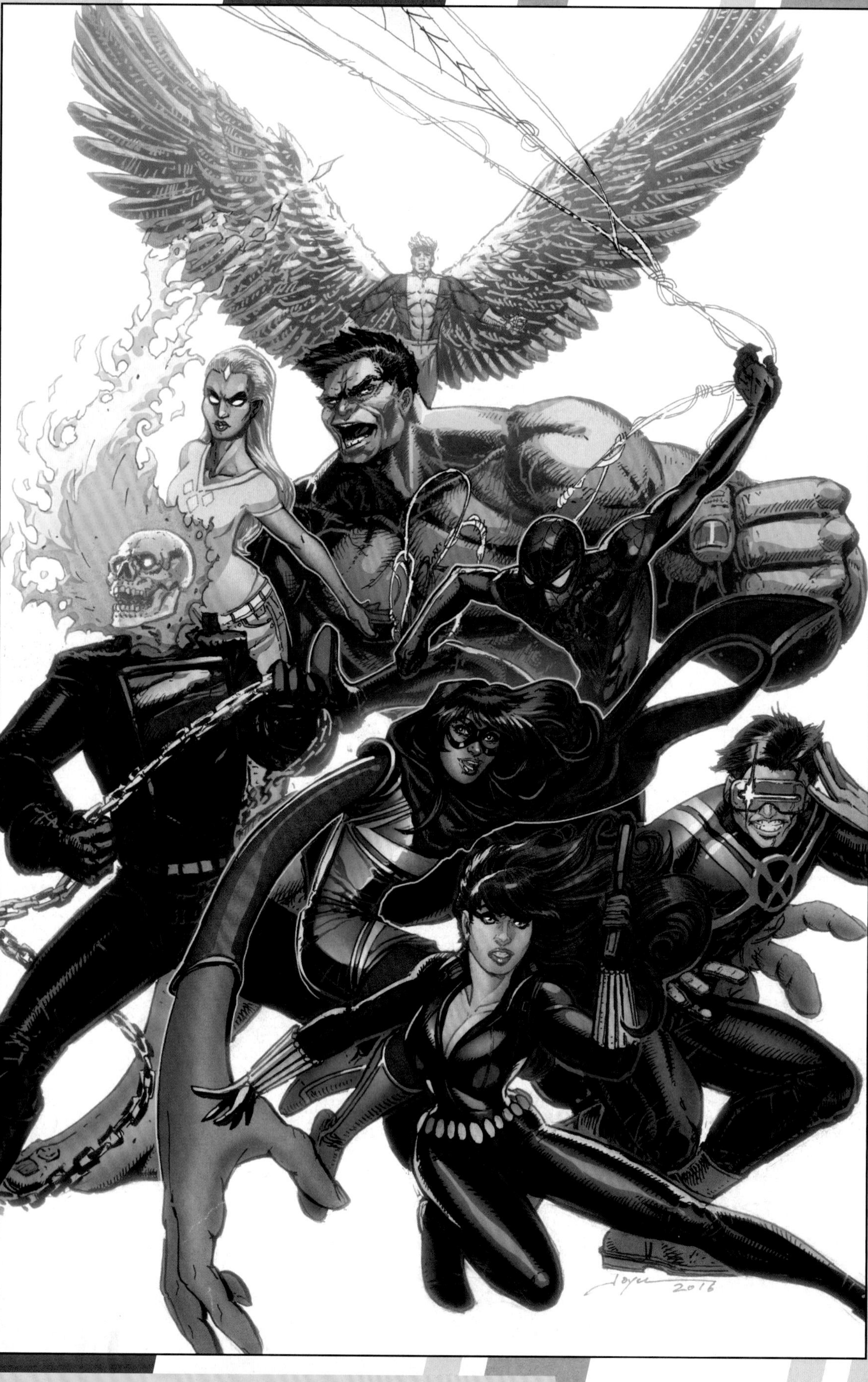
Joyce 2016

DOCTOR STRANGE #12 BY **JOYCE CHIN & MARTE GRACIA**

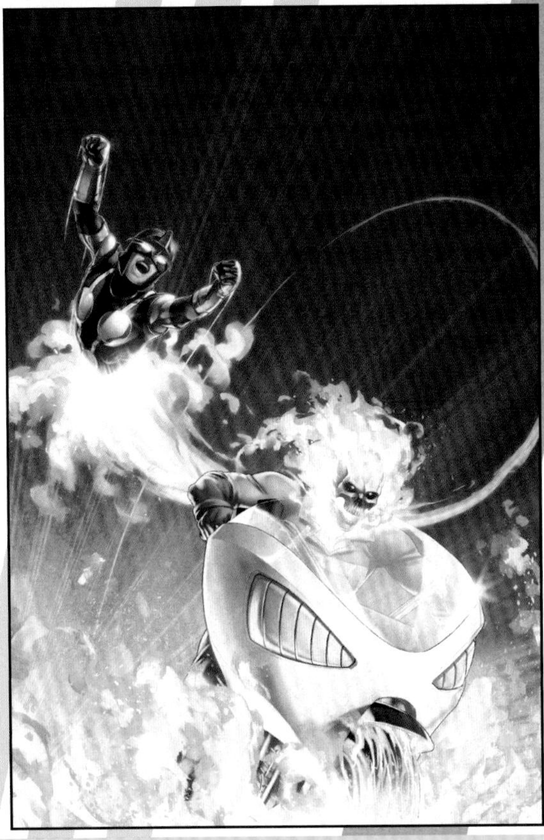

DOCTOR STRANGE AND THE SORCERERS SUPREME #1 BY **JAMAL CAMPBELL**

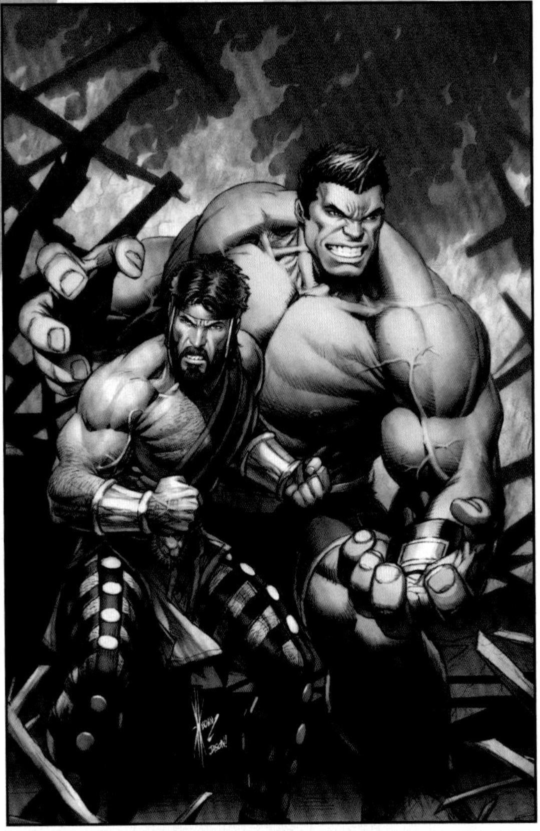

GREAT LAKES AVENGERS #1 BY **DALE KEOWN & JASON KEITH**

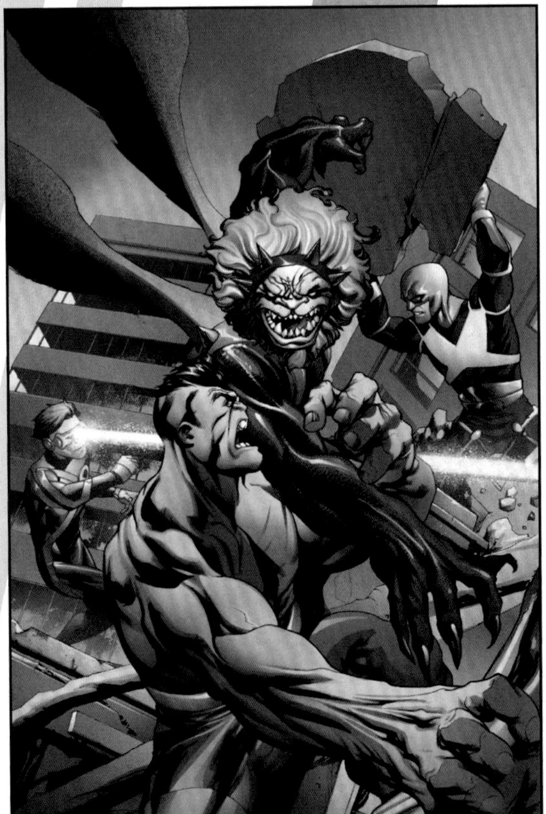

INFAMOUS IRON MAN #1 BY **MIKE McKONE & RICHARD ISANOVE**

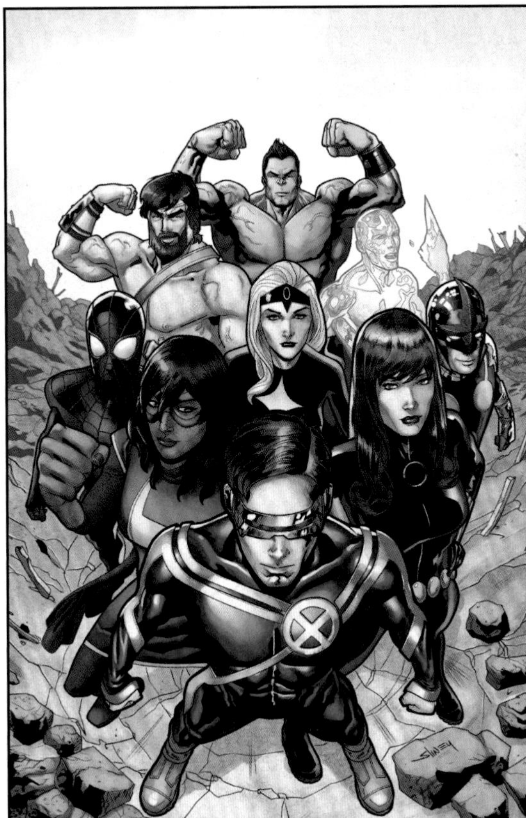

JESSICA JONES #1 BY **WILL SLINEY & CHRIS SOTOMAYOR**

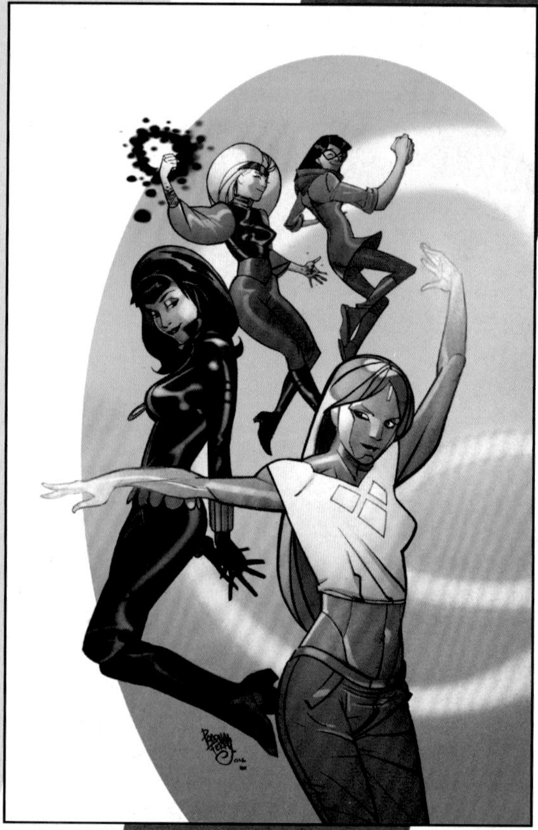

MOSAIC #1 BY
PASQUAL FERRY & FRANK D'ARMATA

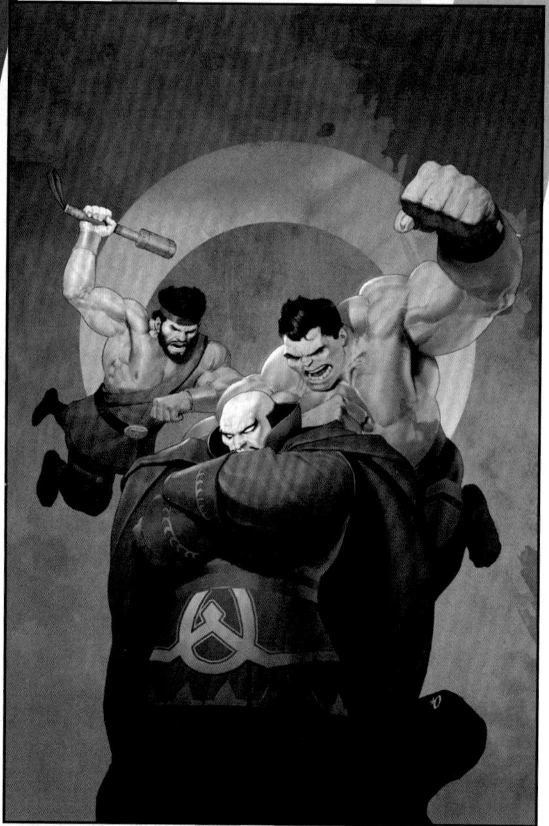

MS. MARVEL #12 BY
ARIEL OLIVETTI

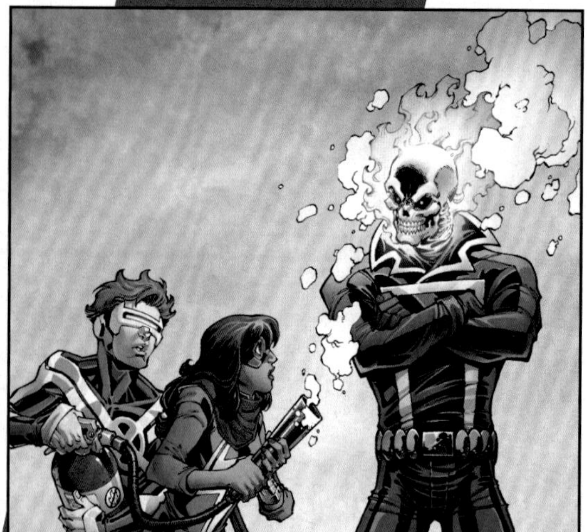
NAUCK

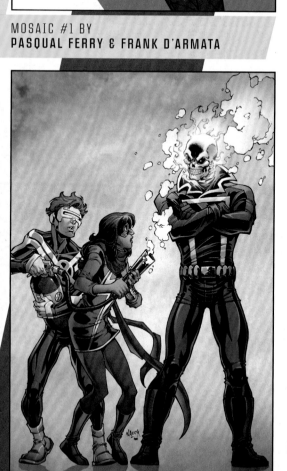

PATSY WALKER, A.K.A. HELLCAT! #7 BY
TODD NAUCK & FRANK D'ARMATA

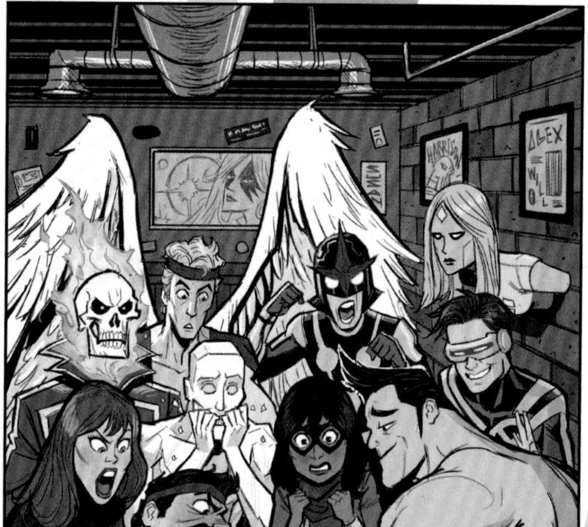
RUBIO

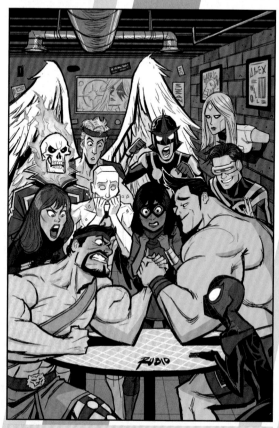

PROWLER #1 BY
BOBBY RUBIO

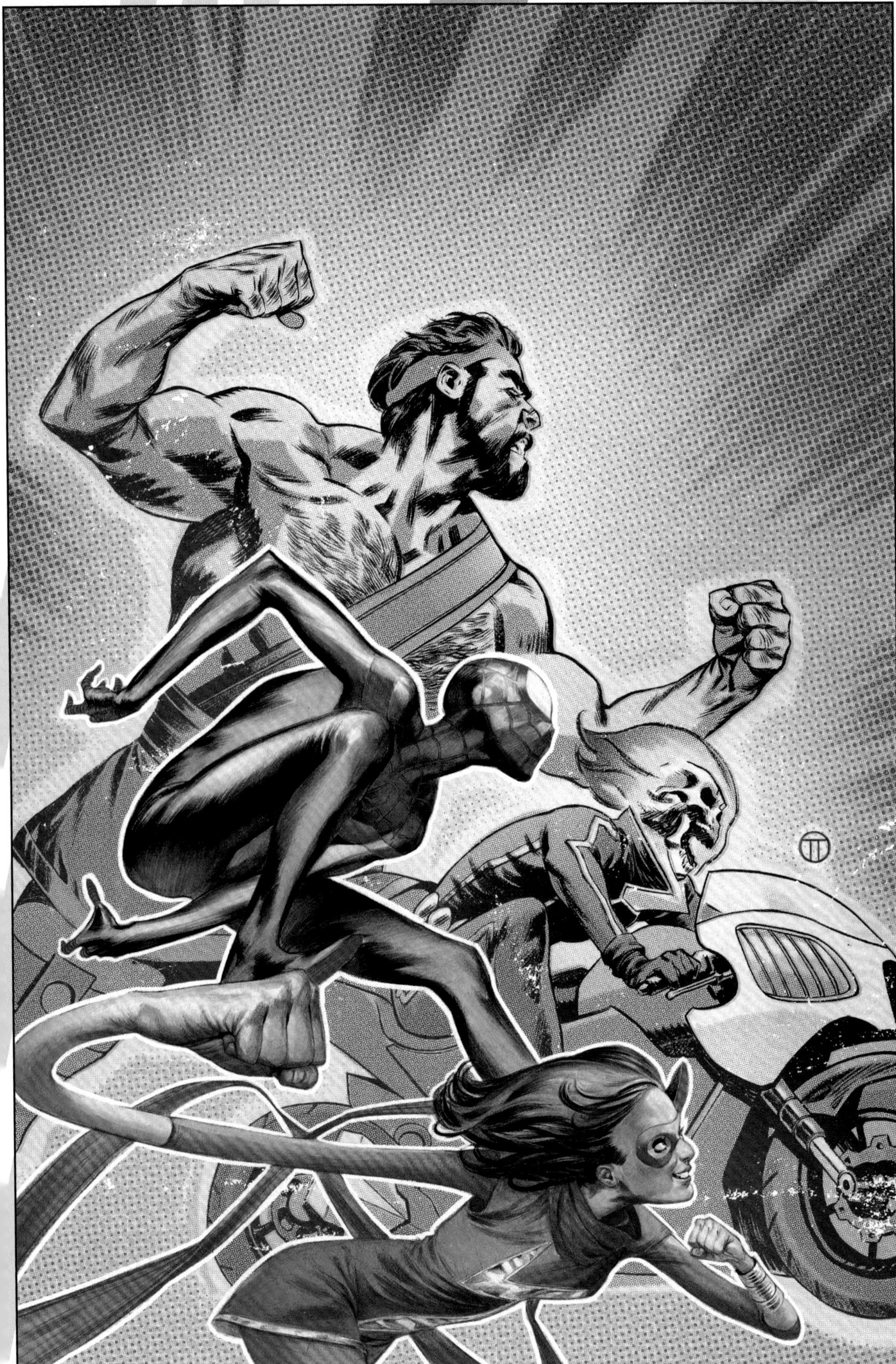

SOLO #1 BY **JULIAN TOTINO TEDESCO**

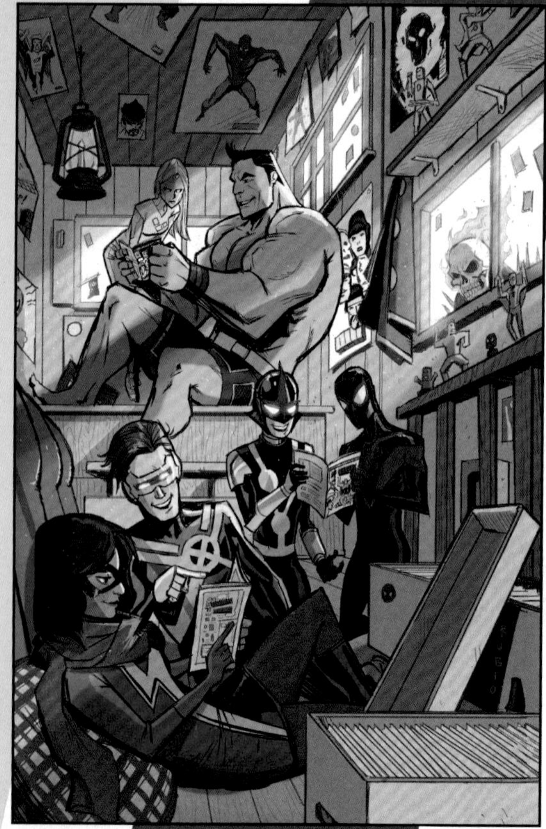

THE UNBEATABLE SQUIRREL GIRL #13 BY
BOBBY RUBIO

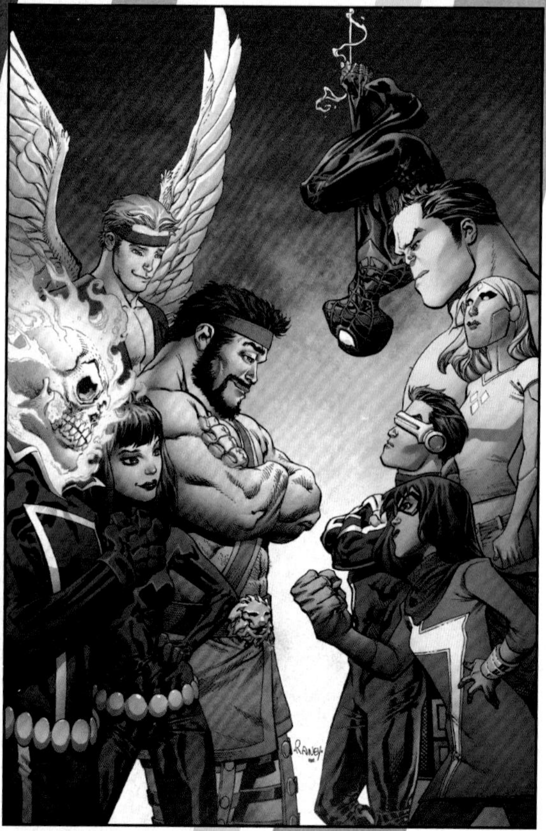

THE UNBELIEVABLE GWENPOOL #7 BY
TOM RANEY & FRANK D'ARMATA

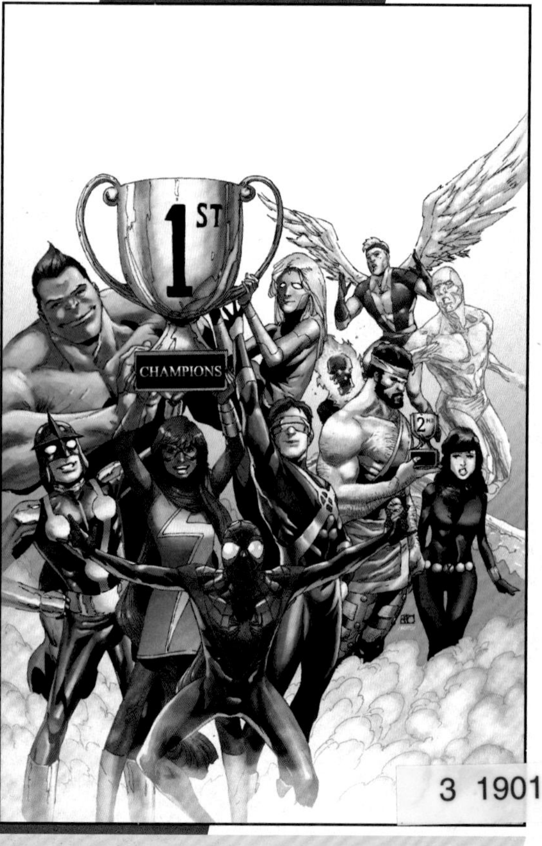
1ST
CHAMPIONS

UNCANNY AVENGERS #15 BY
KHOI PHAM & CHRIS SOTOMAYOR

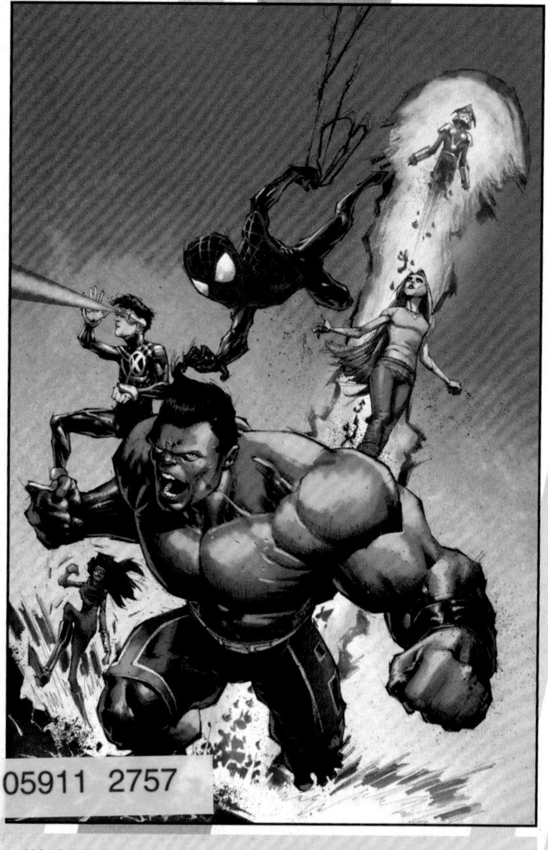

UNCANNY INHUMANS #15 BY
WHILCE PORTACIO & CHRIS SOTOMAYOR